RIDING FURY HOME

CHANA WILSON

A MEMOIR

SEAL PRESS

Riding Fury Home
A Memoir

Published by
Seal Press
A Member of the Perseus Books Group
1700 Fourth Street
Berkeley, California

Library of Congress Cataloging-in-Publication Data

Wilson, Chana, 1951-
Riding fury home : a memoir / by Chana Wilson.
p. cm.
ISBN 978-1-58005-432-4
1. Wilson, Chana, 1951- 2. Lesbians—United States—Biography. 3. Homophobia—United States—History. 4. Mothers and daughters—United States—History. I. Title.
HQ75.4.W54A3 2012
306.76'63092--dc23
[B]

2011043773

10 9 8 7 6 5 4 3 2 1

Cover design by Elke Barter
Interior design by Tabitha Lahr
Printed in the United States of America
Distributed by Publishers Group West

In order to respect the privacy of individuals mentioned in the book, the author has changed their names.

For Dana—brilliant thinker,
advocate for justice—my love always.

CONTENTS

PART ONE: Millstone, New Jersey

Chapter 1. White Plains 13
Chapter 2. Before She Left 16
Chapter 3. Carrier Clinic 20
Chapter 4. University Heights 24
Chapter 5. Millstone 31
Chapter 6. School Days 34
Chapter 7. Atlantic City 38
Chapter 8. Bellyache 43
Chapter 9. Life with Dad 46
Chapter 10. Sweetie 52
Chapter 11. Mom Returns 57
Chapter 12. Alone with Mom 61
Chapter 13. Barbie 71
Chapter 14. Undertow 73
Chapter 15. Overdose 76
Chapter 16. Riding Fury Home 87
Chapter 17. Happy 91
Chapter 18. Return 93
Chapter 19. Perry Mason 98
Chapter 20. Crossing the Demilitarized Zone 103
Chapter 21. Hayride 111
Chapter 22. Leaving Millstone 117
Chapter 23. Englewood 124

PART TWO: Identity House

Chapter 24. Iowa Nights 135
Chapter 25. The Great Divide 153
Chapter 26. Freedom School. 161
Chapter 27. By the Bay 166
Chapter 28. Older Women's Liberation. 178
Chapter 29. FBI 187
Chapter 30. Icebox Canyon 198
Chapter 31. Fire Escape 215
Chapter 32. The Village 224
Chapter 33. Immigrants. 231
Chapter 34. Mother Courage 236
Chapter 35. Unlearning to Not Speak 245
Chapter 36. Woman Share 258
Chapter 37. Identity House 270
Chapter 38. Promised Land 278
Chapter 39. T-Bone 288
Chapter 40. Wilderness. 296
Chapter 41. Leaving Clarke Street 303

PART THREE: Sinai

Chapter 42. Rheumatoid 315
Chapter 43. Diagnosis 319
Chapter 44. Intensive Care 326
Chapter 45. Halcion Daze 332
Chapter 46. Spreading 339

Chapter 47. Devil's Slide 344
Chapter 48. Hospice 351
Chapter 49. Submarine 357
Chapter 50. Sinai 359
Chapter 51. Shiva 362
Chapter 52. Thermals 364

Epilogue 369
Reader's Guide 372
Acknowledgments 375
About the Author 377

"Whatever is unnamed, undepicted in images, whatever is omitted from biography, censored in collection of letters, whatever is misnamed as something else, made difficult-to-come-by, whatever is buried in the memory by collapse of meaning under an inadequate or lying language—this will become, not merely unspoken, but unspeakable."

—Adrienne Rich, *On Lies, Secrets, and Silence*

Until I was twenty five, my first name was Karen. Chana, my Hebrew name, in English is pronounced Hah-nah.

PART ONE: MILLSTONE, NEW JERSEY

Chapter 1. White Plains

I WAS THE FIRST CHILD ever allowed to visit a patient at the private mental hospital where my mother was being treated. Before our first trip there, Dad said, "The doctors think your mother will get better if she can keep seeing you."

Visiting hours were on Sundays, so I had to drop out of Jewish Sunday school, which I had just begun six months earlier. Though I was seven, they had put me with the six-year-olds because I didn't read any Hebrew. The odd-shaped letters blurred before my eyes, and I made no attempt to decipher them. But I loved the singing, humming along to the guttural language. On the easy songs, like "Hava Nagila," I belted the words. After songs, we got to eat exotic treats: dates, figs, and rugelach—buttery spirals of dough with raisins and cinnamon.

My father and I sang on the two-hour drive to the hospital, up the New Jersey Turnpike, over the Tappan Zee Bridge. He taught me his favorite: *"I'll build a bungalow, big enough for two, big enough for two my honey, big enough for two, and when we're married, happy we'll be, under the bamboo, under the bamboo tree."* Dad and I sang and sang: ballads, show tunes, and spirituals, as our old brown Hudson lumbered along.

Going to see my mother who was not a mother. My need of her was frozen, clamped down against any thaw. But she needed me. Maybe if I loved her enough, my mother would heal.

I REMEMBER THE GROUNDS, the front lawn an expanse of green with a curving drive. The visitors gathered outside the front entrance, waiting for the appointed hour. The gates were locked until then, and there was a quiet hush among us, the waiting families. Dad held my hand. In my imagination, the buildings are dark and gothic, hovering like some dragon ready to pounce.

That first time—and every Sunday afterward—I met my mother at the foot of a stairwell. As she came down the stairs, I looked up at her face, puffy and sallow. She leaned over to hug me, and I reached up my arms, willing myself not to pull away, but I flinched a little. She took my hand and we ambled onto the back lawn, my father trailing behind. Mom moved slowly, and she stumbled now and then. We walked past the tennis courts. "Fancy schmancy, huh?" Mom said. Then she laughed, but it didn't sound happy. I knew Mom tried to play. She told me that all the patients were on so many drugs that they missed a lot of balls.

I always brought Happy, my favorite stuffed animal, with me. One day, Mom and I were sitting on some steps outdoors, when another patient came over. He leaned over and put his face close to mine. I could smell his foul breath. He pointed at Happy. "What a nice bunny!" Happy's long, floppy ears must have misled him.

"He's not a bunny, he's a dog!" I protested, in an outburst of anger that was taboo to express around my mother. She was sick, it was not her fault, and I knew I must not get angry at her.

Mom put her hand on my back. "It's okay, honey," she said. The man scowled at me, turned abruptly, and stormed away.

ONE TIME, MY FATHER had a meeting with my mother's psychiatrist while I waited in the car. I watched him walk back, hands in his pockets, head down. He got in, sat behind the steering wheel, put his face in his hands, and wept. Then, finally, he said, "The doctor says your mother will never get well. He says she is incurable." I looked down at my hands. Happy had dropped to the floor. Somewhere inside I knew I must not be doing a good enough job.

On winter days the hospital gave my mother a pass, and we went into town. We always went to the movies. I remember seeing Peter Sellers in *The Mouse That Roared,* a zany film about a tiny country that invades America. In that dark cinema, I could enter another world and forget the bloated stranger called Mother who sat beside me.

After the movies, we always went to a local steak house, and the three of us ordered the same thing: T-bone steak with french fries. How I lived for the dessert—parfait in a tall glass, layers of vanilla ice cream and frozen strawberries in syrup, gleaming red and white. I would spy the parfait on other diners' tables, anticipating its soft, tart sweetness in my mouth.

Chapter 2. Before She Left

BEFORE SHE LEFT, MY MOTHER read to me. Hundreds and hundreds of my mother's books lined the shelves of our living room in the house we'd moved into when I was five. Mom would pull the book of Greek myths down from the shelf. How I loved those stories: Arachne in the guise of a spider weaving her web, Icarus flying toward the sun until his wings melted. Sometimes, she would read me a paragraph in Latin. I loved the cadence of my mother's voice, first the Latin—which seemed so foreign and mythic—and then her English translation.

My mother sprinkled her speech with bits of other languages: the Yiddish primal cry of woe—*Oy gevalt! Vay is mir!*—delivered with a melodramatic wringing of hands; the German she had learned as a scientist; and her love, French. She had a French ditty that she often said to me, declaimed in a low alto with one hand fisted on her breastbone, one hand gesturing outward: "*Je t'aime, je t'adore. Que veux tu?Depuis encore!!!*" (She translated this for me as: "I love you. I *adore* you. What do you want? What more *is* there?") Somehow, even at five, I understood this wasn't about me, and wasn't about my father, but was directed to some mysterious, unnamed person.

My mother adored song: Opera was her first love, musicals second. When she played opera on the hi-fi, sometimes I felt like covering my ears, but after Mom took me to my first opera—*Carmen,* at New York's City Center—I would sing along with her, "*Toréador, en garde! Toréador! Toréador!*" imagining myself a bullfighter in a fancy gold-and-red jacket and that funny hat, waving my cape—"Olé!"—as the bull charged.

In the afternoons, I would come home from kindergarten, and then first grade, filled with stories of my day. I chattered to Mom over a snack, showed her whatever I'd created in class. Then, I got to pick out one of our musicals, *My Fair Lady, Oklahoma,* or *South Pacific*, sitting at the dining room table, crayoning in my coloring book. Together, Mom and I would croon: "I'm gonna wash that man right outta my hair and send him on his way."

All the words that were spoken, that my mother read and sang to me, left so many words unspoken. The silence of what was happening to her. The grief that was pulling her under. It wouldn't be until I was twenty that she would tell me the secret of her anguish, a secret whose impact would shape both our lives.

ONE DAY IN MAY OF 1958, just after my seventh birthday, my mother was gone. I didn't know that while I was at school she had gone into the bathroom and held my father's rifle to her head. I didn't know she'd pulled the trigger, and that, by some fluke, the rifle had jammed. All I knew was that my mother had been taken from me.

Years later, when I was an adult, my father told me about that day.

"I was in the kitchen, home from work for lunch, when I heard the clank of metal hitting the floor and your mother yelling, 'Shit! It didn't work!'"

My father ran to the hall outside the bathroom. My mother was no longer there, but his rifle lay on the floor. He knelt down and opened the gun. A round fell out. He picked it up and stared at where the firing pin had left a dent in the case.

"I thought, *Oh my God, she pulled the trigger!* I put the rifle down and called out, 'Gloria?' She didn't answer. But then I realized we were beyond talking now. I went to the phone and called her psychiatrist. 'Take her to Carrier Clinic, Abe,' he told me. 'I'll call ahead and arrange her admission.'"

After that, my father took over storytelling. At night, he lay next to me in my bed, mesmerizing me with his made-up tales. There were no Greek myths, but I loved his stories, too. One was about a white butterfly who is lonely and longs for friendship. He sees a white fluttering shape far away in a distant field and is drawn toward it, searching and searching. After a long journey, he reaches the shape. Ah, it's a lady butterfly. They fall in love and are both very happy.

A few days after my mother left, Dad explained, "The doctors are fixing Mom. It's her head, not her body, that is sick. She's in a special hospital for people just like her, called a mental hospital."

I interrupted his discourse. "Dad, what's 'mental' mean?"

"It means how you think in your head. Understand?"

I nodded, even though I didn't really get it.

"Anyway, the doctors are using electricity to cure her. It will help her. It will fix her head."

I stared at him, blinking hard, but said nothing.

During the day, I tried to be very good and not complain. But sometimes I would wake in the night, crying, "Mommy, I want

Mommy! Where's Mommy? I want my mommy." Dad would come to my bedroom and try to comfort me, but I would not be consoled.

My mother came home two and a half years later, her New Jersey accent thickly slurred from psychiatric drugs, her eyes dark with desolation. The electroshock treatments had wiped out her knowledge of Yiddish, German, French, and Latin. She told me no stories, sang me no songs. And I had tucked away my daily stories, my longings and need of her, tucked it all far away into some wordless place.

Chapter 3. Carrier Clinic

BEFORE OUR FIRST VISIT to Carrier Clinic, Dad sat me down at the dining room table.

"Do you remember what I told you about Mom's treatments at the hospital? How the doctors are helping Mom by connecting her head to electricity?"

I nodded, fidgeting. My hands picked at the woven place mat.

My father paused, looked at me, and then away. He looked back and cleared his throat. "Sometimes after the electricity, people don't remember things too well. It probably won't happen, but when we go to see Mom today, she may not know who you are."

I stared at my father while what he had said seeped into my body. Then I leapt up and ran. "Karen!" I heard my father call after me, but I didn't stop as I raced up the stairs and down the hall to my parents' bedroom. I flung open their closet door and stood facing myself in their full-length mirror. Yes, there was my reflection. I looked into my eyes, amazed and puzzled; I was still there. *But how can I be? How can I be here if Mom doesn't know who I am?*

CARRIER CLINIC WAS A modern building, with double doors leading to long white corridors smelling of disinfectant. Dad held my hand as we walked down the hall, until we got to a room where Mom was waiting in a chair. I held back, grabbing onto Dad's pants leg. Mom rose, and exclaimed, "My darling girl!" Dad's hand was on my back, pushing me toward her. Mom enveloped me in a hug, but she smelled wrong; instead of her usual flowery scent of Chanel No. 5, she was sour with sweat and stale smoke.

Mom always remembered who I was during those four months of her electroshock treatments. We weren't allowed to bring anything for her, but sometimes I would show her pictures I had drawn in my first-grade class: a yellow sun shining gold rays between purple mountains, or a box house with a triangle roof, smoke spiraling from its chimney. "Wonderful, sweetheart, wonderful," she praised me, but quietly, like she was very tired.

On our visits, Mom, Dad, and I would go out onto the wide green front lawn and walk around the building. Out back, there were horses belonging to one of the doctors. The long wooden row of box stalls smelled sweetly of manure and hay. We walked along to the thumps of hooves against wood as the high-strung horses kicked the walls, until we found a horse to our liking, ears flicked forward in curiosity. Dad carried a bag of carrots he had brought from home. He handed me a carrot. I gingerly held it up to the big gnashing teeth, entranced by the huge face with deep brown eyes, the chestnut coat, the long thick neck, the gigantic musky animalness so close at hand.

On one visit, Mom gave me a pin she had made in occupational therapy. It was a turtle, created out of a circle of alligator skin, with a round leather head that had two glass beads for eyes. Mom had glued a pin clasp to its underbelly. I wore it to school every day until one of its glass eyes fell off, and then I carefully stored it in my pink jewelry box.

I have no memory of our goodbyes. Each visit must have ended in some kind of parting. Did Mom hug me so tight I could barely breathe? Or did she just let me go, waving a limp farewell?

WHEN I WAS IN MY TWENTIES, my mother told me what Carrier Clinic had been like for her. After each electroshock treatment, when she had recovered enough to move her stiff and sore body down the hall to the pay phone, when she wasn't so disoriented that she couldn't remember the names of friends, my mother would call anyone she could think of—my father, her parents, her friends—and beg, "Please, my God, they're killing me—you have to get me out of here!"

The response was always the same: murmurs of sympathy, and "The doctors say you need to be there. This will help you in the long run. I'm sorry, Gloria."

My father recounted to me a time she called him between her weekly electroshocks. "Abe, Abe, get me out of here," she pleaded. "I can't bear this . . . please, PLEASE!"

He tried to placate her. "Gloria, only the doctor can do that. But it will be all right, you'll see." Somewhere in the midst of speaking, he found he was talking to an empty phone. "Gloria . . . GLORIA . . . ?"

"Mr. Wilson?" The voice of a male orderly came on the phone. "Your wife has climbed out the window of her room onto the roof. She says she will jump unless we agree not to give her any more treatments, but don't worry. We'll get her in. We'll call you back."

In spite of her depression, in defiance of all that was bearing down on her, there were moments when my mother's feistiness and leftist politics rallied. One time, my father was in the hospital administration office straightening out some insurance paperwork. He was startled when Gloria marched resolutely into the office. It was several days after her latest treatment, so she was at her pinnacle of alertness.

"What are you doing here?" Abe asked.

"Oh, hi, Abe, don't have time to talk," she replied. "I'm here to let these people know that the food is atrocious! If they don't do something to improve it, I plan to organize the patients to demonstrate."

SOMETIME DURING THE SUMMER at Carrier Clinic, my mother discovered she was pregnant. She had come home on a weekend pass and been with my father. Years later, I'd learn that by then my parents' sex life was practically nonexistent, so perhaps she reached for him in a desperate need of comfort, or maybe she hoped that if they connected sexually, he'd relent and help her get out. When the psychiatrists found out, they had a conference with my father and mother. The doctors were adamant: She was not competent, not in a state to have another child. My mother wanted that baby, but she went for the abortion, beaten. She was taken by ambulance to a hospital, where they dilated her and scraped her uterus. That summer, I lost my chance for a sister or brother.

After the abortion, more electroshocks. She had one after the other—until they had given her eighteen. But she was not cured. In fact, she was more severely depressed than ever. They could do no more for her because electroshock was the only treatment at Carrier Clinic. That fall of 1958, she was transferred to a private mental hospital in upstate New York, about two hours from our house.

Chapter 4. University Heights

BEFORE SHE MET MY FATHER, my mother was feeling age pressing against her with its looming horror of spinsterhood. At twenty-seven, she was living in her parents' attic. She had moved back home after a brief, failed marriage to her college boyfriend. Since her return, she had immersed herself in photography, spending hours in the basement darkroom she'd set up during high school.

One day, her sister, Rita, called. "Gloria, come to dinner tonight. Monte is bringing this guy Abe over after the Rutgers football game."

"Nah, I'm in the middle of a good book."

"Oh, come on, Glor! He's supposed to be a nice guy, and *really* smart. He's getting a doctorate in chemistry."

My mother pushed herself against her own reluctance. "Oh, what the heck, okay."

After that, Gloria and Abe started going out. They had quite a bit in common: Both were children of Jewish immigrants, both were first in their families to go to college, both were science majors and lovers of music and art. Their dates evolved from awkward to companionable. They wandered the Museum of Modern Art, went to free concerts in Central Park, sometimes splurged on the symphony. He made no moves to kiss. Neither did she.

When Abe met Gloria, his experiences with women consisted of a few disastrous interludes during his military service in World War II. Short, terribly shy with girls, and cerebral, he'd met his first girlfriend on weekend leave from the army. He'd gone to a concert and fallen asleep, and was startled awake when an attractive, young woman in the next seat poked him and smiled. They started dating. Once, they took a boat ride up the Hudson River, necking against the deck rail, wind in their hair. He felt wildly exhilarated, dizzy almost. But when she wrote and suggested he rent them a hotel room for the night, he was so terrified he never wrote her back.

He met another woman as his unit was in training to ship out to Japan, and they became engaged. There was one condition: She insisted that he wear Adler's Elevated Shoes to pump up his height. He went as far as going to the shoe store and trying them on. As he clomped around the store, the thought of living like that was humiliating. *I'd be living a lie*, he said to himself. When he told her he wouldn't wear them, she called off the engagement. He left for Japan with a stunned heart.

With Gloria, Abe didn't run into the same problems: At five foot two, she was slightly shorter than he was, and she'd been married, meaning she'd had sexual experiences, and could show him what to do.

Gloria pondered: Here was Abe, a nice guy, a decent, educated guy. As someone to marry, he seemed her best bet. She knew he was shy, and a virgin. She invited him to her attic, where she lit candles and put Frank Sinatra on the portable record player. She took his hand, and they rolled onto her twin bed. The act was simple and quick, without lingering foreplay or delighted exploration.

A few days later, Gloria blurted, "So, what are your intentions? What do you plan to do with me?"

Abe stared at her, and then stammered, "Well . . . um . . . I guess I'll ask you to marry me."

"Okay," she said. It was done.

A few weeks later, during a classical concert, Gloria stared over at Abe in the dim light of the hall, assaulted by a panic of second thoughts. His head tipped forward as he nodded, half-asleep, his glasses having slipped partway down his nose. *What the hell have I done?*

The next weekend, she drove alone to a Jewish resort in the Catskill Mountains where singles gathered. She flirted with men over breakfast, at the pool, in the bar at night. But she found no one that she felt any real connection with, and she returned home, resigned.

GLORIA DIDN'T WANT A BIG deal made about the wedding, her second. They invited no friends, and had no reception. Their only witnesses were her sister, Rita, and Rita's husband, Monte, Abe's younger sister, Sophie, and both sets of parents. Afterward, the group ate dinner at a nearby restaurant.

The humid summer air was stifling as Gloria and Abe checked into a Newark motel on their wedding night. Fans were blowing in the lobby. It wasn't until they got to their room and unlocked the door to a blast of heat that they realized their terrible error: They'd never checked whether the motel was air-conditioned. They turned on the ceiling fan, which circulated the steamy air round and round.

Just before clicking the bedside light off, Abe had reached over, tentatively, and touched Gloria's shoulder. "It's too damn hot for anything," she said. He pulled his hand back. They lay on their backs in the motel bed with the lights out, naked and sweating.

Sleep was impossible. The hours ticked by. In Gloria's chest, a heavy weight gathered. She thought of her mother's bitterness about being stuck with a husband she considered an uneducated Polish greenhorn, and beneath her. She hadn't made her mother's mistake: Abe was bright and educated. But she felt no spark. His insecurity, the thing that had made him so reachable, now repelled her. Rage at her stupidity collected along with her sweat.

At 4:00 AM, Gloria announced in the sweltering dark, "Let's get the hell out of here!" They threw back the sheet and gathered their things. For their honeymoon they were going to Tanglewood in Massachusetts, where the Boston Symphony played outdoor concerts.

They rented a housekeeping cabin in a row of dilapidated motel bungalows. For their first dinner, Gloria was inside making a salad as Abe leaned over a hibachi on the cabin's porch, grilling a steak. He stepped inside for a moment to grab a potholder. As he came back out, he caught a blur of movement. A scruffy mutt was trotting across the lawn, steak in its mouth. "Shit!" he yelled. *This thing is just going from bad to worse.* His shoulders sagged with yet another failure

The best moments of the honeymoon were the concerts, the great swell of music uplifting them. The worst were their nights in bed. My mother offered my father no further assistance after that first time. She lay there, waiting for him to act, her frustration that he wasn't satisfying her more and more apparent. Gloria's angry disappointment and Abe's sense of inadequacy pooled in the bed's hollow between them.

After the honeymoon, they moved into University Heights, where, as a GI, my father was eligible for married-student housing. Two-unit wooden cottages formed a rectangle around a common grassy area. In the evenings, they gathered with the other chemistry students and their wives, dipping cubes of French bread into pots of fondue, and getting smashed on alcohol my father distilled on the sly in the school lab.

The congeniality of their community did nothing to warm my parents' private life. They had furnished their new place in part by borrowing an interior decorator friend's professional discount to purchase a high-quality bed and couch. The bed was comfortable, but each night, they turned away from each other to sleep. After a celibate year, they decided it was time for a child, and they made the effort. Gloria became pregnant with me.

GLORIA'S YOUNGER BROTHER, Marvin, was the person she loved more than anyone else. Marvin was living an artist's life as an apprentice at Taliesin, Frank Lloyd Wright's school of architecture. Since childhood, he and my mother had been artistic oddballs. As teens they went together every week into New York City and bought cheap standing-room tickets at the Metropolitan Opera House, visited Manhattan art museums, or lined up for two-for-one tickets to the ballet and Martha Graham.

Just two weeks after giving birth, my mother left me with my father for ten days and went to visit Marvin. It was the first of her leavings of me.

Dad had just completed his PhD and was home full-time before starting a new job. He quickly learned how to diaper me, rock me, and bottle-feed me. Like a duckling, I imprinted the smell of his neck, the feel of his hands, his voice singing me lullabies.

Two months after that visit, Marvin was killed by a drunk driver. After the funeral, relatives and friends filled my grandparents' house for the week of sitting shiva, the Jewish mourning ritual, but my grandparents would not speak the name of their only son, or allow my mother to, either, as if naming him might shatter their hearts in a million pieces. The grief that filled my mother flowed through the bottle she held to my nursing mouth.

As my parents were driving home from the week of sitting shiva, my mother burst out, "Abe, you must go back to school to become an architect!" For once, my father found his voice, and refused. "Absolutely not, Gloria, that's crazy! I can't become Marvin."

Instead, they petitioned Frank Lloyd Wright to design them a house, asking for one of his scaled-down models adapted for the middle class. They wrote to the elderly Mr. Wright using the combination of my mother's maiden name and my father's surname, in the hopes that "Bachman" would remind him of their connection to Marvin. He was absorbed in work on the Guggenheim Museum, but eventually responded to their request for a modest design, "My dear Wilsons: I suppose I am still here to try to do houses for such as you."

When the plans arrived, my parents sent several letters, pleading for changes to make it less expensive. Finally, new plans removed a basement, and they felt they could proceed. They had already bought a plot of land in Millstone, a tiny colonial-era New Jersey town not far from American Cyanamid, the company where my father had begun work as a research chemist.

My parents hired three Italian masons, two Dutch carpenters, and a German father-son crew of electricians. They rented an apartment right around the corner from the lot. My mother did the bookkeeping for the project—switching the materials for one wall of the main living room from brick to cement blocks to fit their budget.

On nights and weekends, my father climbed a scaffold and sealed and stained the mahogany boards the carpenters had erected that day. Now and then, he paused and looked down at the two story-high living area, overtaken by awe. *Holy shit, I'm doing this, creating a work of art! Incredible, I'm part of it!*

DURING THE YEAR THE HOUSE was under construction, Gloria met with a psychiatrist. She felt hopeless with failure. Her sorrow was leaden, the weight of her disappointment like stones in her belly. As the futility of her marriage became more and more obvious—there would never be any passion—she told herself, *Let's not pretend anymore.* Since they had a child, she had no intention of leaving.

One day, she said to Abe, "Let's stay married, but live like brother and sister."

Abe stared, mouth open, numb with hurt. The shock of this truth, so stark. A memory came to him: He was fifteen, working at Cohen's Rumanian Restaurant as a busboy, where his father worked as headwaiter. A waitress beckoned to him as he was walking past her with a tray. She leaned close and whispered, "Your mother is not so good to your father." He understood this to mean that his mom had stopped having sex with his dad, who for years had been sleeping on the couch.

Abe thought about leaving Gloria, but he couldn't imagine losing his only child. When his mother had kicked his father out of the bedroom, his dad had stayed. The shame of his failure burned in his chest. Already withdrawn, he stayed, and retreated further.

As the construction of the house neared completion, my mother arranged to sell her sister Rita their double bed. She planned to replace the marital bed with two twins.

On moving day, my parents set up the twin beds in a house of mahogany and glass, a house of beauty and light, filled with estrangement and regret.

Chapter 5. Millstone

OUR ULTRA-MODERN HOUSE, with its flat roof—wedged between two pre-Revolutionary colonial houses—looked as out of place as my Jewish parents felt in this small town, populated largely by the Protestant descendents of Dutch settlers. Only fifty miles from teeming, multicultural Manhattan, the center of 1950s Millstone, all four blocks of it, was frozen in a colonial time warp, oblivious that it was poised on the edge of changing demographics.

Along the uneven slate sidewalks there still remained white wooden hitching posts for horses, while the town boasted the oldest working blacksmith shop in the United States. Directly across from our house on Main Street stood the Hillsborough Reformed Church. In its front yard, the town's namesake rested in the grass—a waist-high gray boulder with a hollow depression in its top for grinding grains. A bronze plaque read: "THIS MILLSTONE WAS FOUND ON THE JACOB VAN DOREN FARM 1000 FEET SOUTH OF THIS CHURCH, ON THE SITE OF A LARGE INDIAN VILLAGE." The plaque left unnamed that village's native people, the Lenni Lenape. Of their disappearance—whether they were massacred, relocated, or died from exposure to European germs—nothing was ever said.

IN SMALL-TOWN MILLSTONE, GOSSIP flew like dandelion spores, yet the burn of history went unspoken. My parents had purchased the vacant lot in 1953, two years before the house was built, since Frank Lloyd Wright always required that a structure be designed for its site. In Millstone, they discovered a prime lot right in the center of town. The property had a blackened hole, the charred remnants of the basement of a historic inn that had burned down in 1928.

One afternoon, several years after we moved into our house, elderly Mr. Brezniak, a Slovak, who felt a common bond with Dad as an outsider, told him the story of the old inn's fire. Dad and the old man were alone in his little grocery store, but even so, Mr. Brezniak looked out the front window to make sure no one was about to enter, and lowered his voice.

One early morning before dawn, he was driving down Main Street in his truck, loaded with vegetables that he grew on his farm on the town's outskirts. As he drove past the inn, orange flames lit the dark sky. Several men were dancing around the incinerating inn, roaring with laughter, their heads flung back. He thanked God they were too caught up to notice him witnessing their act of destruction. The vacant and decrepit inn had been bought by a Jewish couple who were renovating it. They were just about to move in and reopen the inn for business. Those men were making sure no Jews moved into town.

No one attempted to burn our house down. But one morning, during the year our house was being built, my father found these words scrawled on the dust of his trunk: "Dirty Jews—Get out of town."

My parents never spoke to me about the hatred someone's finger had etched onto Dad's car. Just as I never told them that now and then on the school playground at recess a boy would come up to me and hiss, "You Jews killed Christ!"

We had our own defense. Unlike our neighbors' colonial houses that brightly faced the street with their open-shuttered windows, our house was set back from the road. A long curved driveway led to the front of the house, where a windowless cement-block facade squatted fortresslike against the intruding world while the back of the house opened to acres of light and green.

On that back side, an open living space was framed by a two-story wall of floor-to-ceiling glass, interspersed with several tall French doors leading to a patio. From within, the view shimmered with green foliage: A lawn edged with mulberry, apple, and pine trees sloped to a woods of tall black walnut trees, maples, and oaks. Through the middle of the woods, a path led to the river, where we had a dock and a tethered rowboat.

It was a life facing nature, turned away from community. My parents played classical music on the Heathkit record player my father had assembled. Every night, in order to go to sleep, I needed my lullaby: Bach's Brandenburg Concerto No. 5 played full blast on the living room hi-fi so I could hear it in my bedroom. I lay in bed with my door open as the record spun, washed by the rhythmic beat of the violins, their frenetic optimism lulling me.

Even at five, I sensed that we were different from our neighbors, and that difference seemed better. We were more elevated and cultured, and I felt lifted, wrapped in the protection of superiority.

We had lived in the house two years the day it all shattered. The day my mother held my father's rifle to her head and pulled the trigger.

Chapter 6. School Days

WITH MOM GONE, EACH day after the school bus dropped me off there was a gap of two unsupervised hours before Dad arrived home from work. Dad's first attempt to cover that gap was to hire thirteen-year-old Judy Gifford to baby-sit me. It didn't last a week. For the first couple days, I went over to the Giffords' after school, but I didn't like their house because it smelled like cat pee and Judy's younger sister was mean and teased me.

Dad then said that all I had to do was stop over at the Giffords', a half-block from our house, and report to Judy my plans, and after that I was free to go home to play by myself. Although I was barely seven, having to check in with Judy offended me. If Mom wasn't there to take care of me, I would allow no one else to. *I can take care of myself,* I thought fiercely. For several days, I didn't show up at Judy's, running from the school bus straight to our backyard. She gave up the job in disgust, and my father relented.

We made a new arrangement. As soon as I got home, I went into the front hall, where the black rotary phone sat on an end table, and called my father at the lab. Once I checked in, I would go up to my room and play with my plastic palomino horse, making up elaborate tales while I cantered him over my bedspread.

As time went on, my father arranged for me to stay after school with different families who had kids my age. For a while, I went to a family out on River Road after school, but Dad stopped letting me go there after the father was charged with shooting his rifle at some neighbor kids who were pestering him.

Over time, I stayed with quite a few families. I watched the mothers.

Ann's mom was a school bus driver. On the days I went to stay with them, after school, I boarded her mom's bus to go home with Ann instead of to my own house. Ann lived on a dairy farm out in the rolling land beyond the encroaching tract homes of Hillsborough. We would ride through the flatlands, dropping kids off at their pastel ranch homes until the bus was empty of all but Ann and me. Then it was like we got our own special ride in the big bus. I loved to watch her mom's back as she drove, the decisive pull of her shoulder and arm as she reached for the long metal handle and opened and closed the squeaky bus door.

At last, we would pull into their driveway and park the yellow bus in the roundabout in front of the barn, next to the green John Deere tractor. Ann and I spent the afternoons running and playing in the weathered red barn or in the sorghum fields behind their house.

Once, we were exploring the barn. All the cows were still out grazing in the pasture. The pungent odor of cow manure and hay filled the dimly lit barn as we clambered among the metal milking stations. I climbed up on top of a metal gate. I sat on the top bar, one leg dangling on each side, and then I looked down, anticipating my descent. It seemed so high up. "Ann," I whimpered, "I'm stuck! I can't get down."

"Aw, come on," Ann replied, squinting up at me.

I started to cry. "Go get your mom, get her!"

I can still remember her mom's arms reaching up to grab me down, the salty smell of her neck as I clung to her chest, my legs around her waist. The feel of her hand, gently patting my back. "See, you're fine now."

THE SCHMITZ GIRLS, all four of them, had long hair, and they all wore it in the same style: parted in the middle with a single long braid dangling down their back. They were a big family—four girls and one boy—and we loved to play hide-and-seek and tag in the woods behind their house.

Sometimes, I stayed overnight. I shared a lower bunk bed with Nancy, who was my age. In the morning, Mrs. Schmitz placed a stool in the middle of the living room. One by one, she called each daughter in turn. They sat on the stool while their mother combed their hair with a bristly brush. First, Mrs. Schmitz would brush the hair, then carefully divide it in three sections, braid the three plaits together, and secure the end with a stretchy band with two colored balls attached. I watched from the living room doorway, my chest tight, silenced and riveted by the crackle of static and the repeated strokes of mothering.

MY SITUATION WAS TABOO IN so many ways: a mother gone, and what had happened to her. I talked about it at first. Once, standing next to the metal jungle gym at recess, I repeated to a girl what Dad had told me. I told her matter-of-factly, "My mom's in a hospital, but it's not her body that's sick, it's her head. The doctors are fixing her." She stared at me, her eyes wide, mouth open. I felt I'd made some terrible mistake. A chill of shame overcame me: Mom's condition was not like having a broken leg; something bad was wrong with her.

Over time, I would learn other words to describe my mother's condition. No one shouted them at me. Instead, like radio waves, the words hung in the air, unseen and ever-present: crazy, nutcase, loony, mad, psycho, mental, wacko, bonkers. There was no end to the names.

Chapter 7. Atlantic City

THE SUMMER AFTER MY mother left, my father drove me to Atlantic City so I could spend the break from school with his parents. We drove down the Garden State Parkway, stopping for lunch at Howard Johnson's halfway through the two-hour drive, where I devoured a plate of fried clams, slathered with ketchup. "Hey, Ketchup Kid! Ready to go?" Dad asked, when I was down to the last clam. I picked up the clam with my fingers and popped it in my mouth, nodding at him.

Our lunch stop and the sights along the way were familiar from all the visits Mom, Dad, and I had made several weekends every summer. Only now, instead of Mom, I was sitting in the front seat next to Dad as he slowed the car to throw a quarter in the Garden State tollbooths. I gazed at the unending bank of oaks and maples and sycamores lining the road, until those woods finally gave way to the stunted South Jersey Pine Barrens, then the marshland and causeways leading to Atlantic City. As we approached the city skyline, I leaned my head out the open window and inhaled the sea air.

My grandparents owned a kosher dairy restaurant a block inland from the famous wide Atlantic City boardwalk. I loved the sight of the pink neon sign blazing Wilson's Dairy Restaurant in the front window, as if we Wilsons were famous. In truth, that family surname was barely a generation old, since my grandfather had anglicized "Viloshin" after he and my grandmother arrived at Ellis Island, the end of their flight from the pogroms and upheaval of Bolshevik Russia.

In America, things had not gone that well. Grandpa Isaac had studied to be a concert violinist in his hometown in the Ukraine, but in the United States, he could never find a job in an orchestra. Once, I had asked Grandpa to play the violin for me. We went into my grandparents' bedroom and he took his violin down from a high shelf in the closet, gently opened the case, and began to move the bow back and forth across the strings. The notes had a rough, sawing edge. He put down the violin and wept. I never heard him play again.

WILSON'S WAS IN A SMALL, narrow storefront with an apartment above it where my grandparents lived. It was a mom-and-pop operation: My grandmother was the cook, my grandfather the waiter. There was a second waiter for the lunch and dinner shifts, a man with a huge belly who always seemed to be sweating. During the summer, a skinny old Ukrainian man with a sunken chest sat outside the kitchen door on a stool in the alley, peeling potatoes for the latkes. Summer was the height of tourism at the shore, and my grandparents worked seven days a week. My grandmother rose at 5:00 AM to begin cooking huge pots of split pea and chicken noodle soup, and to make preparations for the breakfast rush. They ended their workday at 10:00 PM.

During the day, I would be on my own. My grandparents were raised in a world where kids were expected to be independent. At seven years old, I was one year older than my father had been when he started taking the streetcar by himself in Philadelphia.

Before Dad left, he made sure I knew how to walk the back way to the boardwalk. We traced the route together: out the back door of the restaurant kitchen into the alley, around the corner on the sidewalk, and up the ramp to the boardwalk. "You don't have to cross any streets," he said, "so you'll be okay." I stood on the sidewalk and waved goodbye as Dad drove away, my throat tight.

IN THE MORNINGS, I WOKE in the upstairs apartment to the distant clanks of dishes from below. Opening the apartment door at the top of the stairs, I inhaled the warm buttery smells of frying eggs, potato pancakes, and cheese blintzes. I stumbled half-asleep down the stairs and into the small dark kitchen, where Grandma was furiously juggling fry pans, her tiny body dwarfed by the massive cast-iron industrial stove. She looked a bit like a bug: a round, thick middle with spindly legs and arms. I watched her hand beat some eggs and scramble them in a pan, or drop spoonfuls of potato latkes into sizzling oil. Then I wandered out to the restaurant. I sat at an empty table, and Grandpa came to take my order, just like I was a real customer. When he brought me scrambled eggs, he would solemnly plop down a bottle of Heinz ketchup without my asking.

After breakfast, I would go out through the back alley to the boardwalk. I stayed there all day, just running back to the restaurant for lunch and dinner. I was forbidden to swim alone, so that left me the boardwalk to amuse myself. On the boardwalk, there was endless activity. The loud voices of the hawkers, selling cotton candy, popcorn, and saltwater taffy, were backdrop to the swirling mix of working-class tourists in shorts and T-shirts, and wealthy promenaders who came out of the massive grand hotels, the women wearing cardigans with rhinestone clasps and fox stoles.

My father had taught me how the carny men who ran the penny arcade would drop the change in your hand, and then palm some of it back. His boardwalk survival tip was "always count your change." Armed with this knowledge, I felt worldly and self-sufficient, unlike the dumb tourists. But because I had only a small allowance, I mostly stood and watched people at the carnival booths shooting guns at moving targets or throwing balls into point-bearing baskets and collecting their stuffed animals.

Sometimes I would wander out to one of the amusement piers, the Million Dollar Pier or the Steel Pier. I'd watch the kids smash each other in the bumper cars, or look on as brothers and sisters clambered onto the Ferris wheel, aching with a terrible loneliness.

Most local kids ran around together in groups and seemed completely unapproachable. Once, I played with a girl my age who was also by herself. We walked underneath the boardwalk and sat on the cool sand, using discarded Popsicle sticks as dolls in stories we created. She said she lived on Atlantic Avenue, just a couple blocks from the beach. After that, I looked for her every day, but I never found her again.

I became a regular at certain arcade booths, just standing and staring. Often, I tried to look especially waiflike, mournfully frowning, eyes big with an unspeakable sorrow. I was sure that after days of this pose, one of the barkers would recognize me for the orphan I was. I imagined that he would suddenly lean over and say, "Do you want to play for free, little girl?" but no one ever did.

Chapter 8. Bellyache

IT STARTED WITH A bellyache at school. My second-grade teacher sent me to the nurse, who took my temperature and called my father. He had to leave work since he was now my sole caregiver. Dad took me to Dr. Chase's office, who immediately pronounced that I needed to be taken to the hospital.

At the hospital, another doctor in a white coat pushed on my belly. "Does it hurt here, or here?" I almost threw up when he pressed on me.

"Her appendix could rupture," the doctor told my Dad. "We need to operate right away." Dad squeezed my hand as I was wheeled on a gurney into a room with bright lights. A big black mask came down over my face. I woke with a horrible taste in my parched mouth. Dad leaned over and wet my lips with a washcloth. "I know you're thirsty, honey, but you're not allowed to drink anything."

During the night, I dozed and woke, startled in between nurses' rounds by strange noises: beeps, feet scuffing the floor, wheels rolling down the hall, and the astringent smell of disinfectant. Light from the hall came in through my partially open door, and I clenched my free hand around the cold metal of my bed rails to brace myself against the pain.

In the morning, Dad was there. "A special visitor is coming to see you today," he told me. "It's a surprise. Your visitor will be here at one o'clock." Dad went off to work, leaving me to wonder. I had no idea who might be coming. Perhaps Aunt Rita or one of the neighbor ladies. At noon, a nurse brought my lunch of chicken bouillon and orange Jell-O. When she pressed the button on the bed to tilt me up, I yelped from the sharp stabbing in my side.

After lunch, I watched the clock, ears tuned to the door, waiting for my visitor. Each minute of the afternoon pulsed slowly through sixty seconds as I anticipated who was coming. One ten, one thirty-three, two o'clock. At two thirty, I heard my door swing open.

My mother stood in the doorway, "My baby, how are you?"

My mouth fell open. I glared at her.

She was wearing a heavy wool overcoat, and her hair was ruffled, like she'd been in a big wind. Her face was puffy, and she hesitated on the threshold. She staggered a little as she came toward the bed, bending over to peer at me.

I was furious, could barely look at her. All that waiting. It had never occurred to me that she would come, that she *could* come, from the mental hospital.

"Dad said someone was coming to visit at *one!*"

"I'm sorry, honey. I had to get special permission. I had to take a train, but the driver didn't get me to the station in time for that train."

I was mute with rage. I had no words, no understanding of my truncated heart, my child's thwarted longing for a mom able to give comfort, or how I had clamped down against hoping for the impossible. I turned my face from my mother, would not look at her again. I could feel her hand on my brow, fluttering there briefly. I turned my head farther away. I heard the creak of the chair as she sat next to the bed, speaking words that did not penetrate.

She sat quietly for a while. I may have drifted to a half-sleep. I startled awake to her deep sigh, her lips brushing my forehead, the whispered words "I have to leave now, sweetie; I have to go back," and the sound of the door closing as she left the room.

Chapter 9. Life with Dad

ON WEEKENDS, DAD AND I made homemade TV dinners using aluminum pans we had saved from Swanson's frozen meals. Often, we made meatloaf by squishing breadcrumbs into cold hamburger beef. We boiled and mashed potatoes, and defrosted a carton of peas. We'd slice the meatloaf and spoon the potatoes and peas into the triangular sections of the silver pans, cover the dinners with foil, and freeze the week's supply. It felt good, helping Dad get ready for the week.

Our groceries came free from Grandpa Isidor, Mom's father. Every weekend he delivered a box of food from his corner grocery store in South Orange. Money and time were tight for Dad, with the hospital bills and being a single parent. I knew Grandpa was arriving by the heavy rumble of our driveway gravel churning under the wheels of his big green delivery van with its gold letters proclaiming Bachman's Grocery: Quality Meats and Produce. Grandpa never said much, and he didn't stay. He would just carry the box inside, nod at Dad, hug me with his thick butcher's arms, and leave.

One moment, I would be enfolded in his clothes, smelling of pipe tobacco, and the next he was gone.

MOM FIRST WENT TO the mental hospital in spring. As the days warmed, in the evenings after supper, Dad and I would meander down the path through our backyard woods to the little Millstone River that ran along the back of our property. The river was narrow and muddy. Trees leaned out over the water from its banks.

Dad had made a floating dock out of empty oil drums overlaid with planks, and guy wires tethered it to the bank. Our aging wooden rowboat was tied to the dock. Sometimes, Dad and I clambered into the rowboat, Dad at the oars, me in the stern, bailing the slow leak of water. We rowed jaggedly upriver a ways, then turned around and drifted back. I trailed my hand in the water and looked at the ducks skidding to a water landing.

One evening, we pulled up to the dock. Night was coming, but I didn't want to leave the river world. It wasn't a thought, just a reluctance in my body. Climbing out of the boat and onto the dock, my feet dragged against going back to a house filled with the echoes of no Mom. The first fireflies blinked over the water. Dad lingered with me on the dock, shining his flashlight into the shallows, illuminating the tadpoles and minnows. There was a loud splash. "Look!" Dad said, pointing to just beyond the riverbank. A muskrat's head, smooth with wet fur, poked above the water as he dog-paddled toward midriver in the quickening darkness.

My father had taught me to swim in the river when I was five, holding me around my belly, showing me the churning movements of arms and legs, how to turn my head to breathe. Dad was a great swimmer, having grown up at the Jersey shore. His prowess led him to the swim team in high school, and he passed his confidence on to me. The river was my second home. Later, I was puzzled by my suburban cousins' reactions as we stood in our bathing suits at the muddy water's edge. I had led them proudly to my river. "Yuck! It's dirty! You've gotta be kidding! We're not swimming in that!"

Dirty? To me the river was a living entity, its water rich with mud and water creatures and the animals who lived along its shores. They were part of that forest-river world, the other world behind our house that seemed so far away from the town. It was that magical place that me and Dad and the animals all inhabited together.

IN SEPTEMBER, JUST AS Mom was transferred to a mental hospital in upstate New York, I started second grade and Dad was elected to the Millstone town council, the first Democrat since anyone could remember. Dad said that since World War II had ended, times were changing, even in such a Republican stronghold. Some assertive part of my father had emerged when Mrs. Gifford, an ardent Democrat, had exhorted him to run. In fact, civic life was an arena where he was confident. To win votes, Dad had walked door to door, talking to the neighbors and shaking hands. He said the old-timer Republicans never did that, just figured they'd be reelected. Sometimes I went with him. Dad gabbed in a friendly, earnest way to whomever was home.

The first Christmas after Dad was elected, we received an invitation to the yearly Christmas party at the Stevenses' house. Mr. Stevens was some big shot at Squibb Pharmaceuticals, and his house was the grandest in town.

On the day of the party, Dad and I walked through the gate in the white picket fence and up the snowy walk. We waited at the front door for someone to answer the doorbell, staring at a holly wreath with red berries. From inside came the muffled plunks of a piano and voices singing "We Three Kings."

The door swung open, and we stepped into the living room. We'd never been to anything like this, but it was a scene made familiar from picture books at my school, and Christmas advertising images. Christmas cards lined the Stevens' fireplace mantel, stockings hung above a fire, and an enormous Christmas tree stood in one corner. The guests were gathered around the grand piano, where Mrs. Stevens was playing carols. Everyone held glasses of eggnog and was singing along. We joined the group.

I loved to sing, and of course had learned all the carols in school over the years. My parents had never said I couldn't sing them, but somehow I felt there was a line I shouldn't cross: I would not say the word "Christ" or "Jesus." This meant that I would be singing along with gusto, and then suddenly mumble or drop out on the forbidden word. Here, among all these tall adults, no one seemed to notice a child going mute in the midst of a song.

I looked over at Dad. He was belting out "Silent Night" along with the rest, word for word: *Christ the savior is born; Chri-ist the savior is born.*

THE FOLLOWING SPRING, AS a present for my eighth birthday, Dad brought a puppy home from work. Dad's coworker had a scientist wife who worked at a drug company where they used dogs in experiments. She'd rescued one puppy from a lab litter for Dad.

"What should we name him?" Dad asked as he handed me the ball of short brown, black, and white fur. I hugged him to my chest and smelled his puppy breath. With no hesitation, I said, "Happy."

I was naming him after my favorite stuffed animal, the battered tan dog.

Happy was a foxhound. As he grew, his hunting instincts emerged; he loved to root around, nose close to the earth. Often, he would dig up moles from our backyard, legs frantically pawing the earth, dirt flying. Once he caught it, Happy would hold the mole gently in his teeth and then flip it in the air, breaking its neck. I felt sorry for those little moles, blind to the sun, flying into the light, and sometimes yelled at Happy to *quit that,* but I must admit, it was a sight to see.

The following summer, when Happy was one, Dad and I were swimming in the river. We waded in from our next-door neighbors' yard because they had a sandbar that made getting in easier. I was near the shore when I heard Happy's deep low growl, and I scrambled out of the river. His warning sound made my bones quiver, but the brambles along the river edge were too thick and I couldn't see him. I was wearing only my wet bathing suit, leaving my exposed legs too vulnerable to go plunging through the blackberry thorns. Then I heard another sound—the snarls of some strange, unseen animal—followed by a yelp that sent my breast pounding: Happy's cry of pain. What animal had he cornered? "Happy, here boy, *COME HERE!*" I called desperately.

I looked up to see the Reformed Church minister approaching. It was his yard, two over from ours, where Happy was engaged in battle. The minister wasn't wearing his black suit with the white collar today, just an ordinary shirt and work pants.

"Reverend Reverend (I wasn't sure what you called a minister, but it was the closest I could think of). My dog's fighting some animal . . . can you see?" The minister pushed his way partly into the undergrowth, disappeared for a couple minutes, and then reappeared from the bushes. "Your dog's cornered a coon. Nothing to be done. They fight to the death, you know."

The world was spinning, trees and sky, and then I steadied myself with hate, glaring at the minister. *You coward,* I thought, *you're not even going to try to help!* I wheeled then, running to the riverbank to Dad. He hadn't heard Happy's bark when I had taken off to see what that sound was. I hadn't stopped to explain.

I yelled to him about Happy's being in a fight with a raccoon. He treaded water and yelled back, "Run to the Jansens' and ask them for their hunting rifle. Tell them to put the safety on and bring it to me."

My hummingbird heart thrummed as I ran, dripping river water. Breathless, my tale spilled out to Mrs. Jansen. The small, blond woman bent her face close to mine, then yelled for her husband Malcolm. He was her opposite, a tall giant who strode into the kitchen on his long legs. "We can't give a rifle to an eight-year-old girl!" she said, frowning toward him, not looking at me.

"Please, please, it's for my dad, I'll be careful, I'll be real careful," I pleaded. *My Happy, don't let him die.*

"Jenny, go get her the gun from the cabinet," Malcolm commanded. "I'll put the safety on. Abe won't let her get hurt."

The rifle was almost as long as me. I held it cradled in both arms, hefting the weight that could be my dog's savior. When I got to the brambles, I careened to a halt. Dad was waiting, holding Happy by the collar. "It's okay," he said. Happy looked fine; only a few drops of blood splattered on one side of his face, red against his white muzzle, and I couldn't tell if they were his or the coon's.

I gave Dad the rifle, sank to my knees next to Happy, my face against his neck, inhaling his sweet dog odor. "You bad dog," I cried, muffled, into his coat. I squeezed him tighter. "You bad, bad dog."

Chapter 10. Sweetie

JUST AS I STARTED third grade, the old woman next door, recently widowed, moved out of her big house. When a huge moving van stopped on our street, I stood in our driveway, watching the commotion. A wood-paneled station wagon pulled up behind the moving van; a mom, a dad, and five kids piled out—two girls close to my age and three big teenage boys.

I retreated down our driveway, too shy to meet them. But the next day, when I heard the sound of girls yelling and giggling, I made myself go out and stand by the fence bordering our yards. The sisters stopped their game of tag and came over to the fence to invite me to play with them.

Sharon, eight like me, and Kim, a year older, became my best friends. Dad didn't have to worry anymore about what family I would be staying with after school; I was right next door at the O'Briens' every day when he got home from work.

After school, Kim, Sharon, and I played horses in their backyard. We would drag out three chopped-off sawhorses that their dad stored in the small barn on their property. We faced the low sawhorses, snorting and pawing the ground with our feet, neighing like wild mares and stallions. One by one, we cantered and leapt over the sawhorses. "Naaaaaay," we bellowed after each triumphant leap, tossing our heads back.

On Sundays, Dad and I visited Mom. She'd been moved to the county mental hospital after the insurance ran out. Now, all pretext of a country club setting was completely absent. There was a Plexiglas window in the front nurses' station where visitors were required to hand over any bags to be searched. Then we were buzzed through the locked door. Dad and I walked down a long hall reeking of disinfectant to the ward's common room, which was thick with cigarette smoke. All I remember of my mother on those visits were her eyes: dull and glassy, with drooping eyelids. I never spoke to Kim and Sharon about my visits to the mental hospital, and by some unspoken agreement they never asked about my absent mother.

THAT WINTER, KIM GOT the most incredible birthday present: an actual horse. Sweetie was a chestnut quarter horse, so ancient that her spine was deeply swayback. She was stabled in their barn. After school, the three of us cleaned the stable and gave Sweetie fresh hay, feed, and water, currying her while she docilely chomped her oats. I loved the pungent horse smell as I brushed her, leaning my face close to her warm, brown coat.

Sweetie was so old that Kim's parents said only Kim was allowed to ride her, for fear that if we all took turns, we might give the poor horse a heart attack. Sharon and I would watch mournfully as Kim astride Sweetie disappeared slowly down the path to the river, and then we would go off and play our pretend horse game.

THE NEXT SUMMER, BETWEEN third and fourth grade, Kim, Sharon, and I got the idea of putting on a circus, inspired by the swaybacked Sweetie, who was to be our star attraction. We recruited Barbie, a girl who lived two houses down. Barbie's backyard had the perfect circus setting: a large, flat meadow. Barbie also had a hand-me-down drum majorette costume with a yellow and maroon pleated miniskirt and a tall hat with a grand yellow plume. That outfit earned her the honor of being the ringmaster.

Kim, Sharon, Barbie, and I practiced in Barbie's meadow. We enlisted Cheryl Ann, Barbie's younger sister, to be our percussionist; her job was to beat on a bongo drum with a stick. We made tickets on colored construction paper and walked door-to-door through town, selling them to other kids and a few parents.

The day of the circus we were all in a frenzy, barely able to contain ourselves. "Hurry up! Hurry up!" we yelled to each other as we ran back and forth from the shed to the adjacent meadow, setting up folding chairs in a circle. In Barbie's kitchen, we made two pitchers of Minute Maid frozen lemonade and cooked four pans of Jiffy Pop over her mom's stovetop. The kitchen was thick with the smell of burnt popcorn kernels. Barbie's younger brother, Bob Junior, would be selling our refreshments at a wobbly folding table just outside the circle of chairs.

We each tore home to put on our costumes. I was playing Weary Willie, the sad clown, a hobo in tattered clothing with a forlorn face. I'd seen the famous Emmett Kelly play him at Ringling Brothers Circus one time. Now, I raced in our front door and down the hall into the living room.

Dad had told me Mom would be coming home on a weekend pass, and when I got there, Mom was sitting on the couch.

"Honey, go get your outfit on, and then I'll put on your clown face," Mom said.

I nodded, and bolted up the stairs. Dad had given me an old shirt and pants of his, and had helped me cut the sleeves and legs shorter; then we'd shredded the remaining arms and legs in strips to make a tramp costume. I tucked in the shirt and clipped red suspenders onto the oversize pants to hold them up.

Downstairs, Mom took me into our tiny half-bathroom. She set her lit cigarette in an ashtray balanced on the corner of the sink. Smoke spiraled up in a gray wisp. While I sat on the toilet, she leaned in close. Her hands shook, but she got my frown on okay. I leapt up to stare in the mirror and pop on my red clown nose. Around this mother who'd become a stranger, I stayed withdrawn. "Thanks, Mom," I mumbled as I raced from the house.

BARBIE STOOD POISED in the center of the ring in her drum majorette outfit, her baton raised. "Ladies and gentlemen, we present to you the Greatest Show on Earth! And for our first act we bring you, straight from Barnum and Bailey Circus: Weary Willie!"

I stepped into the ring, and for a moment just looked around. Every seat was filled, and there were even some parents standing behind their kid's chairs. The squirming kids with their hands deep in bags of popcorn got still and stared in my direction. The hush of the audience's attention hit me like an electric charge. I marched to the center, where a bucket waited. I jammed my foot into the plastic bucket, then tried to walk, dragging it along. Giggles erupted around me. I tried to shake the bucket off, tripped, rolled around on the ground, and staggered up with it still on my foot, throwing my hands in the air. From all sides came loud *ha ha has*! Elated, I plunged into a double somersault, then limped off, bucket still attached.

After several other acts came our finale: Kim riding Sweetie bareback. Flutophone blast, drum-banging hailed our pièce de résistance: Kim hoisted herself to kneel on Sweetie's bare back, arms raised triumphantly, while Sweetie walked once around the ring, our spectators clapping and whistling.

All the performers gathered in the center of the ring, grabbed hands, and took our bows. As the audience rose and began milling around, Kim and Sharon and I kept laughing and banging each other on our backs. We had done it!

DURING THE WINTER holiday came terrible news: Mr. O'Brien, Kim and Sharon's dad, was taking a new job in California. It was a mythic place as far away from New Jersey as Oz, and I would lose my friends to the land of Hollywood and orange groves. Kim's parents told her some other horrible news: She couldn't bring Sweetie. They sold Sweetie to another family, along with her gear and the horse trailer. Sharon and I stood on either side of a sobbing Kim, crying ourselves, as we watched Sweetie get loaded into the trailer and hauled away.

Just before Valentine's Day, the moving van pulled up outside their house. Kim and Sharon and I had given each other our Valentine's cards the week before. We stood next to their car, hugging each other and crying, when Mr. O'Brien yelled, "Let's get going!"

I watched the O'Briens pile into their station wagon and head for the sun.

Chapter 11. Mom Returns

THE MOTHER WHO CAME home after more than two years away was terribly altered from the mother I had known, although I could barely remember that mother. I was in the middle of fourth grade when she returned. Her body was a different shape: The slender, petite mom was now fat and puffy from drugs. She was sent home with a pharmacy-load of pills: barbiturates, tranquilizers, and sleeping pills. I learned words like "Miltown," "Librium," "Doriden." She staggered around the house, eyelids drooping, slurring her words when she did speak, but more often silently puffing on a cigarette.

My father knew it was time to put her to bed in the evenings after she'd taken her sleeping pills when she could no longer coordinate bringing the cigarette to her mouth, hitting her cheek or chin with the unlit end.

Some nights I could hear them arguing in their bedroom while lying in the dark in my bedroom. Dad would be pleading, "Come on, Glor, put out the cigarette. You gotta go to sleep now." I could tell he was trying to be nice, but he sounded mad.

"Not yet, Abe, pleeease, jus' one more cigarette," Mom cajoled.

"Jesus Christ, Gloria!" Now he really was mad.

"Jus' one more pu . . ." Mom's voice dropped off as she nodded off.

ONE DAY, I CAME HOME from school to find Mom sitting at the dining table; all her cameras and lenses lay on the table. She had a strange, lost expression, staring at the cameras like she couldn't quite see them.

"Hi, Mom."

She looked up, as if startled out of a daydream. "I'm waiting for the man from the photography shop in Somerville. He's coming to buy my cameras."

I wanted to ask why, but just then there was the crunching sound of a car coming down our gravel driveway. Mom got up.

Before she married Dad, my mother had had two careers: one as a laboratory chemist, the other as a portrait photographer. During the week, she worked in a research laboratory. On the weekends, she worked in her photography studio and darkroom in the basement of her parents' home. After she married Dad, she stopped doing much photography. There were almost no photos of me or Dad.

When Mom was away, I used to look through the cardboard box of her black-and-white photographs stashed in our back room. I was especially intrigued by the ones of Uncle Marvin, the brother Mom had been so close to. In his black turtleneck and beret, he looked like a beatnik artist. I stared at the photos, as if I could learn something of Mom that way.

Mom led the man to the table. I watched him pick up the cameras and lenses and the flash attachments, the wide-angle and telephoto lenses, and examine them one by one. "Nice," he said under his breath, as if he were alone and talking to himself, "Very nice." Then louder, "Mrs. Wilson, I'll give you seventy-five bucks for the lot."

Mom didn't argue, just stood there silently while he counted out the money into her hand.

TOWARD THE END OF fourth grade, I began to brag at school that my family was spending the next year in England. My father had been awarded a research grant to work abroad for a year. The plan was for us all to move to London. I was wild with excitement, imagining that Mom and Dad and I would live in an exotic foreign country with Big Ben and people who talked with funny accents, where everything would be different, including us.

But then Mom began to get worse. She was weak from an increased dosage of pills and stumbling around the house. She began to say she didn't want to go. Mom's psychiatrist called Dad and said he doubted Mom could cope with such change. It was decided: Mom and I would stay in Millstone; Dad would go alone to England. Dad hired a neighbor woman, an elderly widow, to come live with us, to cook and be a companion to Mom.

At the beginning of the summer, Mom and I saw Dad off. He was traveling on the *Queen Elizabeth,* the largest ocean liner in the world. We took the train into New York City, and a taxi to the harbor. At the dock, the gigantic ship loomed with its rows and rows of windows, smoke already rising from its two red smokestacks tipped with black. We went on board with Dad for the hour they let the friends of travelers visit. We wandered the huge ship, along its teak decks, into ballrooms with elaborate wood trim and gilt chandeliers as if on a family outing, as if I wasn't about to lose a father, the one parent who had taken care of me for as long as I could remember.

The deep bass warning whistle blew—*all visitors ashore*. I was numb as Dad hugged me goodbye. Mom took my hand and we walked down the gangplank. We stood on the pier, looking up, and waving. My hand fluttered in the air, as if detached from my body. The tugboats pushed the great ship into the New York harbor until the people on deck became tiny figures.

I kept waving. *Bye, Dad, bye.*

Chapter 12. Alone with Mom

MRS. KELLER, THE WIDOW Dad had hired to live with Mom and me, never showed up. Her adult children talked her out of it. "What if something happens?" they asked. "You'd be held responsible. It's not worth it."

It took two weeks for that news to cross the Atlantic Ocean and reach my father. He left his laboratory at Imperial College and made his way to the Thames, where he sat on a stone barricade, weeping. Then, he paced the London streets. *What to do?* Years later, in my thirties, I confronted him: "How could you have left me there, alone with Mom?" Dad answered, "I was desperate. I was drowning. I would have thrown my own mother to the dogs."

My father left me with a mother I barely knew. During the year he was gone, I formed an intense, fierce attachment with her.

Each night, after my mother took her sleeping pills, she resisted sleep. Even as the medication dragged her under, some fear in her battled against tumbling into her dreams. She sat up in bed, a lit cigarette dangling from her lips as her head began to nod. I sounded just like Dad: "Come on, Mom, put it out!" I'd plead. "Jusss one more puff," she slurred. When I switched off her bedroom light, the burning orange orb of her Tareyton glowed in the dark room. I'd go back, grab the cigarette, and smash it in the ashtray. Sometimes I'd swipe her pack of Tareytons out of reach. "Goddamnit, Mom, no more!"

After Dad left, Mom started sleeping downstairs in the study. Upstairs in my bed I worried about fire, slept with my nostrils flared for the smell of a smoldering mattress. With Mom that far away, I had to listen hard. My body became a tuning fork; even in sleep, my ears stayed alert for the stagger and thud of Mom's falling on the uncarpeted floor in her midnight forays to the toilet. I'd jolt up in response, racing downstairs to haul Mom up off the floor, grabbing her under the armpits. With one of her arms over my shoulder, we'd lurch to the bathroom and back to her bed.

Once under the covers, if Mom was restless or insisting on a cigarette, I started to do something my father had not done: crawl in bed next to her. I bribed her with a promise. "Lie down, Mom. I'll help you get to sleep." She'd turn on her side and I would spoon behind her, stroking her damp, sweaty hair, singing quietly. If I started to doze, I was startled awake as soon as Mom fell asleep. *Your mother has a deviated septum,* Dad had said when I asked about her incredibly loud snoring. Her snores rattled sleep from me. I'd slip out from under the covers and stumble upstairs. So tired.

Back in my bed, the spirals of sleep pulled on me, but trees creaked as the wind came up. The faces of wolves hovered at my second story window, just out of sight. Some part of me knew they weren't real. A branch hit my window, and I stifled a scream. No matter how piercing my yell, I knew Mom would never hear me. She was totally deaf in one ear, and she was sleeping the death sleep of

Doriden. Better to huddle under the covers, clamped and shivering, than to give voice to fear.

DURING THE DAY, MOM was relatively able—sometimes more, sometimes less, depending on what, I never knew. Her daytime medications, the sedatives and tranquilizers, didn't knock her down into staggering oblivion like the nightly sleeping pills. She managed to keep us fed. After school, I came home to my mother's kiss, her welcome of "Hi, darling," and a snack—apple slices with Cracker Barrel cheddar cheese, Pepperidge Farm goldfish, and a glass of milk, or sour cream and blueberries sprinkled with sugar. Then there was my after-school routine of doing homework and a half hour of piano practice, after which I would run over to Barbie's—two houses away—and play until dinner.

When we were alone, the protectiveness I felt toward my mother around others ebbed away. The anger that I tried to bury would erupt, but only at insignificant matters. I hated the noises Mom made when she ate. Her teeth had rotted while she was in the hospital, and the dentist there had extracted all her upper and some lower teeth. She had come home, at thirty-eight, with a full upper set of dentures and a partial bridge. The false teeth clicked as she chewed. Sometimes I'd yell, "What are you, *a pig!?*" When she simply shrugged, or her eyes got moist with tears, I felt terribly guilty. But I couldn't seem to stop my nasty remarks.

Sometimes on the weekends, we would go to the movies in Princeton. Once, Mom and I were breezing along River Road, a windy two-lane. It was a crisp fall afternoon and we were going to a matinee. My mother was in a reasonably good mood, and her driving phobia hadn't kicked in, so I relaxed in the passenger seat of our

Hudson and watched the orange and gold foliage pass by, trailing my hand out the side of the car, feeling the rush of air. As always, my mother was smoking a cigarette. When she was down to the filter, she stabbed it in the ashtray with her right hand, her left hand on the wheel; then, flinging her right arm across her chest, she flicked the butt out the window. This interrupted my reverie because I had to dig another Tareyton out of her purse while she punched in the cigarette lighter.

Princeton's only movie theater stood in the center of the small, neat upper-class town with its Gothic university buildings. It was almost as if a cloak of hush had been draped over the town, an air of restraint epitomized in the muted plaids and dull tans of expensive preppie outfits. It made me feel especially conscious to act right and not stick out.

We parked in the lot behind the theater, stopped in the lobby for refreshments. When the theater lights dimmed, I was swept into the cinema world—the aroma of salty butter, the crunch of popcorn, the sweetness of Coca-Cola, the sound of Raisinets running along their cardboard container into my hand.

After a matinee, there was always the shock to find it still daylight. But that was nothing compared with what Mom and I found when we got to our car. Firemen in their black helmets and yellow raincoats had pulled the back seat onto the parking lot asphalt, and they were just finishing spraying it with fire extinguishers. Stinking black smoke wafted up. The seat was incinerated, and I could see its metal springs poking through the charred padding. Our car was a spectacle, and a cluster of people was gawking in silence.

One of the firemen came over to my mother, as we stood staring at the car seat. "Ma'am, this your car?"

Mom nodded and smiled weakly.

"Did you have a lit cigarette that you didn't put out properly?"

Shame flamed in me, prickling my skin.

"I thought I had," she answered. "I stubbed it out and threw it out the window."

"Well, Ma'am, be more careful next time." He stated the obvious, like my mother was some kind of simpleton. I wanted to escape, disappear. Here we were again, Mom and me, standing out, looking weird. *Is it both of us, or just my mother?*

As the spectators began to drift away, the firemen loaded the charred frame of the seat into its place in the back of our car. The one who had talked to Mom raised his hand to his brim and wiggled his hat at Mom before they left.

"Let's get the hell out of here," Mom said.

ON SATURDAYS, GRANDMA MIRIAM and Grandpa Isidor often showed up, not in Grandpa's green grocery van, but gliding down our driveway in their huge boat of an Oldsmobile. Grandma was too elegant to ride in a van. They always came with groceries from Grandpa's store, and the makings of brunch from Tabachnick's, a Jewish deli near their house.

One Saturday, they bustled in, Grandpa unpacking the groceries into our fridge and freezer, while Grandma set out the spread of lox, bagels, cream cheese, whitefish, pickled herring, potato salad, and coleslaw. Like every visit, Grandma looked Mom over, frowning. Most days, Mom wore a dirty gray sweatshirt over jeans or sweatpants. Grandma prided herself in being a sharp dresser. She encased her fleshy torso in a full-length girdle, over which she wore fitted dresses, always adorned with a necklace and matching earrings. "Why don't you fix yourself up, Gloria?"

Mom glared at her. "We're not going to the opera here. Don't forget, Pop and I are going to work on the yard."

As soon as brunch was over, Mom, Grandpa, and I went outside. Grandpa did the heavier chores: cutting back blackberry vines, bleeding air from the well, chopping firewood from the now-seasoned black walnut tree a groundhog had felled. His bald head would shine with sweat as he swung the axe, splitting logs. Grandpa was not a talker. Once, I had asked what his life had been like, before, in Poland. But all he said was, "We were ignorant peasants. We knew nothing. There's nothing to tell." Now, I found comfort in Grandpa's steady practicality, his silence, the *swish* and *whap* of the axe hitting wood.

Nearby, Mom and I had our own project, planting pachysandra against the front of the house. Mom and I each knelt with our trowels, digging little holes in the earth. Aunt Rita, an avid gardener, had donated the groundcover from her large suburban garden. The pachysandra had fluted, dark green leaves and a single root. Over and over, Mom and I repeated the same action: twisting the root into a tight circle, holding it that way with one hand in the hole while troweling dirt with the other, then, with two hands, leaning into the dirt with the weight of our bodies, pressing it down. It was a boring and soothing task. I daydreamed as we planted, relaxing in the safety of the mundane.

Inside the house, Grandma had a pot roast baking in the oven. While it cooked, she straightened up the disorder of our daily life, the clutter of newspapers left on the floor, the unopened mail. We had an early dinner together, and before she and Grandpa left, she'd look around the tidied-up house and say, "There, isn't that better!" as if all would be well.

SOMETIMES GRANDMA stayed with us overnight. She slept upstairs in my parents' bedroom, which Mom had vacated. I worried that she would hear Mom at night, but Grandma was a sound sleeper. I could creep downstairs and haul Mom back to bed without Grandma ever knowing.

The first overnight, after breakfast, Grandma announced we were going to do the laundry. "Go get your sheets," she told me.

"I don't have any," I told her, smiling.

"What?" she asked.

I told Grandma proudly my ingenious method of bedmaking. On top of my bed, there was an orange corduroy bedspread, looking prim and neat. There were no sheets underneath it. Instead, I slept on top of the orange spread with the comforter over me that I pulled out of the closet just before going to sleep. In the morning, I threw the comforter in a wad back in my closet. My plan meant that I never had to make the bed and no sheets had to be washed.

"Let's go see," Grandma said. Her tight face made my chest clench up.

Upstairs, Grandma had me drag the comforter from the closet and drape it across the bed. As we stared at it together, I suddenly saw how frayed it had become, and a bit blackened. It had been a present from Grandma, and had once been a glowing gold satin, soft as a lamb's nose. My grandmother's horror struck a chord of shame in me, as if she had discovered the secret chaos under the exterior of things—*We're not normal, me and Mom.* And it reinforced my unspoken rule: *Don't bring anyone home, don't let them see Mom.* Suddenly, I saw that I was patching things together, and I didn't know what the hell I was doing.

That morning, Grandma taught me how to make a bed *properly*. She demonstrated how to put a pillowcase on and how to make hospital corners with the top sheet, tucking it just so. But that night, after Grandma went home, I left the sheets on the bed, covered by the bedspread, and resumed my old method. To sleep, I needed that comforter right against my skin.

ONE TIME, GRANDMA stayed with us over a whole weekend. When Grandpa came to pick her up on Sunday, Grandma and I were standing on the red concrete landing outside our front door while Grandpa put her bags in the trunk. Mom was somewhere in the house. I watched Grandpa open the passenger door for Grandma. He revved the engine and I raised my hand to wave goodbye. As their car started up the driveway, something broke loose in me, and I found myself running after their car, screaming, "STOP! COME BACK! STOP!"

Grandpa braked and I ran to Grandma's door. She opened it and looked at me, squinting, her forehead creased. "What is it?"

"Don't go-o-o!" I was crying.

Grandma sounded tired as she said, "Isidor, get my things from the trunk." She got out and patted me on the shoulder. "Don't worry; I'll stay with you."

And for a few days, she did.

EVERY FEW WEEKS, when I reached into our postal box in the Biddle's musty porch that served as the Millstone post office, my hand pulled out a blue envelope with foreign stamps and PAR AVION printed in the lower left corner. *Dad!* My body fluttering, I raced home along the slate sidewalk and in the front door, yelling, "Mom! Mom! A letter from Dad!" I ignored her unsmiling face, her lack of excitement as she took the letter and slowly unfolded it, laying it open on our dining table, where we both leaned over, reading it to ourselves.

Dad's familiar handwriting looping across the blue paper brought an ache to my chest, but his writing was dry and matter-of-fact: He told about his fellow scientists at the research project, his visits to museums, plays, and concerts in London. I tried to picture him at these British haunts, but the images were blurry. We couldn't call him, because he had no phone in his rooming house, and even if he did, international calls cost too much.

Mom and I wrote him back, sharing the aerogram, the thinnest of blue paper that folded into its self-made envelope. I wrote Dad about my science fair project making natural dyes using grapes, walnut bark, and goldenrod pollen; about how I had caught a little sunfish from our dock, watched the beautiful iridescent fish swim in our bathtub, and then brought him back in my pail to his home in the river. But there was one thing I *never* wrote about: how hard things were with Mom. Somehow, I'd gotten that my father didn't want to hear the truth. My job was to protect him from Mom, and Mom from everyone.

RELIGIOUS STUDENTS FROM Zarephath, a nearby evangelical Christian community with its own college, sometimes volunteered to spend time during the day with Mom. They believed in good deeds. The teachers knew my mother from her days studying Latin at their school. The volunteers always left before I got home. Once, I found a remnant from a visit. On the piano, someone had left the sheet music to "Jesus Loves Me."

Apparently that day's volunteer had played Christian hymns for Mom with missionary zeal and encouraged her to sing along.

Chapter 13. Barbie

NOT LONG AFTER MY BEST friends Kim and Sharon left for California, I started spending a lot more time with Barbie.

I didn't like Barbie that much, but I was desperate for a friend. As it turned out, our friendship was easy. Barbie had a physical prowess that surpassed mine, and a fearless streak that pushed me in our adventures. She had a small, compact body, a perky, upturned nose, and nonstop energy. We became adventurers together: building forts in the woods, riding our bikes for miles through the neighboring dairyland. She nimbly crossed logs suspended over streams, and I followed, my quaking legs inching along, my arms out for balance, as she waited for me to catch up. In the summer, I leapt screaming from her family's rope hung from a tree on the riverbank into the Millstone River.

On rainy days, we played board games and cards: Clue, Monopoly, Go Fish. On Halloween, she thought up pranks that I joined: We sat in a tree and dropped water balloons on kids in their Halloween costumes, stifling our giggles as they screamed; we ran a dummy made of old clothes stuffed with newspaper up the post office flagpole. In the fall, we raked leaf mazes and played tag in our creations with her sister and brother, and took turns jumping in a huge pile of leaves. In the winter, we skated on the local pond, racing at each other, joining hands, and spinning in a circle.

The year my father was gone, I tried to never have Barbie over. If she and I had to get something from my house, I would race in and out as fast as possible. I prayed that Mom would be secluded in the back room, out of sight.

At Barbie's, I surrendered to child's play, completely absorbed in Kick the Can or Monopoly, my body tingling from running or my attention focused on the roll of the dice and moving my plastic token. But somewhere in me lived my other life, held in a breathless tension of what couldn't be said: how every night I put my mother to bed, how I fought her to stub out her cigarette, how I hovered all night half-awake, listening for her to fall on her way to the bathroom. My secret, hidden life.

Every now and then, right in the midst of the hardest play—say when I was It, racing after Barbie or her little sister Cheryl Ann—my other self would creep up on me and take me by the throat. Breathless, I'd stop in my tracks, halted by an inexpressible anxiety. "Gotta go," I'd say to a puzzled Barbie.

I'd take off running and wouldn't stop until I'd torn into the house, yelling, "Mom, Mom are you okay?" and she answered me.

Chapter 14. Undertow

I WOKE TO THE SOUND OF knocking coming from somewhere below me. I stumbled out of bed and down the stairs, shivering and flicking on lights as I went. The knocking became pounding, not at the front of the house, but at the back. My heart raced as I neared the door.

I turned on the outside light and looked through the glass of the French door. The light made the snow gleam a cold blue. I opened the door. Our next-door neighbor, Mr. Jansen, was holding my mother, who stood swaying and shivering in her dripping pajamas.

Mr. Jansen was saying something, but at first it was as if a roaring filled my ears. All I could hear was the *creak, creak* of the black walnut trees that lined the path to the river, their tall thin trunks swaying in the winter wind. Then his words finally reached me. " . . . and I found her down at the river; guess she jumped in," he said simply. He was a tall, thin man, and my mother seemed very little huddling hunched and sodden under his arm. He said nothing more, holding her out with his long arms as if offering a gift, launching her toward me. My arms were stiff like two bowling pins as I caught her there inside the doorway, the frigid winter air swirling around us.

I stared at Mr. Jansen. Words formed inside me, filled me. I wanted to ask, *What should I do?*

But Mr. Jansen was backing away. His eyes would not meet mine. My mind was scrambling to think: *Could I ask him to help me put her to bed or give her a bath?* But he was a man; he should not see my mother naked. Silence crackled between us. As he walked away, I would not cry out, *Help!*

INSIDE ME THERE WAS just a cold sensation of tightness, as if all of my muscles had drawn inward, as if my breath were a tiny moth beating its wings in my chest. *Just do whatever has to be done.*

I managed to get my mother upstairs, hauling her with one of her arms over my shoulder, my other arm around her waist. I'd decided to run a warm bath. I dumped her on the toilet and struggled with her to remove the soaked pajamas. Her lips were blue, her teeth chattering nonstop. I didn't know if the hot water would shock her, so I made the bath mildly warm. Pressing her hand on my shoulder, she dipped her foot in, then screamed slurrily, "Isss bloody burning hot!"

I added more cold water. She finally plunked in, her body smacking the bottom of the tub as I lost my grip on her. I gradually added more and more warm water, as she could stand it, until it was a regular hot bath. After she seemed warmed enough, I leaned over and grabbed her under the armpits, helping her steady herself as she lurched out of the tub. I toweled her dry, helped her get on other pajamas, and put her in bed. She lay there, teeth still chattering. I got in next to her and lay spooned against her, willing her my warmth.

THERE IS A PHRASE I clearly remember telling myself in my childhood, repeating it like a mantra, a vow, a motto: "I am so strong, I can get through anything." I had no idea of the cost of such survival, the suppressed longings, the anxiety that became like a second skin. The alternative, to not cope, *to possibly let my mother die,* was too terrifying.

If there was rage, in the moment of crisis it was pushed so far down that I couldn't even feel its simmer. It wasn't until adulthood that the immensity of the desertion occurred to me. My mother had left me, a ten-year-old, alone in a house in the middle of the night in the middle of the winter and jumped into the icy Millstone River. She left no note, not even the barest goodbye. Did my mother even think of me as she plunged herself into a cold death, or was her despair so great it overshadowed all other thoughts?

Chapter 15. Overdose

I SAT, NOT MOVING, in the big overstuffed chair in the silent house. It felt like time had stopped, but the sky was darkening, the shadows of the open curtains deepened across the living room. There was a sound of the front door opening, and a woman's voice called, "Karen . . . ? Hello . . . ? Are you there . . . ?" I recognized that voice: Mrs. Fredrickson, Barbie's Mom.

I sat mutely as seconds ticked. The whole sequence of the afternoon flashed through me.

I had walked in our front door after school, as usual calling out, "Hi Mom! I'm home!" Dead silence. I called again. Nothing. I found Mom in the living room, lying on the couch on her side, her arms dangling off the edge. Something was wrong; she had never been a napper. I shook her. Her arms flopped heavily; her eyes fluttered open briefly. Drugged, watery eyes. I shook her shoulder harder, "Mom, how many pills did you take? How many?"

She slurred the words. "Doooon . . . don't let them take me. Not again!" Her eyelids closed.

God, what do I do? If I don't call, something terrible might happen. She could die.

I moved the coffee table up against the couch and stacked pillows on it, in case Mom started to roll. Then I ran. Out our front door, up our driveway, next door to Mrs. Summers. She opened the front door, and I sputtered, "Mom on couch . . . sleeping pills . . . don't know how many . . ." She put her arms around me, pulled me into the hall. She patted my back as I kept talking.

Then, from across the river, the town siren began to wail. *Who could have called? Who could already know what happened to Mom?* I tore myself from Mrs. Summers, ran out her door, and back down our driveway. The front door was ajar.

In the dim hall, I encountered our other neighbor: small, blond Mrs. Jansen. Her sad eyes met mine. "I came by to see your mother, Karen, and found her on the couch. I've called the ambulance."

The crunching of wheels on the driveway gravel, the slamming of doors. Two men carrying a stretcher. I followed them as they carried my mother out the front door. I stepped outside. The light was very bright. Townspeople had gathered in the driveway and all over the front yard. No one spoke, but their eyes pierced me. My mother was loaded in the ambulance, and the red light on its roof started flashing.

I started to run. Around the back of our house, down the path to the river. Running and running, the trees blurred by my tears, until I came to the river and leaned against an old sycamore, my breath heaving. The river ran dark and muddy. It was early March, two months after my mother had jumped in. I stared into the waters, my spine against the tree, until I was numb with cold. Then I made my way back to the empty house.

MRS. FREDRICKSON called out again, "Karen, are you home?"

"I'm here!" I yelled back.

She came into the living room. "Dear, let's go up to your room and get some of your things. Pajamas, underwear, clothes, school books. You can come stay with us."

Mrs. Fredrickson put me in Barbie's room. Barbie shared the room with her little sister Cheryl Ann, so that meant Cheryl Ann got booted into Monica's room.

That night, after Barbie and I had settled into our twin beds, Mrs. Fredrickson came in to say goodnight. There were two windows, and she went over and opened each one halfway. Frigid air swirled through the room. "Could you close the windows?" I asked, "It's really cold in here."

"Fresh air is good for you. It will make you strong," she replied. She left the room, but returned with an extra blanket, which she laid on my bed. I felt embarrassed, needing more than the others, but I didn't know how they stood such cold.

This was a house of rules. Every day when Barbie and I got off the school bus, Mrs. Fredrickson made us a snack. As soon as we were done, she said, "You have to do your homework now." Kids had a set bedtime; dishwashing duty was rotated among the girls. In a way, it was a relief to know just what I was supposed to do. Here, kids were kids and grownups were grownups. But I didn't like being bossed around so much.

Dinner was strange. Not what they ate, but how they did it. Mr. Fredrickson came home from his job as a big-shot executive at Johnson & Johnson and changed out of his business suit into slacks and a plaid flannel shirt. One of the girls set the table. Mrs. Fredrickson sat at the end nearest the kitchen, the father at the head, the kids along the sides. Mr. Fredrickson said a prayer, and I had to bow my head, too. Then Monica, because she was the oldest, was the first to hand her plate to her mother, who spooned vegetables and potatoes on the plate. Then the plate was passed down one side of the table from kid to kid until it reached Mr. Fredrickson, who put a piece of meat on the plate, which was passed back to Monica. There was no sound the whole time except for the chink of the serving spoon hitting the plate. The Fredricksons believed that children should not talk at the table unless spoken to, so no one said a word unless asked. I felt like I had landed on some icy planet, and my breath hung in the air, frozen.

One night at dinner, Mrs. Fredrickson gave me a look and said, "Karen, if you're too lazy to keep your elbows off the table, then you're too lazy to eat. Lift up those elbows!" The roots of my hair were burning, and I could barely see my plate. I hated her, this house, this prison. I blushed with shame as I lifted my elbows. Mrs. Fredrickson told me she was teaching me manners and that it was for my own good. The Fredrickson kids were silent, but I could tell they were sniggering.

One day after Barbie and I had finished our homework, Mrs. Fredrickson told Barbie to go outside to play. Once we were alone, she talked to me about my figure. My thighs were too fat and my tush too round. Only she didn't say "tush"; she said "derriere." All the Hendriksens were tall and square-jawed, with long narrow legs and flat rear ends, like models. Mrs. Fredrickson taught me an exercise to flatten my tush: I sat on the floor with my legs stretched out in front of me and I moved forward by walking on my butt cheeks, one cheek and then the other. Mrs. Fredrickson walked behind me to make sure that I did it.

I missed Happy. Because of the Fredrickson's poodle, Happy had to be boarded with the vet out in Hillsborough. It was too far away for me to see him. He loved to run, and hated to be penned up, so I wondered how he was doing.

In the two months I lived with her, Barbie never once asked me about my mother, about what happened. I think her mom must have told her not to talk about it. And I didn't say anything, either.

EVERY SATURDAY GRANDPA Isidor came to pick me up to drive me to Aunt Rita's, where I spent the weekend. I listened for his knock on the Fredricksons' back door, my overnight bag packed and ready. He always waited for me on the steps. Often, he would be holding a package of meat: steaks, a roast beef, or a chicken. I would take the package from him and bring it inside to give Mrs. Fredrickson. She would come with me to the door, lean out, and say, "Thank you, Mr. Bachman."

Grandpa stood holding his hat in his big square hands, and he answered Mrs. Fredrickson, "You're welcome. It's the least we can do," as he tipped his bald head to her and bowed.

When she closed the door, Grandpa put on his hat, leaned over, and squeezed me in a big hug. Then he took my hand and we walked to his old van, which looked very big parked next to Mr. Fredrickson's white sports car.

Grandpa opened the side door for me, and I clambered into the back. There were no windows in the back, so it was dark and cool where I sat on the wooden floor. The passenger seat had been removed to give more room for storing goods. My body rocked in the swaying van. I inhaled aromas of produce and meat, remnant odors from market day when Grandpa went at 4:00 AM to pick out food for the store.

During the forty-five-minute drive, Grandpa was always quiet. Sometimes I sang to myself or my eyes drooped and I curled up and napped. Or I would just sit and daydream, riding between my week of the Fredricksons' rules and the coming weekend, where I never knew if my cousin Deborah would be in one of her mean moods. In the van, I had no rules to obey. Grandpa's silence enveloped me as I rocked in the cool dark.

UNCLE MONTE ALWAYS greeted me the same way: He smiled a broad grin, grabbed the soft flesh on the underside of my arm between his thumb and forefinger, and twisted hard. For a couple seconds, it hurt like hell, but I didn't yelp. Uncle Monte was a children's doctor and he thought he had a way with kids. "Howya doing, kiddo?" he asked. "Okay," I always said.

Aunt Rita called from the kitchen where she was making lunch, "Go find the girls." I searched down the hall of the ranch-style house. Outside Deborah's closed door, I heard muffled voices. I knocked. The door swung open, and Deborah stuck her head out. She was on the verge of thirteen, two years older than me, and the boss of Abbey, eight, and Ezra, three and a half. "Oh, *you,*" Deborah scowled. "We're busy! Go play with the baby." And she closed the door. It wasn't so bad, because I liked playing with Ezra. He was sweet and agreeable.

Aunt Rita crackled with anger. I didn't know that she had a husband who constantly cheated on her, who had slept with her best friend while she was pregnant with Ezra, but her tight face, her clipped voice, made me stand back. She was always in a hurry. When driving, she screeched around corners. Cars had no seatbelts in 1962, so we kids lurched forward and back as she slammed on the brakes, then gunned it on the green light.

Aunt Rita always had me take a bath. The smell of Dial soap permeated their bathroom. Once, Aunt Rita came in while I was washing and stood above me, looking down. She pointed at my crotch. "You have to wash it all, very well, with lots of soap on the washcloth. You have to do the outside and then go inside all the folds. You understand?" I nodded, hoping she would leave. But she stood there and watched, to make sure I did it right.

At night, I slept in Uncle Monte's office. It was in a separate building next to the house that was attached to the house by a long hall. Aunt Rita made the couch in the patients' waiting room into a bed for me. When she left, I lay on the couch, paging through the kids' magazines my uncle had in his waiting room.

The house seemed very far away from the office. I could hear the cars passing on the busy road outside the office, their rhythmic *swiiish-swiiiish* carrying them past the house. Their lights crept through the Venetian blinds, casting moving shadows. My throat and chest ached. I lay there wishing that I could jump into one of those cars and ride away.

I SENT MY FATHER LETTERS once a week, the same superficial letters I had been writing, as if nothing had changed. One time, I wrote a different letter, though. I told the truth: *Things are bad here; Mom tried to kill herself with pills; I miss Happy every day.* Then I tore it up and threw it in the wastebasket.

Later, I learned an odd thing. None of the adults ever called or wrote Dad to tell him Mom had attempted suicide and was in the hospital. I guess they figured he was gone and not coming back.

For a while there was one bit of freedom that I had. After I did my homework, Mrs. Fredrickson let me to go over to my house. I was supposed to be practicing piano, only I didn't practice.

The house was quiet and dark when I first came in. Sometimes I went up to my bedroom and lay on my bed, reading one of Walter Farley's *The Black Stallion* books, completely immersed. Sometimes I watched TV in my parents' room. Sometimes I wandered down to the river, even though it was still cold out. Other times I simply sat in the brown nubby Saarinen chair named the Womb. It was the chair Mom always lounged in, her feet up on its hassock. It was only the first few times I came home that I sat in Mom's chair and cried.

My piano teacher told Mrs. Fredrickson that I was not practicing. After that, Mrs. Fredrickson made Monica come with me every day. She did her homework upstairs while I played piano. She didn't know much about piano, so I played arpeggios, chords, and some old easy pieces I liked and she thought I was practicing.

AFTER SCHOOL ONE DAY, I pulled down my underpants to pee in the Fredrickson's bathroom and found a brownish red stain across the crotch. I knew what this was. Our fifth-grade girls' health education class had been shown a film on menstruation. Mom had explained it, too. I had followed her into the bathroom, where she had opened the cabinet to show where sanitary pads were kept. I told Mrs. Fredrickson that I needed to go home to get something. At home, I found one of Mom's old sanitary belts, gray with age. I threaded a pad through it, stashed some pads in a brown bag, and waddled back to the Fredrickson's, my belly cramping. I kept my secret, waiting for my mother. Someday she would come home and I would tell her.

One day, I was doing my homework on the Fredricksons' back porch and I heard Mrs. Fredrickson talking on the phone in the kitchen. "I am trying to civilize her," she said. "It's my Christian duty." I figured she was talking about me, but I wasn't sure what she meant. Did she think my mother's craziness had rubbed off on me, or was it that we were Jews?

Then she said, "I have to do something about the dog. He's been boarded for two months now, and who knows how long it will be. I am going to ask the vet to find a home for him." The air grew thick around my head, and it felt like I couldn't breathe.

"No!" I screamed from the porch, and then I was in the kitchen, running at Mrs. Fredrickson. I careened to a stop a few feet from her, "No, you can't, don't you dare, not Happy, I won't let you, I'll call my father in England . . . no . . . no . . . no!" I was sobbing.

"I'll call you back," Mrs. Fredrickson spoke into the phone, and hung up.

All the indignities of the past two months crowded up and down my spine. I stood wide-legged, feet planted. "You will not give Happy away!" I glared at her. "He's *my* dog! You can't! I won't let you!"

YEARS LATER, IN MY TWENTIES, my mother told me what her two-month stay in the county mental hospital had been like.

After her stomach was pumped in the emergency room, Mom was transferred. At the county hospital, she was in a dormitory with forty women. Some were catatonic, lying in bed unmoving, others were belligerent, yelling and screaming and having fits, and some seemed regular, just like everybody on the outside.

At first, she didn't realize they'd taken her off all her medications, and the withdrawal was giving her the shakes. She was so jumpy she couldn't sit still. Meals were at long metal tables, and whenever the nurse looked away, she'd quickly stand up and sit down. When the nurse caught her she'd yell down the table, "Gloria, sit still!"

In the dayroom, she'd pace until someone would holler, "Stop blocking the TV!" Then she'd sit down for a few minutes, her hands trembling, until her nerves forced her to jump up.

For three nights, she couldn't sleep. Sweat soaked her nightgown and she'd lie there, twisting the sheet between her fists. On the fourth night, the woman in the cot next to hers slipped out of bed when the lights went out. She stood next to my mother's bed. Mom pulled the sheet up around her neck, afraid. Her teeth were chattering as the woman leaned close and whispered gently, "With the help of Jesus, I'm going to help you sleep." She began to stroke my mother's forehead and damp hair. "Shhh . . . shhh . . . you can sleep now," she crooned. "Jesus will help you sleep." My mother drifted off.

Once a week, they got to take a shower. All forty of the women would line up nude with a tiny towel over their shoulders to wait their turn. Mom said the hospital food was so awful that she had her parents bring her peanut butter, jelly, and bread. She kept her cache on her shelf and lived off that. But one day, a nurse took it away. Mom got really upset. During Grandpa's next visit, he paid the nurse a bribe, and suddenly Mom could have her own food again.

One time during a visit from her dad and sister, Mom tried to enlist them in getting her out. They were sitting in the visitors' room at a table, drinking coffee. "This place is terrible! You have to do something. You have to get me out of here," she pleaded.

Grandpa just shrugged. Aunt Rita tried to calm her down. "You need to be here, Gloria."

As her father and sister stood to leave, Mom smashed her coffee cup against the table. It broke in three pieces. She grabbed one and bore down hard against her wrist. Mom told me, "Well, I'm sure that made them think I was really crazy, but I wanted to show them how desperately I hated this place."

Three orderlies grabbed her. As they dragged her away, Grandpa and Aunt Rita were staring at her with shocked looks. She was taken to solitary confinement, a room that was all mattresses wall to wall. She stayed in there several days.

When Mom got out of solitary, she became determined to leave. She watched who got discharged, and it was obvious: You had to behave. She became a docile, complying, model patient. She volunteered to do chores. She scrubbed floors and washed bathroom walls. She made sure not to complain. She told me, "I said as little as possible, afraid of a slip. I kept my rage and my hatred of the place shielded behind my eyes. I acted grateful and obedient, and finally, they let me go."

Chapter 16. Riding Fury Home

MOM RETURNED FROM the county hospital in the beginning of May, three weeks before my eleventh birthday. Aunt Rita called Mrs. Fredrickson to tell her they were on their way, and Mrs. Fredrickson said I could go wait at my house for them. I ran outside when I heard the rumble of gravel as my aunt, driving too fast, as usual, roared up to our front door. Mom got out of the passenger side. They'd put her back on pills before she left the hospital, but not as many, so she seemed less groggy when she leaned over to kiss me. "Hello, sweetheart," she murmured. Aunt Rita lifted two bags of groceries from the back seat. She moved briskly into the house, and as soon as she had unloaded them into our fridge, she was gone.

MRS. JANSEN CAME OVER that first afternoon. "Gloria, let me keep your pills for you," she said.

"Not necessary," Mom said, waving her hand while holding her cigarette as if shooing a fly.

Mrs. Jansen glanced over at me, then back at Mom. "Yes, I think so," she said in a quiet, determined voice.

Mom sighed and shrugged. "Oh, all right."

After that, every morning and evening, Mrs. Jansen walked through the fenceless side yard between our houses to bring Mom her pills.

But whatever help the neighbors gave us, there was no controlling Mom's driving phobia, which was erratic. You would never know when it would happen. We had a new car, a Rambler American convertible, that had replaced the old Hudson with its burned-out back seat from Mom's cigarette butt. Dad had bought the Hudson from a coworker for $25, so it wasn't such a big loss. The Rambler was white, with fire-engine-red seats, a red dashboard, and a black cloth roof. You could roll the roof back by just holding down a switch. Sometimes when we were about to go out, Mom would give me the keys and say, "Go put the top down while I get ready." I would go turn the key in the ignition, then hold the switch down and listen to the whir of the motor that lifted the top and the crackle crackle of the cloth folding. Then I would climb into the back seat, pull the cover over the folded roof, and pop all the snaps down that hold it in place. I loved the feel of the leather seats, even if they were really just vinyl.

I already sort of knew how to drive the Rambler, because once a week all through fifth grade, I loaded up our two silver garbage cans in the open trunk, drove the car from our front door to the end of our long driveway, and deposited the cans on the curb before backing up the driveway again. Mom said since we had no cops in Millstone, just a mayor, there was no one around to arrest a ten-year-old for taking out the garbage.

There were no stores in our town except for Mr. Brezniak's little grocery store, so if we needed anything, we had to get in the car. Mom and I would be driving down the road, going along just fine, when all of a sudden it would happen. I'd feel the car slow way down, then the next second I'd be jerked back as we'd zoom forward, then slow down again. *Fast*/slow, *fast*/slow, sending my head bobbing like one of those Chinese dolls. Mom's face would be squeezed up tight, her arms stiff with her elbows out, her fingers gripping the wheel. Her right foot on the gas pedal was doing a dance of its own—down to the floor, up to the sky, down-up, down-up. How I *hated* that foot.

If there was no traffic behind us, we could go down the road like that for a while—*fast*/slow, *fast*/slow—Mom silent, stiff and sweating, until she somehow got over it and went back to normal. I'd brace my arms against the dash to ease the jerking. Sometimes the person behind us would blow their horn and Mom would pull over. She'd take a Kleenex out of her purse and dab her sweaty face and neck. "Shit, shit, shit!" she'd mutter. I'd pat her shoulder, repeating, "It's okay, it's okay."

Mom said she was never like that before her electroshock treatments. I was too little when she left to remember if she was or she wasn't. She said this fear would just come over her, making her freeze up. Bridges, cliff edges, any kind of heights meant an instant freeze. I could not see an easy way to melt her. And it seemed like it got worse over time.

FOR MY ELEVENTH BIRTHDAY, Mom bought me the best present ever: tickets to a rodeo with a special appearance by Fury, the beautiful black stallion from the TV show that I adored. Fury was wild, and let no one ride him except the orphan boy, Joey.

The rodeo was in Princeton, so of course we had to drive there. On the curvy, wooded road to Princeton, Mom's driving fears attacked her, so we lurched down the road and arrived late. By the time we got there, the only seats left in the bleachers were at the very top. But when Mom tried to climb up those wooden bleachers, she froze again. "I can't, honey!" she told me.

"Come on, Mom!" I pulled on her arm. I just had to see Fury. "You've *got* to, Mom," I demanded in a loud whisper, aware of people staring at us from their seats.

"All right, darling, I'll try." Mom put her hands down onto the steps and climbed up the wooden bleacher stairs on all fours like a dog. I trailed as far behind as I could, trying to act like she wasn't my mom.

Once we got in our seats, she seemed okay. I forgot about her while I watched the men on horses roping cattle, riding in figure eights around oil barrels, being flung from bucking broncos. "Whooeee, yee-haw!" I screamed with the crowd. And then, I was silenced by the announcer's solemn voice, "And now, ladies and gentlemen, we present to you the most famous horse on television for a one and only live performance . . . the black stallion known as Fury!"

Of course, Fury had no rider because he was wild. Wild and beautiful and strong. I knew no one could tame him, and I loved that. He came out by himself, his muscles rippling, his coat so black and shiny. He ran in a circle around the arena, and then rose into the air, pawing and whinnying his stallion call of freedom, before he circled one more time and disappeared.

I floated down the bleacher steps to the car, ignoring Mom and the nice man who helped her down the stairs by holding her arm. On the ride back along the dark wooded road, I was lost in a reverie of remembrance of the black stallion. Then—*bam*—my head jerked backward, jarring me out of dreaming. I awakened to the *fast*/slow, *fast*/slow lurching. I stared at the red dashboard. I could feel the hatred gather in my chest. Mom ruined everything. Ruined it.

Chapter 17. Happy

AFTER MOM CAME HOME, one of the first things I said to her was, "Let's go get Happy." She managed to drive us okay to the vet's office. When he brought Happy out, I wrapped my arms around him, hugging him tight as his tail beat back and forth. "Let's go home, boy," I said.

As much as I loved him, Happy had always been a difficult, restless hound. He loved to run loose, and after being cooped up so long at the vet's, he was wild to go. He'd pace back and forth in front of the door and howl to be let out, fraying our nerves, until Mom or I would relent. Then he'd be off, running into the woods behind our house and out of sight. Neighbors reported sighting him several miles away, running through the fields of the dairy farms outside of town.

One day in midsummer, Happy came limping home. I heard him at the back door, whimpering, and went to let him in. "Oh God, Mom," I yelled over my shoulder, "Happy's hurt bad!" His side was ripped open in a jagged line, with big gashes oozing blood and flesh, blood-caked fur, and a bit of intestines peeking out. I sat next to him in the back seat as we drove to the vet's, holding his head in my lap as he moaned and shivered. I was shaking, too.

After the vet sewed Happy up, Mom and I tried to keep him in, but as he healed, he started that irritating pacing again. One day, someone let him out—was it me or Mom?—and sure enough, Happy came back with his wound reopened. At the vet's, the doctor said he needed to board Happy for a while until he healed better.

A few days later, Mom said, "The veterinarian knows a farmer who is looking for a dog. Happy would have a big farm to live on, and could run all he wanted without getting in trouble. The vet thinks it's best. What do you think?"

I stared at her, chilled into silence. Then I managed to choke out, "I have to think about it."

I went upstairs to my room, closed the door, and lay on my bed. *Happy. My Happy.* I loved him more than anything. He was my pal, my comfort. I didn't want to lose him. But the vet had said that Happy's side had been torn open when he'd leapt over a barbed wire fence. I could see that living with us, he kept getting hurt. A sob burst in me, and I lay there weeping.

After I wiped my tears, I went downstairs and said to Mom, "Tell the vet to give Happy to the farmer. I want him to have a good life."

My mother made no offer to take me to the vet's office to see Happy one last time to say goodbye, and I made no request to see him. Perhaps I understood it would hurt too much to feel him against me, so I just let him go.

Chapter 18. Return

THE MUGGY AUGUST NIGHT before my father was to return, I set my hair. Spiky pink rollers with plastic snap-on covers dug into my scalp as I tried to sleep. I had perfected the art of sleeping with an arm under my neck to relieve the pressure of the rollers, but then my arm would go numb and I'd have to give in to the curlers' prickly pain. Spit curls were Scotch-taped against my cheeks—curls that made an almost full loop along the cheeks were the *in* style—posing a problem for me because I was allergic to Scotch tape. I had to stick on the tape as lightly as possible and then rip it off fast in the morning, hoping not to leave a blazing red tape mark. Sometimes I was lucky.

Mom managed to drive us to the airport. In the international terminal, we waited across from the exit where passengers cleared customs. I was wearing my best dress, a full-skirted silk print with a tight bodice that revealed my new breasts, encased in a training bra. I had even wriggled into stockings held up with a garter belt. I peered toward the exit doors intently, so excited I was shivering, scrutinizing each man crossing the threshold. Someone who looked like Dad was approaching, but he was so short. "Is that *him*?" I asked Mom. "Is that *him*?"

During the year my father had been gone, I had undergone a pubescent spurt; I had grown breasts and bled and lengthened to almost my full adult height of five foot one. Now my father was approaching and he seemed to have shrunk. Dad left as a towering giant and returned a little man.

My father stopped in front of us and set down his two suitcases. "You've sure grown!" He sounded surprised, then reached to hug me.

"Welcome home, Dad!" I threw my arms around his neck and kissed his cheek, scratchy with stubble. I disentangled myself and stepped back so Dad could get a better view. I was hoping he would notice more of the new me, but he turned to Mom. "Hi, Gloria."

"Abe," she nodded. They hugged briefly. "The car's in the garage. This way."

As we walked to the airport garage, Dad kept staring nervously at Mom. It seemed all his attention was on her. I sat alone in the back seat of the Rambler for the first time in a year as my father took the wheel and drove us home.

For years later, remembering that day, my mother would fume, "He didn't even say how nice you looked!" She was right: I had been disappointed and hurt. But it hadn't taken me very long to understand that it was the tension—so thick between them, the bitterness and regret vibrating in the air—that riveted my father's vision and blurred all sight of me.

THE FIRST MORNING OF my father's return, I awoke and sleepily went to my parents' bedroom to say good morning. Mom had moved back upstairs to their bedroom with its twin beds. Their door was closed. I put my hand on the knob and swung the door inward. And then I froze, mouth agape. In the farthest twin bed from the door, up against the bedroom wall, my naked father was lying on top of my naked mother. They both turned their startled faces toward me. I was old enough to know what I had stumbled into and be horrified. No one made any sound in those frozen seconds. Mom's eyes met mine—there was a look in her eyes of some unfathomable pain. That look lanced me beyond the simple shame of my bumbling intrusion. I backed out and pulled the door shut.

Soon afterward we took a family vacation to Cape Cod. Grandma Katie came along. Dad drove all the way to the Cape, my tiny grandmother next to him in the front seat, her head barely rising above the seat back.

Mom and I sat in back, giggling and playing car games, calling out the states of license plates and singsonging aloud the Burma Shave jingles as they came at us sign by wooden sign: BEN—MET ANNA—MADE A HIT—NEGLECTED BEARD—BEN-ANNA SPLIT—BURMA SHAVE.

My parents rented a weather-beaten wooden bungalow a few blocks from the beach for the week. Each day my family packed a picnic lunch, beach towels, and blankets and headed for a day at the sea. To get to the shoreline, we first had to clamber through a gap in the sand dunes. This wasn't a great swimming beach, because the water was frigid, so once we deposited the cooler and arranged the beach blanket, Mom and I went off to climb the huge Cape Cod dunes. We ran down in great leaps, over and over. There was a giddy, almost hysterical sense of abandon as we leapt and sank, leapt and sank, deep in sand. Far away down the beach, my father was a shadow, sitting on a blanket with Grandma.

NOT LONG AFTER DAD returned, we started a new routine: Sunday dinners out at Bucky's Chinese Restaurant. Bucky's was on the far side of Manville, about fifteen minutes from our house. In the restaurant's former incarnation, it had been Italian, and the new owners hadn't bothered to replace the prior decor of ornate red and gold velvet wallpaper. On our first visit, Dad looked around the dark, almost windowless restaurant and declared, "This must have been a Mafia joint."

All the round fake-wood Formica tables had lazy Susans as centerpieces, which I thought was swell—no need to ask anyone to pass the food. The waiter brought us menus, but Mom didn't even bother to open hers. She lit a cigarette and blew the smoke toward the ceiling, looking bored. Dad and I opened our menus and stared. I liked thinking about the different dishes, but the truth was we always ordered the same thing: Family Dinner for Three, which started with eggrolls with plum sauce, then wonton soup followed by "Two Choices from Column A/One from Column B." In our case that meant shrimp with lobster sauce, moo goo gai pan, and green pepper beef.

After we placed our order, the tense silence between my parents became even more prominent. It was like this at home, too, but seemed worse at the restaurant, when we were supposed to be having a fun time. I started frantically babbling, telling whatever story came to mind. "In class today, Mrs. Henderson told us about when she was a girl in Vermont, and how they bled the trees for maple syrup . . ." until the egg rolls arrived and we had a diversion. I was proud that I could grab the egg rolls with my chopsticks. Dad had taught me to use them long ago, when he and I had lived alone together. He'd learned how when he went to Japan with the army at the end of World War II. Now, I tried to teach Mom: "Look, Mom it's easy." I raised my hand, holding the pair of chopsticks. "You just put one inside the crook by your thumb, the other leaning against your third finger." I wiggled the wooden sticks to demonstrate. She shook her head, "I prefer a fork," she said flatly.

The waiter brought the soup. I watched as he ladled out the wontons, spinach, and broth into our bowls. As he spun our soup toward us, I was searching for another story, but my mind was blank.

We started eating as I said, "Here's one: Knock-knock!" This was a true act of desperation, because I considered knock-knock jokes for babies.

Mom looked up. "Who's there?"

I smiled at her. "Orange!"

Mom held her spoon in midair. "Orange who?"

"Orange you glad you came a-knocking!" I gave her a big grin. Dad seemed completely oblivious, focused on his soup. Mom gave me a quick smile and lifted a wonton to her mouth.

By the time the dishes were brought to the table in their silver-lidded platters with pedestals, I had run out of stories and jokes. I focused on the food on my plate. The only noise at the table was the quiet rumble of the lazy Susan as each of us spun it around to claim our shrimp with lobster sauce.

Chapter 19. Perry Mason

MY PARENTS' WORDS were dense and hot. In my pajamas, I was crouched in my eavesdropping spot in the upstairs balcony that overlooked the living room. Mom and Dad thought I was asleep as they argued, their voices rising. Some part of me wanted out of there, bad, but it was too late to move.

Then Mom said a word that hit me in the throat and I stood and cried out, "No!" Both Mom and Dad looked up at me, their mouths open. My bare feet were pounding down the wood stairs, along the concrete floor in the hall, into the living room where Mom and Dad were sitting on opposite ends of the couch.

"No, you can't!" I yelled. "You have to try! Please, please don't get a divorce!"

Back in my bed, I shivered. In spite of the silences between my parents, the stabbing looks, I had told myself a story of my family to hold on to—a story of love. It went: *No matter how bad things are, we all* love *each other. We're together even when we're apart. We'll* always *be together.* There was a desperate fluttering in my chest. Dad had been back from England just over a year, and it was all falling apart.

MY PARENTS DID TRY, for another month or so. During that month of November 1963, John F. Kennedy was shot dead. Grief struck us all. We spent a muted, somber Thanksgiving at Aunt Rita's. One night at bedtime, a couple of weeks after the assassination, my father came into my room to tell me he would be moving out the next day. Dad stood next to my bed and held my hand while I cried. He tried to comfort me: "I promise we'll spend time on the weekends together." He looked unbearably sad. I felt so bad for Dad. I choked off my tears and smiled feebly at him.

After Dad left my bedroom, I lay in my bed, imagining myself in a courtroom. Somehow, I'd gotten the idea that in a divorce children have to testify, and I knew from Perry Mason that you had to swear on the Bible. Like on TV, I saw the scene in black and white. *The judge would be bald, with deep jowls and a black robe. We would all stand for the judge. His gavel would come down with a* whap. *They would call me to the stand. "Who do you love more—your mom or your dad?" Swear it on the Bible. "Who would you choose to live with? Choose! Choose!"*

"I love them both—equally," I would protest.

"No, you must choose," the lawyer in the black suit would say. "Mom or Dad; Mom or Dad? You must *answer!"*

I clutched my sheet in my fists. *Mom needs me more,* I thought, *so I better say her.*

Mom came in to say goodnight. She got into bed and held me while I cried. "I don't want to choose! I don't want to choose between you!" I wailed.

She stroked my hair and explained to me that custody was all settled and there would be no fight. I would live with her and visit with Dad one day each weekend. My body went limp with relief—I would not have to choose.

THE FIRST CHRISTMAS AFTER my parents separated was a bonanza for me. My secular parents didn't celebrate Chanukah but had decided early on that they didn't want me to feel so different and deprived, so they gave me Christmas presents. Dad had just moved out a couple of weeks before the holidays, and he and Mom were vying to outdo each other. Dad bought me a pair of skis, boots, and poles from E. J. Korvette, and Mom bought me a beginner's guitar. I found there was an upside to the tug of loyalties pulling on me—the unspoken *who do you love best?*

On our first excursion to the rather pitiful ski slopes of northern New Jersey, Dad brought along a how to ski book. Neither of us had ever skied. We laced on our boots, clipped on the skis, and grabbed hold of the rope tow to the top of the beginners' run. We wobbled to a spot out of the main traffic. Then my intellectual father, who believed one could learn anything from a book, held the book in the air and read me instructions.

"Basic snowplow for beginners: tips of the skis are pointed together, knees inward, back of the skis flare out in a 'V'. . . "

And then I was off, flying down the hill, unable to hear Dad's voice reading Step 2. He had not gotten as far as "How to Stop," so I flailed down the ski run until I fell on my backside and skidded to a stop near the bottom. My wet rear end confirmed the disappointment that had been growing in me: My father wasn't the all-knowing genius I'd believed him to be. After he careened down the slope, I insisted we get ski lessons.

On our weekend dates, Dad often took me into New York City. Usually we went to a museum, and every now and then we would stand in the half-price ticket line for a Broadway show. It was thrilling to be treated to such special excursions. Alone with Dad, I vibrated with excitement. Then, over dinner in a New York restaurant,

I would stare at Dad's woeful, angry face while he complained about the stress of supporting my mother. "When is she going to get a job?!" was his chronic lament. I shook my head from side to side, my face filled with sympathy.

I carried my father's anger home. More than once, I returned from a date with Dad and launched at Mom, "When are you going to get a *job?* Dad can't keep this up!" Sometimes she would say, "Karen, you know I just can't handle it right now!" and begin crying. Then I would feel awful, churning with guilt and anger and sadness all at once. Other times, she'd yell, "Go live with your father if you feel that way, but don't talk to me about it!" I'd go to my bedroom and slam the door.

I LEARNED TO PLAY guitar from a TV class on the public broadcast channel. I perched on a chair, practicing chords in what had been my parents' bedroom and we now used as a TV room. Mom had moved back downstairs to the study right after Dad left, as if she could not stand to sleep in that room. Soon, I had learned enough chords to accompany myself singing the folk songs and political poetry I learned from records: Peter, Paul and Mary; Bob Dylan; Joan Baez; and Pete Seeger.

Folk music was being rediscovered, with hootenanny clubs opening up where kids went to sing along. Even though I sang alone at home, I felt part of something, a message that was shared. On Saturday nights, Mom and I watched the half-hour *Hootenanny* TV show filmed at college campuses.

Playing guitar and singing was easy and fun compared with my years laboring at the piano, practicing the same fractions of sonatas over and over for meticulous scrutiny by my piano teacher. As I sang,

Chapter 20. Crossing the Demilitarized Zone

THE SUMMER AFTER DAD moved out, I spent a month at Camp Birch Ridge. I'd been going to the small camp in the Kittatinny Mountains of northern New Jersey since I was eight. I loved having other kids to play with all day long, and fell into the familiarity of camp routine with deep pleasure, relieved of responsibility by the structured activities.

Twice a day we swam in the lake. In the morning there were lessons, in the afternoon free swim. I was proud that by my sixth year at camp I'd advanced to training as a junior lifesaver. I swam a crisp crawl as Paddles, the swimming instructor, yelled directions over a megaphone for a practice rescue of a drowning camper. During archery, I stood with legs apart, bowstring drawn back, my focus keenly narrowed to sight along the arrow. All else fell away as I felt the power of letting the arrow fly, listening to the sharp *whap* as it landed somewhere near the bull's-eye of the target.

I even took an odd comfort in the dreaded inspections of our quarters, the check for neatly made hospital corners on our cots and clothes folded in our trunks. Every morning, we stood at attention as the flag was unfurled and raised, then in the evening lowered and folded. At dinner, I ate with great gusto camp meals repeated from the same recipes each year, with ice-cold milk doled out by counselors in half-glass refills. And at night around the campfire, there was the group camaraderie as we sang together, flames sparking the dark.

That summer, I brought my guitar. I had learned quite a few songs from the class on public television. During free period, I perched on my cot in my unit's canvas tent, strumming and singing. Other girls joined me, sitting on the opposite cot. I felt almost giddy being at the center of their attention, leading them in song.

WHILE I WAS GOING ABOUT my days canoeing and making lanyards, back in Millstone, Mr. Fredrickson noticed that Mom's car had not moved in the driveway for two days. He went to check on her. I will never know how it was that my mother was still alive, two days after swallowing rat poison. Was there blood, shit, vomit? Was her skin ashen? Did they pump her stomach again, like with the sleeping pills?

Some things are beyond bearing, and so sink from consciousness, leaving no memory. When my month at camp ended, my father picked me up. Years later, he reminded me how, on the drive home, he told me Mom had attempted suicide again, that she was in a mental hospital again, but I have blocked that moment out. Dad moved back into the house while Mom was in the hospital, but I can recall none of those first weeks of eighth grade when I lived with Dad. What I do remember is this: I kept my focus elsewhere—on school, narrowing my anxiety to worries about getting my homework done.

I coveted straight A's. This was my mother's fourth suicide attempt by every lethal means she could think of: the rifle, the river, the pills, and now the rat poison. Hard as she tried, Mom always lived, and the whole possibility of her actually dying seemed unreal to me.

I have one cloudy memory of going to visit Mom: There was the buzz of the locked door as Dad and I were admitted to the maximum-security ward, the walk down a long, empty green hall that went on forever and ever, and the smell of Lysol. No memory of my mother, her smell, her embrace; no remembrance of the greeting or the parting.

YEARS LATER, MY FATHER told me his part of the story. After the ambulance took my mother to the emergency room, someone called him at work to come to the hospital. When he got there, Gloria was on a gurney in the hall, making incoherent sounds, grunts and groans. Her sister, Rita, was with her, and she stepped toward Abe, blocking him from going close to Gloria. Rita said to him, "Glor wants a divorce on the grounds of extreme cruelty!"

Dad glared at her, "Whose cruelty? Mine or *hers?!*"

Gloria was now moaning, "Ah, ah, ahhhhhhh!"

"Okay, okay," Dad said, "I'll agree to it." He turned and left.

Several days later, the hospital called him to come get Gloria and deliver her to the county mental hospital. He was, after all, still the husband, separated or not. As he drove, she sat glumly next to him in the passenger seat.

There's a gap in my memory: Was I out playing with a friend the day that my grandparents drove up with my mother? Or did I greet her as she stepped from my grandparents' Oldsmobile, and wrap my arms around her? She'd been gone over two months. The adults were having a meeting in the living room, and if I was home, they must have sent me out of earshot. My father listened while Mom's parents made a proposal: Move back for good, Abe, and raise Karen.

My mother had been staying at my grandparents' since her discharge, but they didn't want her to keep living with them—I imagine her despair was too great for them. Gloria would be committed to a mental hospital or a halfway house. While my mother was being discussed, she sat mute and unprotesting, as if resigned to a life locked away. My father told me he got mad at her parents and said, "If you do this, it will be the end of Gloria!" He made a counterproposal: Let Gloria move back, and Karen will be with her and look after her, and I will move away again.

And that is what they did.

AT NIGHT MY VIGILANCE returned as easily as turning on a radio to a pretuned channel. I was programmed to startle awake to any sounds of my mother stumbling down the hall on her bathroom forays. But during the day, my interests were elsewhere; I was swept up in eighth grade, homework, piano practice, playing guitar, and riding my bike the several miles to my new best friend Theresa's house. Theresa had long, dirty-blond hair that she chewed on, a tall, chunky body, and a great smile. Best of all, she was very bright and like I did, loved art. We had animated conversations about books and artists we liked, and ideas we were batting around in our heads. Barbie and I had drifted apart, our friendship lost to her obsession with her looks and with dating boys. So it was amazing to find another girl who was intellectual. We talked about all kinds of things—except, of course, my mother's depression and what it was like for me to live alone with her.

Theresa lived in a small cottage with her many siblings and both parents. Because her house was crammed with people, to get privacy we would walk out into the empty fields near her house, or along the railroad tracks. Immersed in conversation, under the big sky, with clouds scudding overhead, I would feel big and expansive, my body vibrating with energy. I had never felt such freedom and joy in sharing my thoughts with another girl.

NOT LONG AFTER MOM came home, she heard about a doctor who practiced alternative medicine. He kept wacky hours, seeing patients at his office in Trenton from midnight to six in the morning. Mom left me at my grandparents' house, checked into a motel in Trenton, and roused herself for her 4:00 AM appointment. The doctor diagnosed her with severe hypoglycemia and low thyroid, and gave her armloads of vitamins, thyroid medication, and a regimen for reducing some of her psychiatric drugs. Although still addicted to sleeping pills at night, she became less groggy in the daytime.

Mom was rumbling back to life. Years later, she would tell me how defective she had felt when she knew her marriage was ending, like there was something really wrong with her. Somehow she decided to go on. That winter semester, she enrolled in a master's of education program to become an elementary-school teacher. Sometimes I helped with her projects. One day, I came home to find her seated in front of a large blown-up balloon resting on the table, a bucket of papier-mâché next to it. Her ashtray was filled with cigarette stubs, and one smoking cigarette rested on its edge. "Hon, can you help me? I don't have the patience." She was supposed to make a globe. I loved anything to do with art, and I launched in, spreading newspaper on the table under the balloon, layering the papier-mâché around it. After it dried, I painted the continents in green, the ocean in blue, happy to have such a simple way to help Mom.

IN THE SPRING OF 1965, American planes started the bombing raids on North Vietnam dubbed Operation Rolling Thunder, and Mom joined Women Strike for Peace. It threw me into a dilemma: Did I think the war was wrong? In 1965 there was no large peace movement yet, and I knew no other kids who were against the war. I sought out advice from my eighth-grade teacher, Mr. Shelton, whom I adored. He wasn't handsome, but I thought he was the greatest because he challenged his students to think. I hadn't yet learned to dampen my smartness in deference to boys, and I was one of those students always furiously raising a hand. One day after class, I asked Mr. Shelton what he thought about Vietnam. He wouldn't answer. He told me that I had to learn about Vietnam myself and come to my own conclusion. I begged, I pleaded, "What do you think?" but he kept pushing me; "This isn't a decision someone else can make for you. You have to delve into it, and then decide what you believe."

Mr. Shelton's respect for my reasoning abilities made me face the responsibility. It was a scary decision. I hesitated because in some vague way I understood that once I concluded that America was not the righteous purveyor of freedom, many beliefs I'd been taught would come tumbling down.

I had stared at the newspaper pictures of Vietnamese Buddhist monks protesting by immolating themselves in the Saigon streets. Puzzled, horrified, and moved by such an act, I was led by the intensity of those pictures to research more. Mom had bought a couple of books about Vietnam. Reading about the history of foreign interventions in Vietnam and the escalating U.S. role, I became clear. Mr. Shelton was right—I could figure out what I believed. I joined Mom on the picket line.

In front of the New Brunswick Army induction center, there were the handful of Women Strike for Peace housewives marching with picket signs held aloft with one arm, their huge pocketbooks crooked on the opposite elbow, and me, the sole adolescent. I felt nervous and exposed marching along the sidewalk, but also angry about the war and proud to be taking action. For the first time, I witnessed these women as more than housewives and parents. Mom had found kindred spirits, passionate women, committed to a cause.

I decided the United States had not simply made a mistake in Vietnam, but that our foreign policy was deliberately *imperialist*—a word I'd just learned. By then, I had watched black people being attacked by police with fire hoses and police dogs in the Birmingham demonstrations on TV. Right here in America, things were very wrong. But I also saw how courageous people could be, standing up against oppression, and that there was hope for change.

I put away my horse books and launched into reading to deepen my understanding of the world. I read *To Kill a Mockingbird, The Diary of Ann Frank, 1984, The Trial, The Grapes of Wrath, The Crucible, The Jungle,* and *The Autobiography of Malcolm X.* The books widened me, touched me with human experiences that were so different from mine, yet so reverberant with our human pathos.

At meals, Mom and I now discussed politics, history, and current events. I discovered something about my mother, something that had been buried by drugs and depression, lost to electroshock and sorrow in the years since she had read me Greek myths: her sharp, passionate intelligence.

Mom and I had a new bond. As the peace movement grew, we went together to antiwar marches. We boarded buses to Washington, D.C.; Newark, New Jersey; and New York City. We carried signs and screamed slogans with the other marchers. The antiwar movement and the growing social unrest gave us a focus for our discontent, and a place to feel some commonality with others after so much stigma and isolation.

Chapter 21. Hayride

SOMERVILLE HIGH WAS a shock. The three-story, L-shaped brick building had a huge smokestack at its center that made it look like a factory. The grounds were asphalt, with not a blade of grass. But bleaker than the physical setting was the dullness of the classes and the loss of my friends. During seventh and eighth grades, I had been with the same classmates in the top track, in the electric air of teachers who challenged us, and we had bonded as a group. Now, I was in an English class where some kids could barely read. My body sagged in the thick, dull air of the classroom, and sometimes, no matter how hard I fought sleepiness, my eyelids would grow heavy and my head would bob down and then jerk up with a start.

Most of my classmates had stayed on for ninth grade at our old school; only the few of us from Millstone township had to go as freshmen to Somerville High. The worst was that I had lost Theresa. Her family had moved away over the summer, but our friendship had ended before that. Toward the end of eighth grade, Theresa had stopped sitting next to me at lunch and passing me notes in class.

She stopped asking me over. She acted like she didn't know me at all—no longer catching my eye, raising her eyebrows, and grinning that conspiratorial buddy grin. I was completely baffled, and devastated. What had I done? I wondered if it was because I had decided I was against the Vietnam War. Or perhaps I had done something to offend her, or now that she knew me better, she didn't like me. Or maybe it was about my mother. The loss left me hurt and aching, and I stayed away from her. I never asked her what had happened. Shame held me back.

THERE WAS ONE ELECTIVE I chose that was actually interesting. It was Ancient Civilizations, my only class that had upper classmen, which made it exciting and intimidating. In the chapter on the Fertile Crescent and the ancient Middle East, there was a profile of a nose with a huge hump labeled "Semitic Nose." No one else seemed to notice; I was the only Jew in class, one of the few in Somerville High. I went home and stared at myself in the mirror, turning my head sideways. My nose didn't have a hump, but it was not petite or pert. I stared harder, cringing at how huge it was. I took my index finger to my nose, pressing it against the tip, trying to imagine my nose made smaller, less enormous, more pretty.

One day in class when we were studying the Roman Empire, an Italian exchange student came to speak to us about his country. At the end of his talk, he said, "I have a question for the class. How many of you are against the war in Vietnam?" My arm shot up. I looked around and noticed my classmates staring at me. I was the only one with my hand up. There it hung in the cold air. How I hated standing out as different. Blushing, I held my arm up a fraction longer, and then slowly lowered it.

Each day after school I came home to an empty house, since Mom was off at her graduate classes. The first thing I did was go into the kitchen, where I would open the stainless steel freezer, grab the carton of ice cream, and plop it on the kitchen counter. Then I would get a soup spoon from the utensil drawer. I would stand over the carton, eating one spoonful of ice cream after another. There was a great, unfillable void in my belly. At a certain point, I would tell myself, *Okay, this is the last spoonful.* And then I would take another. I couldn't stop.

In my freshman year, I gained thirty pounds.

THE SUMMER BETWEEN ninth and tenth grade, I spent the entire two-month season at Camp Birch Ridge. Money was tight since my parents' divorce, which had just been finalized, so I was paying for half the camp tuition by working as kitchen help. Each day after lunch, the camp codirector, Skipper with her short brown hair, wearing men's pants and work boots, stood at the head of the dining hall and sang out campers' names for mail call. This day had been a bonanza for me: one letter from Mom, and one from Dad. I folded both envelopes and shoved them in the back pocket of my shorts, because it was my turn to scrape, wash, and dry all the lunch dishes.

The problem for me in the kitchen was that I was slow and distractible. Left on my own with my rubber-gloved hands in the steamy, soapy water of the double metal sink, I would easily slip into reverie, my sponge moving more and more slowly over the white plates. I never finished before the end of the after-lunch rest period. Today, right after lunch, my unit was going on a hayride. When the camp bell rang, signaling the period change, I rushed to finish up, ripped off my gloves and hung up the dish towel, and raced outside.

In the camp meadow, Skipper was already sitting on the tractor hitched to a wagon filled with hay, and my unit, the Beavers, were all aboard the wagon. "Hurry up!" Skipper yelled toward me as I crossed the meadow. I broke from a trot into a run and leapt into the hay. We lurched forward, across the meadow and into a dirt track through the woods. Someone suggested singing "Kookaburra," and everyone launched in but me.

Kookaburra sits on the old gum tree
Merry merry king of the bush is he
Laugh, Kookaburra, laugh, Kookaburra
Gay your life must be

I PULLED MY MAIL out of my back pocket. The straw smelled musty and was itchy against my bare legs, but I ignored that. I leaned against the side of the wagon and opened my mother's letter first. It was all about her antiwar activities with her group, Women Strike for Peace. Mom wrote that she had come close to being arrested at a demonstration, and that a son of a friend had fled to Canada to avoid the draft. Things were serious, and sad. I got teary thinking of that boy having to run.

I put Mom's letter back in the envelope, shoved it in my pocket, and opened Dad's. The wagon hit a bump; yelps and shrieks interspersed the singing. I read the first couple sentences: "Dear Karen, Last week I married Catherine. It was a simple ceremony with just two witnesses and a judge . . ." I leaned back hard, my throat a lump, looking skyward, the passing trees a blur. *Catherine?* She was a co-worker of Dad's, in the chemistry group he headed. Once, Dad had taken me to the lab and introduced me to her, disappearing for a while, leaving me alone with her. But he'd said nothing more about her. I didn't even know they were dating. She had knit me a ski sweater and matching hat, and I had just thought she was a nice lady who liked to knit. Why hadn't he told me? Why would he think I wouldn't wish him well? Hadn't I listened to all his complaints about Mom, nodding my head in sympathy? Didn't he know I was there for him? My indignation covered the deeper pain that I couldn't let myself acknowledge: the terrible loss of being Dad's one and only, his special girl he poured his heart out to. I couldn't let myself think that he was deserting me again, but my chest beat and pulsed, my throat ached with hurt.

IN THE FALL OF TENTH grade, there were no more special excursions with Dad. Instead, every other weekend I stayed at the two-bedroom apartment he now shared with Catherine in Highland Park, about twenty minutes from Millstone. From camp, I had sent them a letter of congratulations, written with forced good cheer. I had stuffed my rage behind phony good wishes, terrified of seeming resentful, but now, sitting with them at meals, my cheeriness wilted to a withdrawn, sullen silence. All I could manage were occasional compliments to Catherine on her cooking.

Catherine, with her big bones, small eyes, and wide Slavic face, was twenty-six, only eleven years older than me. Dad had mumbled only the barest explanation of why he hadn't told me about his marriage until afterward, saying their courtship had been kept a secret from Catherine's family. They were Catholic Ukrainians who'd emigrated to America when Catherine and her sister were children. It was easy for me to guess why they wouldn't find Dad suitable: He was divorced, a Jew, almost twenty years Catherine's senior, and burdened with alimony payments for an unemployed, mentally ill ex-wife and child support for me, his fifteen-year-old daughter, who in a few years would need money to go to college.

In any case, Catherine seemed to have made up with her family, because she was often on the phone for a long time, speaking in Ukrainian. After dinner, Dad and I would move into the living room, decorated in Danish modern, while Catherine talked on the phone in the kitchen. Dad sat in a recliner, reading *The New Yorker* or the newspaper. I sat on the couch with my own book or sketchpad. After some uncomfortable interval of sitting in the living room, I would say, "I've got homework to do" and withdraw to the spare bedroom I used.

But I rarely did my homework. I had developed a bad habit of procrastinating, and forced myself to do it only at the last moment. Instead, I lay on the bed reading. Once the apartment fell quiet, and I could tell that Dad and Catherine had gone to bed, I turned on the old black-and-white TV. I watched through the late-night movies, exhausted, but too restless to sleep. Eventually, I drifted off, the voices from the screen weaving into my dreams. Other times, I turned off the TV to stare out the window. Across the way blinked the pink neon sign of a Dunkin' Donuts. The shop was closed, but the sign was lit through the night. I stared numbly at the pink glow, mesmerized by its rhythmic beat as it flashed on and off, on and off.

Chapter 22. Leaving Millstone

MY RIVER, THE MUDDY Millstone, was dying. Several years before, Dad had replaced our rotting wooden rowboat with an aluminum canoe. In the spring, summer, and fall, I often took the canoe out, paddling upriver. Occasionally, Mom came with me, but most often, I was alone. The trees that lined the riverbank reflected in the brown water, their leaves evolving from the pale green of spring to deep green summer foliage to autumn golds and rust. I would paddle upriver for a good hour, then drift back downstream, steering with my paddle, watching the ripples, relaxed and daydreamy. I knew the river's bends, where to avoid the old trees that had fallen in and lurked underwater, knew the patterns of bird migrations, the season of the geese's return.

The changes were subtle at first, just a few suds along the shoreline where the water lapped against the banks. Upriver, toward Princeton, there was a new housing development whose soapy runoff was invading the river. Over the course of my freshman year, the bubbles grew to great white foamy swatches swelling against the riverbanks. Then the algae bloomed bright green, coating my paddle with each stroke. By the fall of my sophomore year, the stench began. The fish died en masse. They floated belly-up, their silver undersides coated with algae. I stopped canoeing, stopped going down to the river at all.

I retreated indoors. I still had no friends at Somerville High, no one with whom to share my antiwar activism or political beliefs. I was out of sync with most other girls' obsessions with makeup, fashion, and boys. That no boys showed any interest in me didn't bother me; I told myself they were bumpkins and idiots and that when I got to college I would meet my equal: a mature, politically passionate, brilliant boy who would adore me. After school and on the weekends, when I wasn't at Dad and Catherine's apartment, I lay on the couch reading or sat playing my guitar. I had assigned myself Dostoevsky's *Crime and Punishment,* and I was struggling through it without understanding much. I had added the more cynical and militant antiwar songs of Phil Ochs to my guitar repertoire, and I sang them with vehemence.

Now and then, I still played piano, even though I had quit piano lessons at the end of ninth grade. My piano teacher had argued hard, telling me I had talent and if I would only practice, I could go on to minor in music in college if I didn't want to major in it. But that was just the problem—I resisted practice, and didn't see that changing, and I wouldn't be swayed. Now, I always played the same thing: Beethoven's Moonlight Sonata. As I leaned over the keyboard, my chest ached with melancholy and yearning, the notes echoing in the silent room over the soft pump of the pedal and the lonesome creaking of the black walnut trees that swayed outside in the wind. The sonata was singing my griefs, and the sorrows of the messed-up world, its high notes reaching for hope, then descending back to dolefulness. Sometimes, I played it over and over again.

MOM WORRIED ABOUT money, especially after the divorce. Sometimes I came home to find her at the dining room table, bills spread across it—the electric bill, the psychiatrist's bill, the pharmacy bill. In front of her would always be a yellow lined pad where she listed expenses in a column, checking off what had been paid. The weight of the bills creased her brow as she pondered which to pay first.

Since Mom wasn't working, our only income was Dad's alimony payments. After she got her teaching credential, she substituted at a local elementary school, but they'd stopped calling her. For months, she hadn't paid Grandpa Bachman the mortgage. He'd put up the loan for my parents to build the house. One day in the fall of tenth grade, Mom said, "Grandpa wants his money. He says we have to sell the house."

I stared at her, stunned. Our house was a work of art. I felt nourished by its beauty. But Grandpa had never liked the house. He was a butcher, a peasant from Poland; he didn't understand modern art, felt ill at ease in a house without many rooms, just one vast open living space.

"Man, he has money!" I protested. "He doesn't need it! He just hates this house, Mom!"

"Honey, there's nothing I can do. I tried to argue, but he wouldn't listen. Maybe it's for the best."

It wasn't until Mom began to ready the house for sale that I realized we could move anywhere, except that I didn't want to move too far away from Dad. We were unmoored, adrift; there was no one who much mattered to us or who cared about us. This idea held a certain freedom, but most strongly it underscored my loneliness. I decided it would be a relief to get out of this goddamn small town with its nosy-bodies and conservative ideas. Much as I loved our house, I had grown to despise Millstone.

MOM AND I MET Ruth and Brian Walker at a weekend conference on nonviolent civil disobedience held at a Quaker meetinghouse in northern New Jersey. They were communists, which intrigued me and scared me a little. Communists were the bogeymen in those Cold War days, but now that I'd decided I'd been taught a pack of lies, I was curious about what communism really was. Brian had been an actor who was blacklisted during the McCarthy HUAC hearings and lost all his work. Now, he ran an acting school in New York City.

Ruth and Brian came to visit us at the house. Communists or not, they were awed by the fame of its architect, and by its beauty. They stood in the open living space, staring around the two-story main room with its mahogany ceiling and furniture designed by Frank Lloyd Wright, with its wall of twelve-foot glass windows that looked out on the woods. "Won't this place be hard to leave?" Ruth asked. Mom just shrugged, her eyes sad. I felt sad, too. How would I say goodbye to this place, my home? When they heard our dilemma of where to move, they suggested their town: Englewood, New Jersey. It was close to New York City, right across the Hudson River, but quieter and cheaper, and had a good high school, and, of course, they lived there, so Mom would have some friends. And it was only a forty-five-minute drive from Dad's. Now we had a plan.

IN THE SPRING, for the first time since Dad had married Catherine, they invited me to go with them to a special event: a poetry reading in Princeton by the Russian poet Yevgeny Yevtushenko. The thought of hearing a real Russian writer had me jazzed. The Saturday evening of the event, Mom and I sat eating dinner. Our house was on Dad and Catherine's route to Princeton, so they were going to pick me up. Excitement distracted me from whatever Mom was saying, and as soon as I heard the revving of Catherine's VW bug in the driveway, I leapt up from the table, kissed Mom on the cheek, and made a hasty exit. I hated for Dad to come to the door, hated to feel the air crackling between my parents.

I had never heard a poet read, had never thought of poetry as something related to my life. At the packed concert hall in Princeton, Yevtushenko first read his poetry in Russian, his voice vibrating with intensity. I understood nothing, of course, but his passionate intonations thrilled me. I stole glances at Catherine's face to gauge the reaction of someone who understood Russian. Then he read the English translation, and the thrill of meaning emerged.

He began to read a poem called "Babi Yar" in English. Certain words jumped out: *no memorials . . . the steep hillside . . . as old as the Jewish race.* I felt chilled, the whisper of something stirred in me. Then the second stanza, *wild grass . . . one silent cry over the many thousands of the buried . . .* and my growing horror, hearing of another atrocity, one unknown to me, against my own people. And astonishment: here was a man, a Russian—not a Jew—who identified with us and felt the shame of his own country's collaboration.

ON THE RIDE HOME, over the chug of the engine, I asked Dad, "What was Babi Yar; what exactly happened there?" I leaned forward in the back seat to hear his answer.

"It was a ravine outside Kiev where the Nazis shot and massacred thousands of Jews."

Kiev! The horror came closer, became personal. Kiev was where Grandma Wilson had lived with her family. She had been sixteen when she'd left in 1920, simply saying to her mother and father, "I'm going out for a walk," when in fact she was about to cross the border with my grandfather, never to return.

"Dad, what about Grandma's family that she left behind?"

"We don't know what happened," Dad said. "Grandma lost touch with them long before the war because her brother told her to stop writing. It was too dangerous for them to have relatives in America."

I thought about this as the car curved along the dark wooded road, how Dad had never mentioned that possibly his grandparents, uncles, and aunt were in that grave in the ravine of Babi Yar, piled with the other Jews. How there was so much we never talked about.

Dad turned down our driveway and pulled to a stop. I thanked them, bid them goodbye, and stood on the front steps a moment, watching them make a three-point turn and head up the drive.

Then, I opened the front door. Water rushed toward me; several inches of it filled the hall. "What the . . . ?" I gasped. I waded down the hall, the water sloshing around my ankles, yelling, "Mom! Mom!?" Where the low-ceilinged hall opened to the two-story main room, I got my first glimpse of my mother. She was sitting on the floor by the bank of windows in her pajamas, holding a running hose in one hand, water pouring out its nozzle.

"Mom, what the—?"

"Hi honey! I'm washing the windows!" Mom grinned a loopy, lopsided smile. Her speech was slurred; she must have taken her sleeping pills early, sometime after I'd left for Princeton. Perhaps she'd been upset, and had taken an extra one. Or two.

"Christ!" I ran back down the hall and flung open the front door to call my father, but he was long gone.

I slogged back to Mom, bending over her. "Come on, Mom, get up," I pleaded, grabbing her arm hard. *I thought she was better. I thought nothing like this would ever happen again.*

"Ouch!" she bellowed.

"Sorry, come on, let's get you up!" I grabbed her under the armpits and we staggered toward the study where she slept. She plopped onto the twin bed and giggled while I struggled to help her out of her soaked pajamas. "Come on, turn on your side! Lift your legs, Mom. Lift your behind!" I went and got a towel and patted her dry as best I could, then pulled the covers over her naked body. For once, thank God, she fell right asleep.

I went back to the living room, where the hose was still adding water to the lake. I followed it out the French door, where Mom had threaded it through, and turned it off. I waded to the phone; my father should have reached the Highland Park apartment by now. I picked it up and began to dial, but halfway through, I hung up. What was the point? I'd been conditioned not to ask for help, trained for so long by his silence and his absences. Anyway, I didn't want to humiliate Mom and myself by Catherine's knowing.

I got the mop and opened the French doors that led to the terrace and backyard. My feet were cold and soaked, and as I looked down to start mopping, I saw that the leather dress shoes I'd worn for the night out were destroyed. I began to mop, pushing the water out the doors. The terra-cotta concrete floor had been painted the day before as part of the preparation for selling the house. Now, bits of red paint, looking like congealed bits of blood, were bubbling up and floating in the water.

I mopped and mopped. I mopped until the water was gone and I could drag myself to bed, leaving the ruined floor damp and molting.

Chapter 23. Englewood

WE MOVED THE SUMMER between my sophomore and junior years. Our apartment was in an old four-story stucco building that bumped right up against the sidewalk on Grand Avenue, a busy thoroughfare. The hospital was two blocks away, and day and night ambulances blared their sirens, wailing down the street. In the dark, I could see the flash of their pulsing yellow and red lights reflecting off my bedroom wall. Now, we lived in simple boxy rooms with white plaster walls. I couldn't let myself think about having lost a solace deeper than words: a house of ever-changing light, its view connecting me to the bloom and ebb of nature. I told myself the ugliness didn't matter; life would be better here.

That first summer in Englewood, Ruth introduced me to Joan, a girl my age who was a daughter of a friend of hers. Ruth and Mom dropped me off at Joan's for a little while to get acquainted. The house was a small two-bedroom wooden bungalow, where Joan lived with her divorced mom. Joan had long, thick brown hair, parted in the middle and down to her waist, and wore wire-rimmed glasses like I did. I silently admired her hair, since I was trying to grow mine out, but mine was thin and stringy and wouldn't grow much beyond my shoulders. We hung out in her room awhile, but she didn't have much to say to me. Finally, she asked, "Want to smoke a joint?"

"A what?"

"You know, a reefer."

"Oh." I tried to act cool. I was scared of drugs because of watching Mom stagger around on them, and had vowed never to use them, along with cigarettes. Just as I'd vowed never to be suicidal.

"Hey, um, listen," I stammered, "my mom is coming back soon, and I have to help her unpack, so I'll . . . I'll just pass this time. But cool, thanks, gotta go," I mumbled as I left, waiting anxiously on the sidewalk outside her house for Mom and Ruth to return. I felt dizzy, as if things were whirling around me, shifting faster than I could assimilate. It had seemed so hopeful, moving to a new place; now I wasn't sure.

For the rest of the summer, I withdrew to a world where I was more comfortable: the world of adults. Mom and I spent lots of afternoons at Ruth's. Her husband would be off at work in New York City, and the three of us would sit at her kitchen table, drinking Lipton's instant iced tea, eating pretzels, and discussing politics. Ruth had an odd habit: When she was most engrossed in some passionate political argument, perhaps about Vietnam, or unions, or organizing the working class, her hand would reach down her blouse, under the cloth, and rest on her breast, cupping it as to emphasize her point.

"In the whole history of revolution," Ruth was saying—and there it went, her hand reaching under the open collar of her shirt—"there has never been a social experiment like"—now her hand was getting close to her breast as I tried not to gawk—"in the Soviet Union." Bingo, she'd landed home.

"Oh, come on, Ruth," Mom retorted, "it's a totalitarian state! You just don't want to let go of your dream of a communist utopia."

But by now, I was barely listening, instead wondering if Ruth was unaware of her gesture or, if she was aware, feeling fascinated that she made no effort to stop herself.

At night, I took to watching hours of television. The TV was in Mom's room. We would lie on her bed side by side, propped up on pillows, while she smoked nonstop. When her sleeping pills kicked in, her head would start to droop, the cigarette dangling limply from her lips. That was my cue to grab it before it dropped into the bedcovers, and snuff it out in the ashtray. Sometimes I would drift off and wake to stare at the test pattern on the screen. It was often 2:00 AM when I would stumble to my own bed.

DWIGHT MORROW HIGH School was a gothic structure that from the outside resembled my image of an ivy-covered English boys' boarding school. It was much swankier than ugly Somerville High. School was more challenging now that I was again in tracked classes, this time labeled "college prep." It should have been much less boring than Somerville, and in many ways it was, but I had a new obstacle: cynicism. I no longer believed I was being taught information that was relevant or accurate.

I started to cut school. At first, it was just occasional. My homework procrastination worsened, and I sat watching TV with Mom in her bedroom until late before starting on it. Mom had given me the bigger of the two bedrooms so that I had room for a desk, but I hated the room. It seemed so desolate in there. Often, I started working at my desk after Mom was asleep. In the morning, if I hadn't finished an assignment, or if I was too exhausted, I would pretend to be sick. I would lie in bed and say how awful I felt: a headache or a stomachache or nausea or just generally crummy. Mom let me get away with it. But we had to keep up the mutual pretense that I was actually sick, which required that I stay in bed. Mom took care of me, bringing me aspirin, toast, and scrambled eggs in bed. And as I lay there during the day, I often felt more and more ill. It was almost as if Mom and I had a deal: We needed each other for company, and we'd be depressed together.

IT TURNED OUT THE journey to Dad's took a lot longer than forty-five minutes. I visited every other weekend. Dad said he would drive me home, but I had to get there on public transportation, a trek that took two to three hours, depending on connections. There was no direct bus from our New Jersey town to his. Instead, I had to board a bus in Englewood, cross the George Washington Bridge to New York City, descend into the subway and take the A train through Harlem to Port Authority Bus Terminal, and then board another bus to New Brunswick, where I would call from a phone booth and Dad would pick me up. In the underground corridor from the subway to Port Authority, I felt very worldly tramping with the multiethnic crush, past the nun in full habit sitting with her metal cup soliciting donations, up the grimy stairwell. By then, I always needed to use the Port Authority women's room, where I never knew whether there would be some woman slumped to the floor, nodding out against the wall next to the sinks, heroin tracks covering her arms. On the bus ride, the acrid smell of the infamous New Jersey petroleum refineries penetrated the air, and the gray industrial landscape, with its metal pipes and flaming smokestacks, perfectly echoed the bleak place inside me.

At Dad and Catherine's apartment, things felt tense because of the alimony they were still paying for Mom and me. Catherine was pregnant and new expenses loomed. Dad grilled me now and then. "What's with your mother? Is she looking for a job?"

What could I answer? I just shook my head.

ONE DAY IN LATE summer, after I had been in Englewood over a year, I was surprised by a phone call from Barbie. We had not been in touch since I left Millstone. She said that her mom was bringing her to New York City on a shopping expedition for fall school clothes. Did I want to meet them for lunch and then shop together?

On the day of our reunion, I put on the hippest outfit I had: a bright yellow minidress, an A-line that flared widely to its hem halfway up my thighs. I paired this with matching yellow pumps and white fishnet stockings. I wanted to impress Barbie with how groovy I'd become since I'd left our small town.

Over lunch with Mrs. Fredrickson and Barbie, Barbie gabbed about her new boyfriend. She didn't ask me about myself, and I couldn't think of any topic for discussion other than halfheartedly grilling her about her boyfriend. Our common language had been our bodies in movement: playing tag, riding our bikes, building forts. Of course, that discourse was lost forever. I felt a sinking feeling; she didn't really want to meet with me, to know about me. I wondered why she'd called.

Mrs. Fredrickson finally asked, "So, how are you, Karen?" in that stiff, closed-faced way she had.

"Fine." My answer evoked no further probing.

Barbie had grown tall, busty, and long-legged during our separation, more and more like her fashion-model sister, Monica. She had glowing, pale skin set against dark brown hair, a delicately chiseled nose, and long eyelashes. Her mom dropped us at Macy's on Thirty-fourth Street and said she'd meet us outside in two hours. We grabbed clothes from the racks and hauled them into a shared dressing room. There was a momentary flash of very white skin and bright pink nipples as Barbie took off her bra and pulled a yellow tube top over her head.

"So, whaddaya think?" she giggled. This top was a daring and sexy choice. I imagined it was for a date with the boyfriend.

I stood behind her as we both faced the mirror and stared at her. Her lightly freckled complexion was luminous against the yellow cloth, her long slender arms and neck rising elegantly from the clinging tube. Not an inch of fat on her ribs where the tube clung and then rose over her high breasts. "Looks great," I muttered.

And then in the mirror I saw myself behind her. My yellow dress made my olive skin turn its most sallow. My short legs looked pudgy in the minidress, the flaring A-line exaggerating my squat, chunky shape. I realized with horror: This was the most hideous outfit I could have ever worn. I wanted to hide my body, not strip to try clothes on. At that moment, I wasn't sure whether I hated myself or Barbie more. Beautiful, tall, dumb Barbie. I never wanted anything to do with her again.

BY MY SENIOR YEAR, I averaged one to two days absent a week. Mom always wrote me a note. Later, I stopped bothering her and simply forged the notes myself. No one at school confronted me about my absences, perhaps because I still managed to have an A average. No one said the word "depression" to me or asked me what I might be going through.

On my walks to school, I would scan the sidewalk in front of me for bumps and cracks (there were virtually no other pedestrians), and then close my eyes and walk as far as I could with my eyes closed, then open them, scan the sidewalk, close them, over and over. Or I would half-close my lids and walk in a twilight torpor, as if I didn't want to be awake. My body felt heavily weighted, in spite of the fact that I was dieting to ready myself for college and had lost twenty pounds. I was just so weary. I told myself I was being efficient, resting while walking, as if this made sense. As if it were normal to be exhausted.

MOM NEVER DID GET a job during my two years of high school in Englewood. We eked by on alimony supplemented with the modest amount left over from the house sale. She seemed to hover, not getting worse or better. I only had to call the ambulance once in those two years, and that turned out to be a false alarm. One Sunday evening, I came home from my weekend visit to my father's. "Hey, Mom, I'm home!" I called out after I'd let myself in with my key. The lights were blazing throughout the apartment, and it was still early evening. Silence. *Shit.* My belly tightened, my body going into that automatic state of emergency: *No time for fear; just see what has to be done.* I found her lying on the floor next to her bed, already in her pajamas, the bedcovers ripped askew. I shook her by the shoulders. "Mom, Mom." Her eyes fluttered open. "Mom!" I yelled. "Tell me, Mom, how many pills did you take?"

"Arraruh . . ." Her eyes closed again.

I shook her again. No response. *Damn.* I called the ambulance. While I was waiting for them, Mom came to. I was crouched next to her when she opened her eyes. *"How many pills, Mom?"*

She slurred out her answer, "Jus one 'tra one, 's all. Couldn't sleep."

When the doorbell rang, I stared into the face of two blue-uniformed policemen, not the white-coated volunteer squad like in Millstone. I stammered, "Really sorry, officers, I made a mistake. I thought my mom had taken too many sleeping pills."

One policeman turned and looked at the other, who shook his head and threw up his hands. "Okay, miss, don't do that again."

Later, when Mom told Ruth what had happened, almost making a joke of it like it was a silly mistake, Ruth said to me, "You should have called me to come help."

I looked at her, flabbergasted. *She has no idea what Mom is really like, how bad things can get.* No way could I subject Mom or me to such scrutiny—it was just too shameful. The idea of getting help was foreign, but also intriguing, a new idea tickling the back of my mind. *Really? You mean you would come?* some part of me wanted to ask Ruth. Instead, I just stared at her a moment, and then looked down, picking at my thumbnail.

BY THE END OF HIGH school, some part of me knew that I needed to get far away from my mother. I had two viable college choices: a full scholarship to Douglass, the sister school to Dad's alma mater Rutgers, or a pretty good scholarship from a school I'd applied to on a whim: Grinnell, a small liberal arts college in Iowa. I'd heard of it when a recruiter had come to our school, declaring it the Harvard of the Midwest. The thought of staying in New Jersey gave me shivers of claustrophobia. I chose Grinnell, in the middle of nowhere. Just where I needed to be.

I remember the day I left my mother. Dad was waiting at the curb in his car to take me to Newark Airport. Mom helped me drag my things to the elevator. As we stood there, waiting for it to come up, she repeated what she'd said the night before: "Have a wonderful time, darling!" I knew she meant it. I reached for her, and we hugged as the elevator dinged. She threw her arm across the elevator door to keep it from shutting while I shoved my bags in. We stared at each other as the doors closed, my throat tight.

Out on the street, Dad and I hoisted my bags into the trunk. I looked back up at the windows of our apartment. Mom was looking down on me. Even from the distance, it seemed to me her eyes had a look of sorrow and longing that made my heart feel like it was being squeezed. I knew I was never coming back, would never live with my mother again. Would she survive? What if she took another overdose? There'd be no one to come home and find her and call the ambulance. But I knew I had to go, no matter what. I took a long, slow breath, exhaled, and waved Mom a farewell.

PART TWO: IDENTITY HOUSE

Chapter 24. Iowa Nights

DAN AND I HAD CLIMBED naked out of his basement dorm window and were lying on our backs on the grass of the campus lawn, looking up at the vast blaze of stars. The early autumn night was still warm enough for us to lie bare-skinned without shivering, as the smell of dewy grass wafted around us. We had just finished making love in his room in our virginal way, with him moving on top of me, a sheet barring penetration. My first boyfriend ever. I felt almost dizzy with the freedom: so *here and now*—my mother pushed far into the back of my mind. I felt very avant-garde.

I had met Dan a few weeks into the first semester, at a student guerilla-theater group. I'd been intrigued by the idea of political street theater, but nervous at the first meeting. After brief introductions, we stood in a circle and did voice warm-ups and a few stretches. Next, we played a game where one person started a repetitive movement accompanied by a sound that the rest of the circle imitated, then the next person did their version that the group followed. It was so goofy and mindless that my body relaxed. *God, this is fun!*

After that, someone played director and gave us situations to act out in improvisations. The improv skit's demand to *just do it, don't hold back* pushed me past my shy reluctance into exhilaration. Afterward, Dan walked out with me, and we strolled across the campus. My excitement allowed me an even rarer unself-conscious animation with him. I talked and talked, my hands moving in expressive arcs. Dan asked if I wanted to take a bike ride with him the next day.

We'd ridden to a park off campus for what turned out to be our first date of sorts. I was laying down in the grass, looking up at the sky, clouds scudding high overhead, when suddenly Dan was leaning over me, pressing his lips against mine. I raised my hand against his chest, pushed him off me, and mumbled something semicoherent about not trusting people too fast. I didn't understand his urge to kiss me—I didn't even know him—but dating rituals were a complete unknown to me, so perhaps one kissed first and felt something later. In an out-of-body way, I was buzzing with excitement, a kind of generic charge not particular to any feelings for Dan, but for this moment: first kiss, first boyfriend.

Lying back in the grass after our aborted kiss, Dan said, "You're amazing. So bright—I could just tell at the group last night—and so beautiful." Now *that* got me turned on.

We rode our bikes back and stored them in the campus bike shed. As we were walking toward the dorms, Dan asked, "Do you want to come to my room?"

"Do you think I should call my mother first and ask her?" I found myself saying, tossing it off as a joke by adding with a laugh, "Do you think she'd approve?" Pause. *Stupid idiot,* I chided myself. "Okay, just for a bit," I said.

Being an upperclassman, Dan lived in a single. His tiny room was dark with filtered basement light from the one aboveground window. I flopped on my stomach on the twin bed, the only furniture in the room other than a desk and wood chair. I was trying to act nonchalant but was instinctively protecting myself, unable to be face-to-face with Dan. I thought he was exceptionally unattractive: a big hulking guy who moved clumsily, with pasty white skin and straight blond hair.

I could feel the warmth of Dan's hand resting in the small of my back, the sag of the bed as he sat down next to my hips. "Want a back massage?" he asked.

"Mmmph," I muttered into the bedspread.

He took that as a yes. His hands began moving against my T-shirt, kneading me lightly. I tried to will myself to relax, but there was a jangly buzzing throughout my body that coalesced into a painful knot in my stomach. Suddenly, I found myself leaping up. "Uh, it was fun, Dan" was all I could come up with.

He laughed. I didn't know what else to say, so I started for his door.

"So, how about checking out the campus movie tomorrow?" Dan asked.

I turned back toward him and smiled. "Okay," I said.

IN OUR SECOND WEEK of hanging out together, Dan introduced me to pot. He sat at his desk rolling a joint, his hands working the Zig-Zag cigarette paper back and forth. I stared nervously as he brought the joint to his mouth, licked the glue strip, sealed the paper, and twisted the ends. "How 'bout it?" He smiled over at me where I was perched on his twin bed.

Drugs scared me, but everyone said grass was different; it was cool, not like the older generation's horrible alcohol or tranquilizers.

I was wound tight and hated to lose control, but some part of me longed to. I hesitated, then answered, "Sure."

Dan joined me on the bed and we passed the joint back and forth. I coughed after the first inhalation, but persisted. We lay down on our backs, giggling, and then we turned face-to-face. Dan stroked my hair. I looked into his smiling face and saw an expression both sweet and gentle; he no longer seemed quite so homely. After an interlude of kissing, we both sat up and stripped. We lay back down naked, again face-to-face, stroking each other's backs. It was the most delicious sensation, feeling his fingers trailing down my spine, my fingertips following the arc of his shoulder blade. I sighed deeply, skin tingling, amazed at such intimacy. It was wildly exciting that someone wanted me, wanted to feel my body. I thought touching someone was knowing someone, and marveled that we had flung aside superficialities along with our clothes.

I remember writing to my father that Dan and I were cutting right through the mundane, going for deep connection. He wrote back a cautionary note: *Dan sounds nice, but take your time, you could get hurt.*

I wrote Mom about Dan, too. I rarely called her—it was too expensive—but during one phone conversation, my mother casually asked, "What kind of birth control are you using?" I was outraged at her assumption. As if she knew me so exactly that she had no need for asking details, as if she knew my life as it now was.

The truth was, Dan and I were both inexperienced. He'd had a girlfriend or two but was still a virgin also. So we stroked each other's bodies and dry-humped with a sheet between us, and did little else. I thought I was knowledgeable from junior-high sex education, but no one had ever told me I had a clitoris or that women could have orgasms, and I had never discovered it myself.

DAN AND I HAD BEEN together a couple of months when we finally discussed birth control. Dan was adamant that I not use the Pill. He thought it was not natural and potentially harmful to take a bunch of hormones. That was one of the moments I edged closer to loving him, moved that he showed concern for me. Condoms didn't occur to either of us. We settled on a diaphragm.

In 1969, there was only one way for a Grinnell coed to get birth control, and that was to go to Planned Parenthood in Des Moines, a ninety-minute bus ride away. I made a Saturday appointment and Dan agreed to go with me. But on Thursday, he bounded into my room, jubilant. "Kathy's visiting this weekend!" Kathy had been his best friend at Grinnell through their freshman and sophomore years—a platonic relationship, Dan told me. She'd transferred to another school to complete her junior and senior years. Every time he spoke of her and how amazing she was, his eyes would wander off and he'd grin to himself. "Feel free to go to Des Moines," Dan added, "but I want to hang out with Kathy. She's just here for the weekend, and I need to spend all the time I can with her."

I canceled my Planned Parenthood appointment, peeved at Dan and damned if I was going to go without him. We were apart all weekend. Once, from a distance, I saw him and Kathy crossing campus, their blond heads down, immersed in conversation. On Monday, he came by my room after class. He didn't sit down, just stood awkwardly in my doorway. "Listen," he said, "Kathy's visit made me wonder about some things. About you and me. Whether we work. I need some time to think. I'll see you in a couple days, okay?" And he was gone.

When Dan showed up at my room three days later, he sat on the far end of my bed and told me that he'd concluded from Kathy's visit, from how much they had in common, that he couldn't keep on with me. It just wasn't working.

My head felt suddenly heavy. How could I fight what he'd said? I didn't feel he even knew me, but I had no idea how to show myself to him. I could find no words, just looked at the floor.

After a while, Dan asked, "Are you in love with me?"

I had no clue what that meant, to be in love. But strangely, I found myself nodding yes, shrugging as if to take it back, then bursting into tears.

We just both sat there awhile. Then Dan, suddenly the worldly older brother, said, "The first breakup is hard. I remember: It hurts like hell. But you'll see, you'll get over it."

MY JUDGMENT ABOUT my college classes was swift: It seemed the same old conservative drivel as high school, and thus irrelevant. I wanted to roll my eyes when our first assignment in English class was *The Odyssey*; I had read that in ninth grade! Who needed any more Greek tales? I had so hoped for thought-provoking stimulation, but I gave up easily. I reverted to my bad habits of skipping classes and doing papers at the last minute.

I gravitated to the more radical students. My roommate Debbie was lovers with David, a Maoist who was in charge of ordering the films shown on campus. That meant we got to watch the movies before their campus screening. Our leftist group piled into David's living room to watch *The Battle of Algiers* and the films of Godard, Fellini, and Ingmar Bergman. I was gripped by whole new worlds of cultures, characters, and artistic visions.

One day on the spur of the moment, five of us movie fanatics piled into a VW Bug and roared off to the University of Minnesota to go to a reception for Godard. When we arrived five hours later, there Jean-Luc was, sitting on a couch sipping wine and discussing his movies. I worked my way close with my camera, focused the lens on the famous director, and started snapping wildly, pressing the shutter over and over. Godard turned, stared, and chastised me, "Don't waste film; it's a precious thing!" The Great One had spoken to *me,* and I glowed, unfazed that the words were critical. I nodded assent, echoing to myself, *Yes, what a great truth: film is precious!*

I learned to drive stick shift on the way home. Everyone else was pretty wasted, having downed many glasses of free wine while I was snapping photos. David gave me a quick lesson in a parking lot, then everyone crashed asleep while I lurched through the darkened two-stoplight Minnesota towns, stripping gears.

IN MID-NOVEMBER, a caravan of several busses took Grinnell students to Washington, D.C., for the Moratorium, a huge demonstration against the Vietnam War. I sat next to a woman named Kate on the many-hour ride. I had first noticed her in the campus cafeteria, a short blond woman dressed in a pink satin Playboy Bunny suit. Behind her, other women from her feminist street-theater group held up signs protesting the exploitation of women. I couldn't help staring at her large, pale breasts spilling over the low-cut suit.

Kate and I agreed to stick together as buddies as we marched and chanted with the crowd thronging to the Washington Monument. At the rally, we sat jammed elbow to elbow as we half-listened to the speeches muffled by the loudspeakers, both perking up to the songs of Arlo Guthrie and the cast of *Hair*. We sang along with Pete Seeger to "Give Peace a Chance," swaying with the crowd. Here I was, among hundreds of thousands of demonstrators, a long way from my first protests with my mother and the handful of her Women Strike for Peace activists.

As the rally wound down, we wandered the city, turning a corner to find ourselves in the midst of riot police lobbing tear gas at protesters. We ran holding hands, eyes burning and half-closed, to sounds of screams and coughing. We ran blind until the gas fog thinned and we could pour water on handkerchiefs to blot our burning faces. "Bastards!" I said between coughing fits. "Bastard pigs!" Kate echoed.

On the bus home, we were a bedraggled crowd, many of us red-eyed and damp from dousing off tear gas. Between naps, Kate and I talked. She had a kindred passion for politics and guerrilla theater, even if her focus was different than mine. She told me about her women's group, where they talked about female oppression. "You should come," she urged. I could sort of see her point about women's problems, but I felt it was trivial; I had much more important things to focus on, like militarism, imperialism, and colonialism. And finding another boyfriend.

HOMECOMING WEEK WAS the pinnacle of school boosterism. My guerilla-theater group scorned all that: the corny homecoming queen and king, who were paraded around the football field in a pickup truck throne before the game, the overeager cheerleaders who worked up their most elaborate routines, how everyone got oh so teary over "The Star-Spangled Banner."

On game day, my gang gathered clandestinely in an empty field behind the football stadium. We could hear the crowds roar at a play, and then the *boom* of the marching band's bass drum signaling halftime. The tallest man among us carried the Vietcong flag while the other twelve of us marched in a scraggly V behind him. Our tactic: onto the field fast, out even faster. We scrambled across the football field, chanting:

Ho, Ho, Ho Chi Minh
NLF is gonna win!

The roar of boos, hisses, "Go back to Russia!" some scattered clapping and raised fists. A fair number of students were against the Vietnam War, but for many this went too far; we were trampling on sacred turf to disrupt the homecoming game.

My heart beat hard as we crossed the field. All my childhood, I had hated standing out as different. Now, my discomfort at being noticed mixed with an incredible exhilaration. This time, I was not alone but belonging to my group of renegades, and instead of shame, there was pride. My whole body felt electric, buzzing with the charge.

I WENT HOME OVER winter break to a new Mom. Gone was her slurred speech, the nightly sleeping pills. She had done an amazing thing after I left—checked herself into a hospital to go through drug detox. Mom told me the barbiturates and tranquilizers she'd been on were so powerful that withdrawal from them was worse than heroin. She'd had days of sweats and muscle cramps so unrelenting that the nurses had to inject her with muscle relaxants.

When I had left home, I had prayed that she would make it, but that possibility seemed so precarious. I held a belief deep in my bones: *If I am not there to watch over her, she'll die.* Ironically, it took my leaving for her to decide to get off psychiatric medication. Our enmeshment had been destroying us both.

All that first semester in Grinnell, I had repressed my anxiety about my mother so heavily in my consciousness that it had lodged in the pit of my belly, clamoring like a siren. I had taken to drinking milk before and after every meal in a frantic attempt to quell an ulcerous stomach. When I came home to an alive mother, my stomach pains began to ease up. A part of me that had been clenched so tight began to breathe again.

Another part remained wary. How long could this last? Would she revert? It felt completely unnatural to me to let go of worry. And thrilled as I was, there was an underlying resentment, barely audible to my consciousness, like the voices of people in the next room when you can't quite make out their words. It was still too taboo to listen to those whispers: Why couldn't Mom have gotten it together when I lived with her as a child and taken care of me?

Mom had a new therapist, a leftist psychologist she was wild about. She couldn't stop talking about how wonderful this woman was, how much she was helping Mom. In addition to her individual sessions, Mom attended her therapist's group. They met every other week with the therapist and on alternate weeks on their own as a peer group. The leaderless weeks, they met at Mom's apartment.

The night they gathered in Mom's living room, she introduced me to everyone, beaming. Afterward I retreated to my bedroom. When the group ended, Mom came into the bedroom while I was smoking a joint. I didn't worry about her minding, as she rarely chastised me or played that kind of parental role. Anyway, she was such a bohemian I figured she'd be cool, but then she surprised me.

"I'd like to try it; can I have some?" she asked.

It weirded me out, the thought of getting high with my mother, but I passed her the joint, not able to say no. We sat side by side on the bed, taking hits. Then after a while, we were laughing at something someone had said in the group. I confessed that I could hear every word they said through the thin French doors.

We wandered into the kitchen, voracious. Sitting at the kitchen table over peanut butter and jelly sandwiches, our pot-induced silliness escalated until we were howling, tears running down our faces.

"Want some milk, Mom?" I asked, going to the refrigerator. I poured us two glasses, just to unstick the peanut butter from my mouth. Not that my stomach needed it.

I MET MIKE ON A SCAFFOLD. At the beginning of my second semester, I'd seen a sign calling for assistants for a mural being painted in a drama department rehearsal room. When I found the room, there was just one small blond guy with a goatee, painting high on a wall with his legs dangling off the platform. He was engrossed, and it took a couple shouts of "Hi up there!" for him to look down.

I hadn't done any art since high school, where I had taken every art course I could elect. But I had decided with regret that I didn't get to be an artist, because it was too self-indulgent when the world was so messed up. I felt I had no choice but to devote myself to political action, to saving the world. Not that I was doing so much of that here in the middle of Iowa.

"Come to help?" the guy on the scaffold asked. I nodded and he climbed down to get me started. Mike explained that this mural was his homage to Dada. I had no idea what that meant, but when he said the point was to create nonsensical images, I figured I couldn't go too far wrong.

The smell of paint again, the feel of the brush, that familiar intoxication: lush colors moving beneath my hands. Mike and I both worked immersed and silent for several hours, then washed up and went to the cafeteria together for dinner.

There was no formal dating between us, just a moment after several days of painting sessions when we held hands leaving the mural room, and then we kept walking until we got to his room. Without preamble, we made out. Day by day over a week, our make-out sessions progressed: kissing, necking, petting. I explained to Mike that I was still technically a virgin. By now, my virginity felt like a *thing,* not exactly a disease, more like an impediment. I was tired of the tension of that line I had not yet crossed over.

When I mentioned my virginity to Mike, he said, "Don't worry, I would never go ahead without checking with you first. We should decide on this together."

One evening, Mike and I were lying naked side by side on my bed, kissing and touching each other. He rolled on top of me as we kissed. Suddenly, I realized he was inside me. It was an odd moment mixed with relief and anger. Relief that the question was resolved, no going back. A flash of rage: *He didn't ask.* I couldn't linger on that thought, what that might mean. Then he was moving in and out of me. It was damn uncomfortable, because I had a tampon in, something Mike hadn't stopped to notice. I was mute, couldn't find my voice to stop him, but it wasn't that long until he pulled out and came into the sheet.

All I could say was, "That hurt. I had a tampon in!"

"Do you need to take it out?" Mike asked.

"It's a little late for that."

Beyond my moment of inchoate rage, I couldn't or wouldn't name what had happened. After all, I was willingly having sex with him. I didn't want to think about it as a violation. But my fury curled inside me like a cougar in its den, and every now and then, it made brief hunting forays.

We never made any declarations to each other: *like you, love you.* We had sex and slept together in Mike's bed every night.

When we weren't having sex, we talked about Mike's art, or rather, Mike talked about his art. He was a freshman like me, but he was already clear on his purpose: He was majoring in art. One morning when Mike had left before me for an early class, I sat on his floor, twisting metal wire as he'd shown me to around the armature of a five-foot metal sculpture in progress, which was taking up most of the free floor space. I didn't have class that morning, so I spent a couple hours at this. And then an odd flash: I saw myself, as if I were standing outside my body, watching as I meticulously poured myself into Mike's work. Who was this woman, so eager to assist, like one of those housewives Kate's women's group mocked? In that moment, I saw that I had taken in more female role socialization than I cared to admit. And there something else I didn't yet understand: I had artist envy that I channeled into being Mike's assistant.

SEX AFTER THE FIRST TIME, which had hurt as I expected, stunned me with disappointment. *That's it?* I asked myself. *That's all?* What a letdown! Foreplay had been fun, sometimes intensely exciting, but now that I was Doing It, there was less of that. In high school, I had drunk in what the girls in my art club had said about intercourse. They claimed the whole world shook, that it was the most profound experience ever. I had held on to that promise as my beacon guiding me toward the shore of *yes*.

I considered myself liberated because sometimes I was the one on top, but whatever the position, neither the earth nor my body quaked. I started to feel like a fuck machine, just there for Mike's pleasure, servicing him. But I said nothing.

I had never made the trip to Planned Parenthood for birth control, so we were using the pull-out method. Mike seemed to manage every time, and I didn't worry much. Then my period was late. After a week, I told Mike. His face blanched. "How late are you?" he asked. Mike borrowed a car, and we drove to the clinic in Des Moines. I left him in the waiting room, thumbing through magazines.

I waited for my first gynecological exam lying on the narrow exam table in a thin paper gown, chilled. The friendly male doctor seemed quite chipper when he informed me, "It's too soon to test you for pregnancy. But let's get you fitted for that diaphragm!" He plunged into the job while I contemplated a plan: I would leave school and fly to New York, which had just liberalized its abortion laws. Mom and Ruth, who worked at Columbia Presbyterian Hospital, would find me a willing doctor.

I didn't know if I said "abortion" to this doctor, even at liberal Planned Parenthood, whether he would have to throw me out of the clinic or not. *Roe v. Wade* was still three years away. After he handed me my diaphragm and spermicidal jelly, all I managed was a coded plea, "But I need to find out *soon.*"

"Don't worry," the doctor replied breezily, "you have plenty of time."

Mike looked up when I came into the waiting room, "Well?" he asked.

I shrugged. "It's too soon to test me." We drove back to school, tense and silent.

Frantic, I went to my resident advisor, a senior who lived across the hall from me. I stood in her doorway, telling her my plight. "Wait," she told me, "I've got something for that." She disappeared into her room. When she came back, she dropped two pills into my hand. "It's progesterone," she explained. "Take them, then wait three days. If you're not pregnant, it'll bring on your period."

Classes blurred. What took prominence were my forays to the bathroom to check myself. Day three: nothing. Day four: nothing. An agony of hours until day five: nothing. On the evening of day five: red spots on my white underwear. Such relief, the ecstasy of blood.

ONE MORNING IN LATE winter, I woke ill with flu. I tromped across campus through the snow from Mike's room to my dormitory, went into the bathroom, and wrestled my diaphragm out. Then I got in my bed, shivering with fever, queasy with nausea. I stayed there three days. My roommates Debbie and Anne took care of me, brought me soup, and went to the school nurse for pills and advice. Mike showed up on the third day. He was excited, in the midst of a new art project. He stood near the foot of my bed so as not to catch my germs, talking and talking about his latest sculpture.

Through my haze of nausea, I saw something clearly in that moment: his complete self-absorption. I sat up partway. "Mike, would you hand me the wastebasket?" I asked.

He handed me the plastic bag–lined container, and I sat all the way up, vomiting into it. When I looked up, he was gone.

My moment of clarity brought no relief. Leaving the relationship didn't occur to me. I endured, my hatred simmering, my suffering a silent accusation. That familiar state: hating the one you love, the one you're most connected to.

A few days after I more or less recovered from the flu, Mike informed me we were having Sunday dinner with his roommate John, John's girlfriend, Cindy, and his friend Peter. He had signed us up for one of the private dining rooms with an attached kitchen that students could reserve on campus. All us two women had to do was broil up the Sunday steaks, a campus tradition, and reheat the baked potatoes provided by the cafeteria. We didn't have to bother with dessert, because we'd all make our own ice cream sundaes. "Oh, and wear a dress!" Mike added to his monologue.

Unfortunately, over the fall and winter, I had gained quite a bit of weight and none of the dresses I'd brought to school with me fit anymore. The only way to wear my favorite dress, an orange A-line with flaring sleeves, was to dig out a girdle and suck in my breath.

When I got to the dining room, I was a bit late—a bad habit of mine. Mike rushed up, looking peeved. "What took you . . . ?" The others greeted me, and we sat down to eat.

Mike and I usually spent our time together alone, and when seeking company I preferred hanging out with my political comrades, so I hadn't gotten to know his friends. They seemed to admire him. They listened avidly to his description of his latest art project, and praised his previous work. Then they launched into some other subject, but I didn't really bother listening. I was staring at my steak, the puddle of steak sauce and the blob of ketchup next to it. It all looked revolting. I hadn't regained my appetite yet since the flu, and the girdle wasn't helping. In fact, I could barely breathe. It seemed I was breathless with silence, as if the more everyone talked, the quieter and farther away I got. My wind was gone; I could see myself shrinking and shrinking and felt no power to do anything about it.

As disgusted and angry as I was with Mike, my silence bound me. We continued to sleep together in his twin bed, where our nightly sex was rote and quick. No matter that I reassured Mike that my diaphragm was in, he always pulled out to have his orgasm outside me, while his roommate's Led Zeppelin music beat through the alcove door.

THE IOWA SNOW MELTED; the first emerging buds brought the remembrance of green. I had been bragging to my radical friends about my plan to drop out after the end of the school year, but I was incredibly relieved when Kate said she would move with me. Truth was, I was scared. Just in case, we both negotiated a one-year leave of absence, so it felt less irrevocable if the world turned out to be even worse than school.

Over spring break, Kate and I were making an exploratory expedition to California. When we'd discussed where to spend our year off, we had come up with two options: New York City or San Francisco. Kate was also from New Jersey, and we both wanted to avoid being too close to our families, so if we liked California, that's where we'd go.

We bought two cheap one-way student tickets to L.A., planning to travel up the California coast and then search for a ride back to school. It turned out Mike, Kate, and I were on the same plane. He lived in Colorado, where we were changing planes. We disembarked the plane in Denver together, and there was Mike's dad, waiting for him as we exited the gangway. He was compact like Mike, but clean-shaven, with blond hair in a crew cut, wearing a button-down shirt.

"Dad," Mike said, "these two girls are from Grinnell. They're catching another plane. This is Kate, and this is Karen."

Mike's dad smiled. "Hello."

I stood there expectantly, waiting for Mike to elaborate, but he looked right through me.

"Well, see ya!" Mike nodded goodbye.

"Bye, girls," his dad echoed, waving his hand.

Mike and his dad turned away. I grabbed Kate's arm. I was breathless with hurt. Was I nothing to him? I'd been a fool, putting

Chapter 25. The Great Divide

AUNT SOPHIE, MY DAD'S sister, picked us up at LAX and drove south. At her suburban home in Orange County, I wandered into a small backyard fragrant with flowering lemon trees. The air, so warm and different from just-thawing Iowa's, seemed magic and sweet with possibility. I stared, dazed with wonder, at the brilliant purple and magenta bougainvillea climbing the back trellis. My God, we'd landed in Oz.

Kate and I had no plan, except to get to San Francisco and check it out. After we'd spent a couple days hanging out and swimming in the Pacific, Irwin, a friend of my oldest cousin, Aaron, stopped by the house. It turned out he was driving north, back to college in Santa Cruz. From there, we could easily take a bus to San Francisco. The next day, he and another male student picked us up. Beyond L.A.'s freeway maze, I was mesmerized by the strange treeless hills of California rolling by. In the last couple hours of the seven-hour trek, Irwin's friend took over as the driver. Kate was in the passenger seat, and Irwin was in back with me. "I'm beat," he said "Mind if I rest?" And before I could say much, he laid his head in my lap. It startled me, but I let him be. After a while, he started rubbing his hand against my leg. I had no particular attraction to him, but I didn't stop him.

Since the airport scene with Mike, I'd decided if he couldn't acknowledge me as his girlfriend to his dad, I was free to do whatever I pleased. *To hell with him.* That night, Irwin and I went at it under a sleeping bag thrown on the floor while Kate was asleep or not asleep on his twin bed—I didn't really check. I went along with Irwin's moves, which were swift, abrupt, and of the school of *wham, bam, thank you, ma'am.*

In the morning, Kate gave me a rageful, chilling look over breakfast in the campus cafeteria, but said nothing until we'd parted from Irwin. As we walked along the Santa Cruz beach, carrying our duffels, Kate spat out, "Didn't you think of me at all? How could you be so inconsiderate!" I felt lousy about the whole thing, and mumbled an apology.

But as Kate and I traveled, I was intoxicated with my newfound ability to entice men, giddy with the power of it. It was *being* desired that was erotic for me. I didn't know yet that this was no great feat; it was just about a girl trailing pheromones, big eyes, and willingness wherever she went.

IN SAN FRANCISCO, I made out furiously with a high school friend of Kate's while she was in the bathroom. I couldn't seem to stop myself, and didn't really want to.

After a week of sightseeing in the city, we went to the Haight-Ashbury Community Center bulletin board—the Grand Central of hippiedom—looking for a ride. Coincidentally, we bumped into another Grinnell coed, Wendy, while staring at the Haight-Ashbury listings. Among the handwritten signs tacked into the cork was one by a couple with a van driving to Chicago, passing right through Iowa—and the three of us arranged for a ride. When Jim and Mary picked us up, we climbed with one other passenger, Bob, into the back of the white Econoline van, whose rear seats had been removed and replaced with a mattress covered by an Indian print bedspread on a raised platform. We headed due east, leaving the city Kate and I had agreed we loved and would move back to.

All went well as we climbed the Sierras, descended into the Nevada desert, skirted Salt Lake City, and clambered into the Rockies, but the van broke down at the Continental Divide, a few miles outside of Rawlins, Wyoming. The engine coughed and died as we rolled onto the shoulder of the highway. No amount of coaxing would restart it. Jim and Mary were stuck with their van, waiting to be towed, but the rest of us, who'd found this ride from the bulletin board, felt no loyalty.

Kate stated the obvious: "We'd better pair up for hitching. Four is too many." She gave me a dismissive glance and added, "I'm hitching with Wendy."

Kate was pretty disgusted with me for my sex play with every male we met. The last straw for her had apparently been when I fucked Bob, who'd turned out to be a real male-chauvinist creep, in the van while everyone else got out at a rest stop to pee and grab some food. It had to be a real quickie, but we still weren't quite done when the first person returned.

Bob had said something stupid about women-libbers earlier that day, and he and Kate had gotten into a fight. She didn't take crap like that. I thought he was a jerk, too, but later Bob's foot had nudged up against my hip while we were resting on the mattress in the back of the van. He wiggled his toes a little. I reached under the covers and stroked his ankle.

GETTING READY TO HITCHHIKE, we pulled on boots, hats, and gloves and gathered our bags. Wendy and Kate got out first, stood on the shoulder of the interstate with thumbs out in the late-afternoon light, and, being two women, got picked up right away. Bob and I took our turn. Off the side of the highway, there were patches of snow amid the clumps of sagebrush. We stood shivering in an icy wind that buffeted the treeless bowl of prairie and shook the sage bushes. We could see Jim and Mary huddled in the stranded van, waiting for a passing highway patrol car. It came all too soon, red lights flashing.

The cop wore a Stetson, like someone out of a grade-B Western. He motioned his thumb at us. "Get in the patrol car." He waited until Bob and I were seated in back, then leaned his head into the doorway. "Do you know it's illegal to hitch on the interstate?" He let that sink in a minute, in no rush. "Give me your ID. Just may have to take you in."

He sat in the front seat, writing our information down onto something I couldn't see. I was thinking about my Zig-Zag papers, red joint roller, and baggie of pot stashed in my duffel. Inside I had gone cold and still and breathless. Each second buzzed in my head like a swarm of anxious bees as I watched that shoulder.

Finally, the patrol officer got out and opened our door. He handed Bob his ID, casting a disgusted look at his long blond ponytail. "You're no spring chicken, boy! Hell, twenty-seven years old!" He glared at Bob. "You're just lucky she's eighteen." He gestured with his chin in my direction. "Just you watch it," he concluded to Bob.

The cop handed me back my ID. "Young lady, you and this boy are going to get back in that van and wait while I call the tow truck. If I see you set one foot and one thumb out on this highway, you are going to see the inside of Rawlins's jail. Do you understand me?"

"Yes," I muttered quietly.

"Yes, sir," Bob piped up.

THE AUTO REPAIR SHOP said it would take a day or two to order and install a new thingamajigger for the 1961 Ford van. We rented one motel room with two double beds. We were all too beat to go to dinner, so we shared what we had among us: a big bag of Fritos and some string cheese.

Then the four of us all lay sideways across one of the beds and vibrated to one quarter's worth of Magic Fingers, but Mary got up partway through and lay down on the other bed, said it was making her sick. She was still recovering from the abortion she and Jim had driven from Chicago to San Francisco for. Abortions were illegal in Chicago, like they were in most of the country, but they knew someone who knew someone who knew a doctor in San Francisco who would do it.

Bob and I wound up playing around with each other in the bathtub. When we went back into the darkened room, Jim was snoring deeply. For just a moment, I thought of Kate, and wondered if Mary was asleep or lying awake, still nauseous. We got in bed, and Bob was on top of me and at it before I had time to think further about Mary. I hoped he'd remember to pull out. I'd told him that first time in the van that I had left my diaphragm back at school in Iowa, since it hadn't occurred to me I'd be sleeping with anyone on my trip. Part of me knew pulling out wasn't the greatest birth control method, but denial and momentum took over.

In the morning, the four of us walked a few blocks to a coffee shop. Along the way, I noticed the traffic was mainly pickup trucks, and every truck had a gun rack in its cab with one or two rifles resting long and dark across the cab window.

The coffee shop was bustling. The counter had orange vinyl stools, and the padded booths were nearly full, mostly with men. Their hair was cut short and neat beneath their cowboy hats. Pointed cowboy boots were tapping the floor. The waitresses and the few women customers wore heavy makeup and had their hair poufed out, teased, and sprayed. There was an unsettling lull in the din of conversations as we entered and found an empty booth. No one else there looked like us: Bob with his blond ponytail, Jim's curly brown hair shooting out from his center part like an unsheared poodle's, Mary and I in bell-bottom jeans and peasant blouses.

The second night, we all stared at the road map, locating ourselves right on the Continental Divide, gauging how far we had yet to go. We were all antsy to be on our way.

In order to make up time, we agreed that we would just keep driving, stopping only for brief bathroom breaks and to grab some food. Bob and I took the first shift while Mary and Jim dozed against each other in the back seat. Hours later, somewhere in Nebraska, Mary startled awake and yelled, "Would you watch how you drive up there!?" She could feel the car making great lazy swings from lane to lane across the highway.

I laughed, not really caring. "Okay, okay, don't worry." The late-night road was empty, so I felt it didn't matter if I drifted. As I was driving along in the dark, Bob was playing with my nipples and occasionally dipping his hand down to my crotch. Every now and then I reached over and fondled his penis beneath his jeans. Back on the highway after confinement, I felt like a reckless character in a movie, a female *Easy Rider.* Gone was the good girl. The wildness of playing with a near stranger while driving made me aroused and wet. It was terribly distracting, and I steered erratically. Finally, Mary announced, "Pull over. You need us to take our turn."

Bob and I stepped out of the van into a Nebraska night smelling like wheat and clambered into the back. We scrunched down under a sleeping bag, making out and fondling each other, undoing our clothes just enough to have access to each other. Then Bob pulled my pants and underwear off, lowered his jeans around his hips, and was humping on top of me. His belt buckle was digging into my thigh, and, as usual, the act of screwing was a letdown.

Early morning midway across Nebraska, we stopped for breakfast. When I went to the bathroom, Bob followed me, caught me in the hallway. "Gotta tell you something. Last night, I got caught by surprise—came before I could get out in time."

I was furious. I was relying on Bob to pull out, just as I had with Mike. Our route would take us right through Des Moines, so I insisted on calling Planned Parenthood to try to get the Day-After Pill.

Jim and Mary looked concerned when we came back and I said I needed to make the call. The staff worker at Planned Parenthood asked me a series of questions, and then said I wasn't eligible for the Day-After Pill. It was still experimental and possibly dangerous, and they gave it out only in particular cases. I would just have to wait and see.

For the last leg of our journey, Bob and I sat silent and parted in the back. When we got to Grinnell, I had them drop me at the off-campus house of friends. Bob and I said a terse goodbye. I didn't want to go back to the dorm yet, to have to run into Kate or Mike. I needed space to think.

It was early afternoon. I borrowed a bicycle from my friends and rode out into the Iowa cornfields. The rich black earth—among the most fertile in the world—was freshly tilled. The Iowa sky was big, like in Wyoming, but it arched over rolling pastoral fields so unlike the harsh Wyoming range, with its fierce winds. I was thinking not so much with my mind as with my body, my legs pumping the wheels, heart beating hard. I was mad, all right, felt the surge of anger propelling my legs, but was it at Bob or Mike or Irwin or myself? Had I been wild and free or just stupid? Was I being used and duped? It wasn't that I felt bad about what I'd done, but I knew that I'd been reckless and hadn't taken good care of myself.

Something was shifting in me. As I pumped along, I could feel some new kind of determination rising up from my belly, but I couldn't yet name it. My mouth frowned in a bitter grimace. I slowed the bike, leaned over, and spat onto the pavement. Then, as I sped on along the road bordered by telephone poles and fields, a simple certainty came to me: I was done with Mike.

Chapter 26. Freedom School

NOT A WORD FROM MIKE when I got back to campus, and I didn't contact him. A few days into the spring term, I saw him walking and holding hands with Lorrie, a girl who looked a lot like me: long wavy brown hair parted in the middle, no makeup, same bell-bottom jeans. There was one noticeable difference: She was thinner. I couldn't believe he'd replaced me that fast. Even though I was done with him, it irked me.

In early May, school life was jolted by the news that four students at Kent State University had been shot and killed by the National Guard while demonstrating against the bombing of Cambodia. In response, there were nationwide student strikes. At Grinnell, we took over the ROTC building. Male students burned their draft cards in the school's Herrick Chapel. All classes ended, and the school was closed down before commencement. No finals, no final papers. My procrastination of school assignments had me on the verge of flunking several classes, so I heaved a sigh of relief. Kent State had saved my academic ass.

Instead of leaving town, my group of radicals, still energized from the ROTC takeover, decided to stay on over the summer to study theories of revolution. We called ourselves Freedom School. The dorms were closed, but we found places to stay off campus. Kate stayed, too, and we postponed moving to San Francisco until the fall. We'd somehow made up by avoiding all mention of our spring trip.

Our group read Karl Marx, Mao Tse-Tung, and Frantz Fanon and studied the history of the Cuban Revolution and the story of Che Guevara. I did some of the reading, but my bad study habits now seemed to bleed over to even these chosen subjects, and I just couldn't stay focused. My mind would wander off halfway through a paragraph or I would grow sleepy and doze. I came to our daily group discussions ill prepared, which didn't help my confidence. My shoulders tensed up, my breath grew shallow and fast, and I was made shy by my fear of saying the wrong thing. Here was the sharing of political ideas I so longed for, but I couldn't bear to appear unthinking or politically naive among these admired peers. My silence hardly seemed noticed, since the men dominated the discourse anyway. Two guys in particular pontificated constantly about political theory, hurling quotations and rhetoric at each other. I hated conflict, and these diatribes made me cringe.

The women of our group lived together in the house of a sympathetic professor and his family who were away for the summer. On the coffee table, feminist newspapers began to pile up. One day, I was slumped on our living room couch, struggling through *Das Kapital, Volume 1,* my feet up on the coffee table, when I just couldn't bear slogging through any more and so I picked up a women's paper. I idly scanned a column. Suddenly, I found myself immersed, gobbling the feminist analysis of the cultural myths we'd all been raised with. And then—*bang!*—I was thunderstruck. Here was my life, my experiences given name: *women's oppression, patriarchy, male chauvinism*. Given a cultural context that was so much wider than my own individual life. This feminist analysis, laced with my own remembrances—how in sixth grade my newly emerged breasts made swinging a bat awkward and shameful; how in eighth grade I started to hold back my enthusiasm for having all the answers, in favor of letting the boys shine; how I had acted so eagerly as Mike's art assistant—gave me my first glimmer of recognition of how the culture had conditioned us women to capitulate in our relationships with men, and to abandon so much of ourselves.

We, the women of Freedom School, started having separate consciousness-raising meetings to discuss feminist ideas. Our stories poured forth: experiences with men, sexuality, abortions, what it meant to be oppressed as women. The room buzzed with our excitement and anger. Then we read and discussed Anne Koedt's essay, "The Myth of the Vaginal Orgasm." My God, this was why fucking had been so uninspiring—I had a clitoris! My poor clitoris had been neglected on the myth that vaginal penetration automatically brings waves of bliss, and I had felt like a failure. It was a stunning example of a cultural lie that benefited a male-oriented sexuality. Our anger shone in us, a light that overcame depression and shame.

Our women's group decided to confront the men about their domination of our mixed group meetings. As a result, a new policy was instituted: Before each discussion of reading material, each person got dealt two playing cards. When that person spoke, he or she would throw a card into the center. Each person had to use both cards, and no one could speak more than twice or for more than five minutes. In theory, I applauded us women having equal speech, but I took to speaking once briefly, and then slipping the second card underneath my buttock.

One night, we women went to the drive-in movie together. We had no cars among us, but we had discovered a low fence at the back of the local drive-in lot. After the movie started, it was easy to climb the hillock behind the movie field and clamber over the wood fence and sit on the strip of grass uphill from the parked cars. We couldn't really hear, so one of us would make up zany dialogue and we'd all roar.

I leaned back on my elbows, my belly loose from laughing, smelling the sweet summer grass mixed with the acrid odor of cooling blacktop, the Iowa sky showering us with stars. I scanned the row of us silhouetted by the light cast back from the movie screen. We had all made identical shawls, crocheted loops of tan acrylic shaped into a V, and we were all wearing them: seven shawl-clad women looking like septuplets. My connection to these women amazed me. We had told each other everything, shared open-hearted revelations that intoxicated us with our newfound commonality. I had never before felt such a sense of belonging. *Sisters,* I whispered to myself. *My sisters.*

WHEN FREEDOM SCHOOL ended, I cried as I packed, knowing I would never see most of my Iowa friends again.

I went home to New Jersey to see my parents and gather some of my things before Kate and I headed for San Francisco. Mom was still pretty phobic about driving, so Dad met me at the Newark Airport and drove me to Mom's. On the way, I spouted my newly acquired feminist rhetoric about male chauvinism and the unequal power dynamics between men and women. "I'm only going to have secondary relationships with men," I ranted. "I will have my primary relationships with my sisters, with women!"

I glanced over at Dad; saw his hands gripping the wheel, his face clenched tight. Finally, he managed to sputter, "I hope this . . . this . . . phase . . . won't last too long."

WHILE I WAS AWAY, my mother had gotten her first job in several years. It was a tough, heartbreaking job, and I was amazed she could handle it: teaching remedial English composition to African American boys on the verge of dropping out of high school. My mother was still doing individual and group therapy, but I wanted her to go to women's liberation meetings, where she could get support without the premise that there was something wrong with her. I'd tacked up the Manhattan number for Older Women's Liberation on a bulletin board in the kitchen. So far, she'd ignored it.

I called her Gloria now. "No more dehumanizing, oppressive title of 'Mom'!" I told her. Besides, we were Sisters, and I wanted to recognize her personhood. I started calling my dad by his name as well. "Hi, Abe, how ya doin'?" I'd say into the phone, as if he'd become someone else, and not quite my father.

For all my talk of sisterhood, when my mother was around, I didn't pay much attention to her. I walked around humming "California Dreamin'." I wrote in a journal that I had begun at Grinnell and mailed letters to the Freedom School women. More than anything, I needed not to focus too much on my mother, not to resume a role so familiar and deadly. My love for her was too fierce, too consuming, and I couldn't afford it. My vision was turned from her, moving toward a life of my own.

Chapter 27. By the Bay

KATE AND I FLEW INTO the arms of sisterhood. Before leaving New Jersey, we'd called a women's switchboard in San Francisco, so we boarded our flight with the name of a married woman who had volunteered to put up new women arrivals to the City of Love. In the Women's Liberation Movement of 1970, it was as if a huge group of orphans had discovered their lost kin and were gleefully screaming, "Sister! Welcome!"

During the taxi ride to our hostess's house in Diamond Heights, San Francisco Bay gleamed blue and wide like the new life spread before me. I vibrated with an excitement I couldn't admit had fear laced through it. After thirteen years of school, there was no set structure to life. What would I make of it?

Ann, our benefactress and hostess on that first night, escorted us on the following morning to a three-story Victorian mansion in the ultra-rich neighborhood of Pacific Heights, poised on a hill looking down to the bay. Her friend Frances, in her forties, was renting out rooms in a home she shared with her husband, Paul, and two young daughters. Paul, an architect, had lost his job in a firm two years before and was still unemployed, so they had begun taking in boarders. Frances was totally involved in the Women's Movement, and was filling the house with Women's Liberation activists.

The room that was available had once been the master bedroom. It had the formality of an old-style upper-class world I'd seen only in movies: stained-glass windows bracketing the marble fireplace, a crystal chandelier, plush white carpeting, and heavy maroon velvet drapes. Nonetheless, the rent was cheap, and Kate and I decided to join the expanding household.

The first thing we did was to pull apart the double bed. We dragged the mattress onto the floor of the far corner and left the box spring sitting on its metal frame on the other side of the room. We flipped for who got to sleep on the mattress and who was stuck with the box spring. I was the loser.

WHAT HAD BEEN AN upscale nuclear-family home was now a countercultural collective household. The group pooled food money, $10 per week each, and we took turns shopping for our produce at the farmers' market. Refrigerator magnets held two sets of chore wheels, one for household tasks, the other for dinner-cooking duty.

At night, twelve of us ate in the spacious living room, sitting on the floor around a low-slung marble coffee table or perched on the couches and stuffed chairs. Frances was an artist, and her large abstract oil paintings hung throughout the rooms above the oak wainscoting. On the sideboards were Chinese vases, and in a corner, a life-size wooden Buddha. Welcomed into this family, I felt as if I'd entered some avant-garde new age where the rich shared their lives with political activists.

The two daughters didn't seem fazed by the change in their home. They burst in and out of the house, babbling with us all about their day. Paul disappeared for hours into his study, coming out for brief forays where he wandered around the house looking rather lost, but he gamely took his turn at cooking dinner, although it was always the same: hard-boiled egg and tuna salad sandwiches on whole wheat bread with carrot sticks on the side. Paul's lost, sad way reminded me of my dad, and I felt a bit sorry for him.

On Friday nights, Gay Women's Liberation met in the house. The one out lesbian in the household, Donna, a Texan in her late thirties, had invited them. The first Friday after moving in, I could hear murmurs and laughs from below. I knew I was going down there. Since I'd left Grinnell, I couldn't imagine being lovers with men again—that seemed way too oppressive. Logic told me that left only two options: celibacy or lesbianism. It was an intellectual concept, because I wasn't aware of any erotic feelings for women, but I was curious to sit in on the meeting. I waited until Kate went down first. I wanted to go separately, worried that people might assume we were lovers or, for that matter, assume I was a lesbian.

Fear made my legs heavy and weak, and I held on to the oak banister as I descended the staircase. I had never been in a room filled with lesbians before. As far as I knew, I had never met a lesbian. I couldn't remember anyone ever saying anything about lesbians, but there must have been something half-heard and half-forgotten, because somehow I'd soaked up the culture's disgust and repulsion. I thought I was too enlightened and progressive to be affected by such stereotypes, but lurking in the recesses of my mind were noxious images of bulldaggers—rough, swaggering women with slicked-back hair—rousing fear.

And then I was in the room. Sixty-some women were gathered: lively, laughing, all absorbed and facing the speaker in the front of the room. It was easy to unobtrusively slip in and sit on the floor at the back of the room. I looked around. The place was packed. Women were seated on the couches, chairs, and floor, spilling between the living and dining rooms; most were in their twenties, many with long straight hair, wearing bell-bottom jeans or green army surplus pants. Some were in hippie regalia of tie-dyed T-shirts or colorful Indian embroidered tunics laced with little mirrors; there was a smattering of girls in their late teens and older women in their thirties, forties, and fifties. An ex-nun in blue jeans and a flannel shirt was standing in the front of the room, telling her story of leaving the convent. Her tale was greeted with a wave of friendly laughter, as if the group were saying, *Yes, yes, we hear you, sister!*

I sat among the group and heaved a sigh of relief and joy. These were just women, wonderful women. Women who seemed vibrant and self-assured, laughing deep belly laughs. Many looked just like my feminist sisters from Freedom School. Many looked just like me.

ALTHOUGH MY FIRST meeting of Gay Women's Liberation brought a startling recognition, I didn't feel any sexual arousal for women, so it seemed impossible to really call myself a lesbian. I signed up for a one-afternoon course given by Breakaway, a grassroots feminist school, titled The Woman-Identified Woman.

We met in an actual classroom because the teacher, Bev, was a full-time professor at a community college. She wasn't supposed to use her room for an outside meeting, but there we were. Bev, in her thirties, was, in my eyes, an older woman. Her dark hair was cut short around her ears, wire-rimmed glasses resting on her pale, angular face. She wore a white tailored shirt tucked into brown corduroy pants with a thick leather belt and heavy black work boots. Before she started her talk, Bev sat at her desk, tamping pipe tobacco into a pipe bowl, lit up, puffed deeply, and then stood to begin her talk, pipe in hand. The sweet scent of pipe tobacco filled the room.

The lecture began. "Because what uniquely identifies a woman as a lesbian is sexuality," Bev explained, "society has defined lesbians solely as women who have sex with women. But this is too narrow," she continued, waving her pipe as she spoke, "and misses the richness of lesbian experience. Let's think about what are the aspects of being a lesbian."

Bev moved to the blackboard and began writing a list in her neat script, each item given its own line. She'd write a line, then turn and repeat it while facing the class, scanning our faces with her brown eyes that seemed to me deeply intelligent. Along with each of Bev's statements, a gong began ringing in my head.

"A lesbian is," she intoned, "a woman who loves women." *Yep, that's me.*

"A woman who gets her primary emotional support from other women." *Another yep.*

"A woman who shares intellectual ideas with other women." *Check.*

"A woman whose life centers around women, whose daily passions are with women." *Check.*

She kept going, my head nodding enthusiastically, until she got to the final point:

"A woman who has sex with another woman." *Well, nine out of ten. Close enough.*

I left the class joyous. Permission given—I was a lesbian! Phooey on straight society's narrow definition. Now I felt fortified, more sure that my woman-identified love would carry me along until I opened sexually.

During that afternoon, something else shifted in me: The disdain for manly women that I'd absorbed began to lift. Although Bev looked the stereotype of the old-style butch, I found her terribly handsome, beautiful in her confidence, compelling in the assured way she lit her pipe. She was so bright, so alive. I could watch her forever.

A MONTH OR SO AFTER MY first Gay Women's Liberation meeting, Kate and I both proclaimed ourselves lesbians. Neither of us had had any kind of sex with a woman, but that didn't stop us, now that our nineteen-year-old bravado was filled with women-identified lingo.

The meetings began breaking into small discussion groups halfway through each session so that women could develop a stronger connection and share more. Kate and I joined a group of eight who were to become an ongoing unit. Both of us were vocal in our opinions. On the topic of coming out, we declared that women should deal very directly with parents and straight friends, something neither of us had yet done. When, after a few weeks, relationships and sexual experiences became the topic, we both had to admit we'd never had any. "What!" several members burst out. Group discussion grew heated: Was a woman a lesbian just because she said so, even if she'd never slept with another woman? Did we get to stay? Two women said they felt unsafe. I burned with embarrassment and I longed to slip out of the room. But by meeting's end, votes for inclusiveness prevailed.

IT WAS A RELIEF WHEN AN attic suite became available and Kate and I could move out of the ornate master bedroom. The plainer room felt more fitting, with its sloped ceiling and bare wood walls and floor. Kate slept in the large main room, and I had my own turret alcove jutting out from one corner. With curved windows all around, the turret was like a bird's aerie perched above San Francisco Bay. I loved that tiny space. Sleeping on my twin mattress on the floor, I felt wrapped in my own magical nest.

A couple of days before New Year's Eve, Kate and I admitted to each other that each of us had been looking for some experienced dyke to initiate us.

"Kate, um, don't you think it's, you know, oppressive of us, to expect some older lesbian to bring us out?" I asked, glancing at her sideways. I was too ill at ease to look at her directly. And then I did. Right into her startling green eyes, set deep in her pale face. We smiled awkwardly.

"Yeah, it's really not cool," she replied.

I gazed at Kate, the friend who now shared almost every minute of every day with me. We were living very cheaply on our savings, which hadn't yet run out, so we still had the luxury of not working. Our days consisted of feminist classes and events, explorations of the city, Gay Women's Liberation meetings, rehearsals of our newly formed street-theater group, communal dinners, and life in the house, and through it all, we shared a running commentary, digesting our experiences. A shiver went through me; I'd never been this close to anyone.

I opened my mouth, and what poured out was "I love you." I'd startled myself, but there was no going back now. Once I'd said it, to my astonishment, I felt it—something buzzing in my belly, vibrating up into my throat, breaking my face into a smile. *I love her*. Of course. How simple: Kate, right there in front of me all the time.

"I love you, too," Kate smiled weakly. "Sex can't be that difficult to figure out, can it?"

"Nah. You're right, how hard could it be?" Suddenly, I was so scared, everything numbed up again, like a shovelful of dirt dumped on a campfire.

Neither of us made a move. Instead, we both agreed it must be time to go down to dinner. After dinner, we lingered in the living room for a couple of hours with several of our housemates. From a distance, I heard most of what they were saying, and sometimes my mouth moved in response, but my nerves were so jangled I could barely register anything. Finally, the talk ebbed and we all retired to our rooms.

Kate put on her yellow flannel pajamas. They matched her fine blond hair, cut bluntly at chin length. I put on my red flannel nightgown. It was cold in the uninsulated attic. Outside, a thick fog had settled on the bay, and we could hear the foghorns bleating rhythmically. Kate clambered into her twin bed, sat with her knees up as she leaned back against the wall, and pulled the blankets up.

"How about some music?" I asked. Kate nodded. I put Laura Nyro on the record player and sat down in the rocking chair next to her bed. We listened to Laura croon, *"Come on, come on and surry down to a stoned soul picnic. Surry down to a stoned soul picnic. There'll be lots of time and wine . . . "* I was rocking double-time. *Get a grip! Just calm down.* I stilled the rocking chair. Kate was twirling a piece of her hair with her index finger, round and round.

I couldn't stop shivering, I hoped just from the cold. I got up from the rocking chair and went to my pot stash in the cigar box on my dresser. I returned, sat back in the rocker, damped a line of pot into the joint roller, inserted a paper, and concentrated on rolling it out the other end. I lit the joint and handed it to Kate. We passed it back and forth, not speaking.

I knew that I was expected to take the lead because I was the one with sexual experience. Never mind that I barely knew my own body, that I had never had an orgasm, that sex with my boyfriends had been unadventurous and pretty unsatisfying.

"Want to dance?" I blurted, when we had finished the joint down to the roach. Kate nodded slightly, pushed back the covers and swung her legs out of bed. Laura Nyro was singing, plaintive and slow, "*Emily and her love to be, carved in a heart on a berry tree . . .* "

Kate stood next to the bed, hesitating. I'd gotten out of the rocker and was facing her, but my legs were shaky, leaden, so I just reached out my hands toward her. She took one step forward, reached her hands toward mine. I felt dizzy, faint. Fear had me holding my breath. Another step and our hands met, and then our arms wrapped around each other as we leaned our bodies one against the other. We began swaying, then moving slowly in a trancelike two-step. Under my hand, the cozy feel of flannel, the arch of her back moving underneath. With touch, my fear ebbed. The breath I had been holding released. The smell of her neck, salty sweet, mixed with the scent of herbal shampoo. I could feel her large, soft breasts pushing against mine.

We slowed until we were rooted, pressed together. She was short like me, and we fit right together. I kissed her neck and she leaned her head back, sighing. I worked my mouth up her neck, leaving wet marks against her skin. A great heat rose in me. Trembling, I halted, overwhelmed by the intensity that was stirring. And then she moved her face forward and we were kissing, stiffly at first, then softly, then more fiercely.

God, how I want her.

I took Kate's hand and led her into my turret, with its single mattress on the floor. She lay down on the bed while I lit the sand candle on my dresser. I stripped off my nightgown and lay down next to her, unbuttoning her pajama top, stroking her back. She ran her fingers through my hair, and my scalp tingled, electrified. I ran my tongue along the edge of her ear, down her neck, and along her collarbone. *Now what do I do?* In that moment of awkwardness, I looked up at Kate's face—her eyes were closed, mouth in a blissful smile—and I imagined what I would want: tongue moving slowly around my nipples, then faster, then teasing to slowness, then harder. For a moment, the insecurity held me suspended, then I let go: *Yes, her breasts, yes, I could live here, forever.*

I sat up and tugged Kate's pajama bottoms down from her waist. She lifted her hips while I pulled the pants off. Stroking down her belly, my fingers entered the wetness beneath her soft blond pubic hair. Kate moaned, as the long-forbidden touching released a chorus of hallelujahs in me. She reached for me as well. *Oh my God, her hand caressing me, inside me.* I rolled on top of her, pressing, rocking, gathering momentum, our throats crying out as I lost track of whose moans and sighs were whose. There was a great tightening roar and then a glorious floating.

IN THE SHOWER THE NEXT morning, I found myself grinning one of those goofy grins, remembering the double delight: first time with a woman, first orgasm of my life.

I couldn't wait to go downstairs and proclaim my new status: no longer the lesbian virgin. Kate was still asleep, so after my shower I went to the kitchen. Donna was standing at the toaster, plopping two slices of toast onto a plate. I must have still been beaming, because Donna stopped buttering her toast, holding the knife in the air. She stared a moment, then smiled. "Well, good morning, I guess!"

"It sure is!" I paused, not from shyness, but to add drama to my announcement. Donna, at thirty-nine, was one of the two "older women" in the house, and a puzzlement to me. I understood very little of the pain of her early life as a closeted lesbian in Texas in the '50s, how as a practicing Christian and a teacher she had felt even more pressure to hide and pretend not to be queer. Now, she was an activist within the homophile movement, working for civil rights. I often argued with her about her approach. "Donna, why waste your energy? Working within the system is useless—the whole thing has to come down and we have to start over. Revolution, not revisionism." She would smile indulgently at me, the teenage whippersnapper.

Now, Donna simply looked at me expectantly.

"Kate and I became lovers last night!"

Donna's smile deepened so that her eyes crinkled at the corners. "Well, congratulations! I'll bet you two are sweet together. Wonderful!"

KATE AND I KEPT UP our round of activities, bound by a togetherness that now included making love every day and sleeping in the same bed.

One weekend in February, Kate and I went away to a rented cabin in the Sierra foothills. Bringing enough groceries to hunker down, we arrived after dark to a cottage surrounded by pine trees. In the morning, we woke to the muffled quiet of snowfall damping the forest sounds. The cabin was set back from the road, and we could make love with the curtains open, the steadily falling snow a bright white against the dark trunks of the pines. We stayed in bed for hours. We read to each other from a new novel, *Patience and Sarah.* In the story, two women in the 1800s find a way to love each other in spite of all the daunting societal restraints, and create a life together on their own farmstead in New York State. As I listened to Kate read, it was almost as if we were those women, alone in a cabin in the woods, finding their way to an astonishing passion. We'd read a few chapters, make love again.

In the afternoon, we pulled on boots and ran out into the snow and chased each other around the trees. Later on, back in the cabin, we stripped off our snow-encrusted layers, got back in bed, and read some more. At one point, while Kate was reading to me, I reached over to her and caressed her cheek. "Wait, rest a minute," I said. It had struck me how loved I was, how I loved her back. It was scary, and wondrous. It made me breathless, and I needed to lie there quietly and look at her, try to take it in. Suddenly, I could feel in that moment how I'd closed down my heart to not need my mother, to bear losing my father. How I'd been encased in nineteen years of loneliness.

"You love me, don't you?" I half asked, half stated. She put the book away on the nightstand, pulled me to her. I could feel her warm breath against my ear, almost tickling me as she whispered, "I love you so much, sometimes I think I'll burst." Then we both laughed, but I knew she meant it. Something was bursting in me, too.

Chapter 28. Older Women's Liberation

ONE AFTERNOON, KATE and I took a long walk from the Pacific Heights house. We wandered through our neighborhood, with its mansions and foreign embassies, then headed downhill to Fisherman's Wharf and Ghirardelli Square.

On the way back, I stopped at a phone booth to call my mother. After a few rounds of hellos and how-are-yous, I asked, "Hey, listen, there's a piano at our house, so I was wondering, could you ship out some of my piano music? Everything that's in the piano bench?"

"Your piano music? Yeah, sure." Then, with barely a pause, she added, "Something I want to ask you. Are you *gay?*"

Mom's non sequitur hit me with a wave of chest-tightening anxiety. Here it was, that question—no getting around it. I'd been sharing with her steps of my process, and had even told her about attending Gay Women's Liberation, so she'd definitely had clues. Now I took a big breath. "Yes, Mom. I am."

My mother started right in, as if she'd been rehearsing what to say. "I don't agree with this! I think you're limiting yourself by not relating to men; you're copping out. Is this going to become your *cause* now? Are you giving up the rest of your politics?"

I'd never heard her this fierce and sharp, at least not directed at me. Her reaction stung, although I thought I understood it: her friend Ruth, the Communist Party hard-liner, was probably feeding her this "copping out and turning away from true leftist politics" bit. Still, I defended myself: "Glor, you don't get it—feminism is revolutionary! I'm not giving up my politics, I'm expanding them to include personal relationships, men's sexism. Don't you get how liberating this is?"

But it was as if she hadn't heard a word I said. "I've been talking in my sessions with my psychiatrist about you, that maybe you were gay. She told me that your becoming gay is really a plea for me to ask you to come home. Do you want to come home?"

Something in her voice caught me; she sounded tense, almost in a panic. *Goddamn psychiatrist!* "Gloria, listen, your psychiatrist is off her rocker. Kate and I are lovers, and it is the most wonderful thing. I wish you could see the power of women, of getting love and support from other women. I know you've heard the stereotypes about lesbians, but I'm still *me*."

Mom's voice only rose in pitch and urgency. "Darling, I worry that this is a *bad* choice! That it's a lonely and alienating life. And you're taking on a lot of oppression. I don't want you to suffer!"

I tried arguing, but nothing seemed to ease my mother's panic. We agreed to end our argument and talk more another time. After I hung up, I stepped toward Kate, who had been leaning into the phone booth during the whole conversation. Kate reached for me. "Wow," she exclaimed.

"Man, I didn't think she'd take it that badly" was all I could say before Kate folded me in her arms. We walked hand in hand back home, through the windy January streets.

OVER THE NEXT FEW WEEKS, Mom and I wrote each other letters, avoiding the phone. She was not much of a writer, and her letters were short and to the point. In her first two notes, she repeated her concern that with women I was heading for a life of depression and loneliness. I felt bad for her that she was torturing herself over me, that none of my arguments seemed to be changing her mind.

Then came her third letter. I read it out loud to Kate. "My God, listen to this!"

> *Dear Karen,*
>
> *I have quit therapy. Women's Liberation is going to be my therapy from now on. I have joined an Older Women's Liberation consciousness-raising group. It's wonderful—we talk about everything.*
>
> *Love,*
>
> *Mom*

I wrote back a jubilant letter of joy and encouragement.

A few weeks later, another letter:

> *Dear Karen,*
>
> *I read about the gay women's organization Daughters of Bilitis in that terrific book you sent me,* Sisterhood Is Powerful, *and I went to one of their meetings in New York*

City. I now fully approve of everything you are doing. In fact, I feel very close to you.
Love,
Momushka

At first, I thought, *What an incredible, supportive mother I have, going to meet lesbians in order to understand me!* Then I wondered, what was she really saying? Something held me back, though, and I didn't ask. It seemed delicate; if she was wavering on the verge, I didn't want her to react by my pressing her. A couple weeks later:

Dearest Karen,
I have told my Older Women's Liberation group that I am bisexual. Several of the women had negative reactions. I know over time they will come to better understanding. Myself, I wake up in the morning, look in the mirror, and feel so happy to be alive.
Love,
Gloria

That was it—I had to call her. This was incredible, since as far as I knew she'd been celibate for years, at least since she and my dad separated, when I was twelve. As soon as she picked up, I launched right in. "I got your letter about telling the women in Older Women's Liberation that you're bisexual. So, what the heck is going on? Does that mean you're having relationships with women?"

"Yes, sweetheart."

Her voice had a lilt in it I couldn't remember ever hearing. I leaned against the glass wall of the phone booth, digesting that. "Wow! Glor, that's fabulous!" She laughed.

I pushed on. "So, are you having relationships with men?"

"No."

"Are you planning to have relationships with men?"

"No."

"Well, Mom, I hate to tell you, but you're not a bisexual, you're a lesbian! You're just scared of the word, but it's not so scary."

She was pretty damn nonchalant: "Guess so, honey."

SUMMER ARRIVED AND my mother was coming to visit. I was bursting with excitement; I'd get to be with this new, joyful mother at last.

At a meeting of the Gay Liberation Front, a guy stood up and announced that a friend of his had a vacation cabin at the Russian River and was going to be away for a month; did anyone want to use it? Kate and I raised our hands like eager sixth-graders, waving vigorously. *Yes, we do, we do!*

The cabin in Rio Nido was rustic. There was no plumbing, no electricity. Kerosene lamps lit the dark wood interiors, and cooking was done on a cast-iron woodstove. There was no outhouse, so we squatted over holes we dug in the steep hillside of the backyard. We loved the place, the old-world feel of a cabin nestled among redwoods, the homesteading feel of chopping wood for the stove.

My mother was arriving during our last two weeks at the cabin. The day before her flight, Kate and I hitchhiked to the Guerneville Safeway and bought the ingredients for a Russian borscht—just the thing to make my Jewish mother feel at home.

Our friend Stephanie was visiting us from the city, so I borrowed her Datsun and drove to pick my mother up at the San Francisco airport. As I waited for her at the gate, my chest thrummed with anticipation. Then there she was, coming toward me, wearing jeans and the orange and purple tie-dyed T-shirt I had made and sent her. I noticed her formerly gray hair was now dyed dark brown, her short curls the same shade as my long hair. At the sight of me, her round face broke into a wild grin and she bellowed, "Karen!" Her arms flew out, grabbing me into a hug. We fit together, my body the echo of hers: short and pear-shaped, with ample hips and thighs curving from our waists.

I was so eager to show Mom my beautiful California that I took her up the long, windy coast route on Highway 1, forgetting about the jet lag and her fear of heights. As we curved along the precipitous cliffs, she clung to her armrest and turned slightly gray, but she didn't complain.

At the cabin, she and Kate hugged long and hard. "I'm so glad you two are together," Mom said, beaming at us both. Stephanie, Kate, Mom, and I chatted and laughed over the steaming bowls of borscht accompanied by pumpernickel. We even had herring with sour cream, one of Mom's favorite foods and a staple of my childhood.

The day after my mother's arrival, Stephanie, Kate, Gloria, and I spent the afternoon skinny-dipping at our private little beach, just a spit of sand along the Russian River hidden from the road by bushes.

That evening back in the cabin, Mom took me aside. "I'm attracted to Stephanie. Do you mind?" she asked simply.

My mouth hung open a moment. "Do I mind? Glor, she's my *friend,* and she's my age. God, are you kidding? No, don't even think about it."

Mom shrugged. "Okay, honey, it's no big deal, really. I have plenty of other lovers back in New York. Just thought I'd enjoy myself."

"How many lovers do you have?" I asked this with a mixture of awe and chagrin. I was shy, and couldn't imagine finding multiple lovers, but I covered that envy with a self-righteous superiority: I thought my monogamous relationship with Kate trumped Mom's affairs.

"Well, every week I go to the women's bars in New York City and to my Daughters of Bilitis meetings, and I usually go home with a new woman every weekend. But I tell all the women how it is with me, how I was celibate for so many years and now I'm coming back to life. That I'm into pleasure and being close to a woman, but I'm just not serious right now. It's sex, and it's fun, and it's *good.*"

ONE AFTERNOON, MOM and I were alone drinking peppermint tea in the cabin kitchen. My mother reached across the table and took my hand. "I want to ask you something. Do you remember Marian, my friend at University Heights?" Mom was staring at me with a most intense expression.

The question startled me. I reached back with my mind. University Heights was the married-student housing for ex-GIs where my parents and I had lived while Dad was getting his PhD. I remembered a big-boned woman, tall, with long black hair. "Sure, Gloria."

Mom went on, "You and she and I spent every day together for two years, from the time you were two until you were four." My mother hesitated. She let my hand go, looked back at me: "We were lovers," she said.

A memory flashed: *I am standing with my mother in the doorway to Marian's bedroom. Marian has her back to us, and she is sitting at a white dressing table on a backless seat, facing a mirror. Her head is bent slightly to the right, and her long hair cascades down her neck and over her right shoulder as she brushes her hair. Mom leans against the doorsill, and I am pressed against Mom's thigh. We are both spellbound, mesmerized by Marian as she strokes with the hairbrush over and over again. There is some feeling in the room I am too young to name. The room shimmers with it.*

I realized I was gripping the tea mug midchest, and set it on the table.

"At first, we were just friends. But Marian had been in the WACs during the war, and she'd had women lovers there. After we became lovers, I was happier than I'd ever been. I was really happy, and I was really in love."

Mom's face had a faraway smile. Her hand drifted toward her teacup and she took a sip. Then she looked at me again, her smile fading. "We kept it a secret, never told our husbands. I longed to take you and just go away with Marian, but she wouldn't hear of it, and I really couldn't see a way to do that. So, during the day we were lovers, and at night the husbands would come home. Sometimes the four of us would have dinner together and play cards."

I leaned forward in my chair, breathless.

"Then, Marian had a nervous breakdown. I didn't understand what was happening to her. One day she was gone, off to a mental hospital. No one said a thing to me—I had to go ask her husband where she was. When she came back a few weeks later, she said to me, 'Gloria, I'm cured. We can't do this anymore.' She told me, 'Gloria, we just have to be good wives, spread our legs, and be faithful to our husbands.'"

"Oh God, Mom!" A great weight had gathered in me, rooting my body to the chair.

Mom nodded, her brow creased with remembering. "It got worse. When I begged Marian to be with me, she mocked me, called me a dyke, a sicko. I wanted to die, right then. I just wanted to die."

Mom looked down and gripped one hand in the other. She sighed. "Not long afterward, we moved to the apartment in Millstone while your father and I were building the house. I was so depressed, I started seeing a psychiatrist. I thought he might help me. Of course, his whole goal was to get me to adjust to my marriage, and I went along with it because I thought there was something wrong with me."

Mom shook her head, as if she could shake away regret. "But I just got more and more depressed. I can't quite remember when I started getting so depressed that I wanted to kill myself, but it was sometime after the affair with Marian broke up. And then they took me away to the hospital for those shock treatments."

As my mother talked, a fury built in me. My body blazed with it. All those years that Mom and I suffered, all those suicide attempts—the rifle, the river, the rat poison, the overdoses—all the times when I found her half-dead, all those pills tranquilizing her into droopy-eyed sedation . . . all that was now made clear as the aftermath of her love for a woman, forbidden and punished by society.

Another thought hit me: It hadn't been her fault. Relief mixed with my rage: There was a reason. My God, it wasn't our fault!

Chapter 29. FBI

OUR ACTIVIST HOUSEHOLD SET amid the mansions of conservative and wealthy Pacific Heights stood out like a colorful sore thumb. All the comings and goings of braless women in overalls and the occasional long-haired, scruffy man must have alarmed the neighbors, although I never spoke to any of them. Strange occurrences were going on outside our house, and we began to suspect that we were being watched.

One evening, we noticed a Pacific Bell telephone repair truck set up right over the manhole in the middle of our intersection just prior to a Gay Women's Liberation meeting. Every Friday, sixty to eighty women gathered in our living room for those raucous meetings. The first time, none of us paid much attention to the truck. But then it happened the next week. By the third Friday, we started to worry. We'd heard rumors that the government was using utility trucks for spying on people. The bay windows of our living room faced the center of the intersection. I pictured a camera and a shotgun microphone pointed straight at us from inside the van. Creepy.

None of us was completely sure about the truck, and no one wanted to be overly paranoid, so we went about our business in the various groups that met throughout the house: feminist consciousness-raising, gay rights, the anti–Vietnam War movement, my guerilla-theater group, which rehearsed in the attic. What could they do to us anyway?

I was leaving the house early one morning, when I noticed a smaller-than-usual garbage truck stop in front of our house. What was strange was that it only stopped at our house, not at any others on the block. From then on we paid attention, and sure enough, every week we had our very own exclusive garbage pickup. At a house meeting, we talked about being careful not to put marijuana seeds or anything too personal in our garbage.

I WAS LEARNING TO DRAW from Frances. Our landlady offered a drawing class for anyone in the house and she taught us how to see, to really *look,* to feel shape with the eyes and let the hands move from that knowing. I loved my not very realistic but expressive drawings, and hung them proudly on the walls of my turret.

I started carrying around a sketchpad again, as I had in high school. Frances and I made trips to the beach, where she and I sat on the dunes, drawing birds, waves, passersby. In those moments, I was swept up, totally immersed. At last, I was being the artist rather than the artist's assistant, the role I had so easily and resentfully fallen into with Mike. Frances showed me the way, and I adored her for it.

One afternoon, Frances and I returned to the house from a sketching outing to Baker Beach. As we came in the front door, one of Frances's daughters, eleven-year-old Jenny, rushed up to tell us she had seen Bill rifling through papers in Donna's room in the area where she kept membership lists.

Bill had moved in about the same time as Kate and I. He was tall with a long ponytail, living on unemployment benefits. Even though Frances was trying to fill the house with feminists, her first priority was getting renters, so her backup choice was leftist men. I'd been enthralled with Bill's tales of a journey to Cuba. Now, I wondered, who was he, really?

ONE AFTERNOON, TWO different unknown women rang our bell and asked if we had any pot for sale. Frances turned them away, saying firmly, "No one sells drugs here." We noticed that police cars kept passing by. Housemates gathered in the living room and wondered—were we about to get busted? We decided to take everyone's personal stashes and sneak them out of the house.

Bill had been away for several days; we didn't know where, so Kate and I went into his room to check for dope. His stash was beyond easy to find—over two pounds sitting in a large clear plastic bag on his nightstand. What the hell? He had never tried to sell any of us anything. We gathered his baggie along with everyone else's stash, and Paul, the straightest-looking among us, secreted it out of the house.

The next day, when Bill returned and was confronted about his dealer-size stash, he said. "Man, my unemployment's running out, and I just needed some dough. I heard about this great deal, so I went for it. Listen, I'm sorry about that—I'll keep the shit in my car from now on."

Two weeks later, John, Frances's grown son from her previous marriage, was over at the house. Some of us were hanging around the living room, including Bill, when John announced, "Man, I just scored some great smoke, so let me know if any of you guys want to buy weed." The next day, cops showed up at his apartment, searched the place, and arrested him.

Kate and I decided to search Bill's room. He'd been spending more and more time away from the house, and we had no idea what he did during his absences. This time his pot stash was only a little more hidden. In spite of his promise, we found enough pot in his closet to incriminate the whole household.

Furious, Kate and I flushed it bit by bit down the toilet. Then we searched Bill's room further and found a picture of him with short hair and utility bills to another San Francisco address. This supposedly unemployed hippie was maintaining a separate apartment.

Now, Kate and I were completely convinced that we were living with an FBI agent. When Bill showed up the following Monday for our communal dinner, one of the housemates blurted out, "Some people here think you're an agent, Bill. Are you?" I was aghast that she'd blown it like that. Bill laughed. "Oh, come on!" he said.

The next morning, I passed Bill's room as I headed downstairs for breakfast. His door was ajar and I glanced inside. Sometime in the middle of the night, Bill had cleaned out his room and vanished.

NOT LONG AFTER BILL disappeared, the house was put up for sale as part of Frances and Paul's divorce. As a stopgap, Kate and I crashed in our friend Stephanie's commune, where five women were living in an upper flat of a Mission district Victorian. What should have been a dining room and a living room were being used as bedrooms, so the only communal space was the kitchen at the end of the long central hall, where the household gathered for meals and interminable meetings. Kate and I slept in the tiny guest room, actually a walk-in closet off the hall.

We didn't want to commit to a city rental because we were considering moving to the country, saddened by the infighting in our women's groups and wanting respite after the trauma of FBI surveillance. The heady idealism of the women's movement had given way to disappointment. In the lesbian-feminist movement, we'd believed we were creating a new community, one where we could totally trust each other, never be oppressed again. Our personal stories had poured out, each woman's tale its own wondrous revelation, resonating with our experiences in a patriarchal society. But as we went on, this togetherness grew cracks, stresses, and fissures. Our yearning was so intense that there was little room for differences. Each difference, over time, felt like betrayal. Amid the fractures, our hearts sank.

Kate and I began to take periodic breaks from the city, sometimes hitching down the coast and camping at the beach, or taking the bus due east to the Sierra mountains.

We knew we couldn't keep crashing at the crowded commune, so we called Frances and asked if we could camp on land she owned near Point Reyes National Seashore. It would give us time in the country to feel it out, and a base. Frances agreed, so we loaded up our backpacks and hitched over the Golden Gate Bridge and through Marin County, beyond its wealthy suburbs to where the land opened to rolling hills dotted with solitary live oak trees, through valleys with ranches and small towns. Our ride dropped us off on the one main block of Inverness, with a single market, gas station, and post office.

Kate and I said little to each other as we hiked the two miles to Frances's land. Things had become strained between us. Since moving to California, we'd been with each other constantly, and our togetherness had intensified after we'd become lovers. It was difficult to admit that I clung to Kate. Since childhood, I had thought of myself as so independent, but once I was touched by Kate, need rose in me like an oil geyser from a Texas well.

There had been one evening when Kate and I had been alone in the tiny guest room of the flat and she had blurted, "We *have* to spend some time apart, or I'm going to go crazy!" Her outburst shocked me, scared me, *God, don't let me lose her*, but I saw the truth of it. "Okay," I agreed. But this was something we hadn't yet managed to do.

Kate was a determined hiker, while I was a meanderer, but, loaded with my pack, I had no desire to dawdle as we marched side by side in step. Yet, even burdened by the weight, I felt something of the green forest began to seep in, the scents of pine and bay laurel rising up as we crunched tree droppings underfoot. Something held tight in me began to ease. Moving my body through such beauty gave me my breath back.

The dirt road ended at Frances's plot. We set up our pup tent, crammed in our sleeping bags. By the time we got our camp organized, it was early evening. We used Kate's backpacking stove and cooked up macaroni and cheese mix from a box. Kate withdrew into a sullen silence. I had the urge to shake her and yell, *Talk to me!* But instead, after our strained dinner, I got out my flashlight and a paperback, crawled into the tent, and read. That would show her I could give her space.

The next morning, there were no morning kisses. After a mostly silent breakfast, we walked into town.

That evening Kate announced she would be going back to the city the next day, by herself. She wanted to attend a Radicalesbians meeting and would probably stay for a couple days beyond that.

My eyes burned and my heart banged in my chest. I'd hoped that the country would let us relax back into ease with each other. Now, through the knot in my throat, I managed to force out, "Sure, of course. I hope you have a great time."

I WOKE DISORIENTED, no Kate there beside me. She had left just after dawn. Then I remembered: *I'm alone. Kate has left.* A rush of panic made my skin sweat.

When I stumbled out of the tent, I saw that it was late morning; the fog that had poured over the ridge the prior evening had burned off. The details and rhythms of California nature were new to me: the rainless summertime, the chilly coastal fog. I shivered, though it was not especially cold, and made my way to the nearby stream. I crouched among the ferns, splashing water on my face, shocking myself into the present. In my stomach, there was just a dull ache where I'd clamped down against my terror at Kate's departure, closing my ears to its whisper: *She doesn't love you, she'll leave you.* While that mantra beat in the nether regions of my psyche, I assured myself: *We're together; she just needs space.*

After a breakfast of granola and powdered milk, I pulled my sketchpad, pencils, and Cray-Pas from my pack. My anxiety eased a bit with the awakening of something else—a flicker of curiosity. How would I do by myself? I wanted to learn this land, take in its foreign beauty until it became familiar, became my new home. I spent several hours sketching the landscape around me: the meadow bordered by a hillside thick with trees, a close-up of a manzanita bush with its maroon bark, the ferns and foliage along the stream, rocks in the stream bed, my own legs and feet resting on a tree root hanging into the stream. I settled into a trance of solitude, a state so familiar from my solitary play as a child, honed from loneliness.

I did see one person that day—a tall white man in late middle age with gray hair, jogging in a T-shirt and shorts past the meadow. I nodded at him, but he gave only the slightest tip of his head. I tried not to think about being a woman, alone, out in the woods in a flimsy tent, and now some man knew I was here.

I turned back to my journal, a bound, college-ruled notebook with a green and white mottled cover. It was the first journal I had ever kept, begun almost two years before at Grinnell. I wrote in it erratically, but that afternoon I poured my thoughts into its pages. I pondered the current state of sisterhood: There had been the rush of feminist consciousness, the euphoria of coming out, the feeling of belonging, and the hope that we could change the world. Then there began to be struggles and bitter fights. How disappointed and confused I now felt. *How hard it is to live in this fascist world!* I lamented to my journal. The writing both stirred things up and calmed me down.

After dinner, I smoked a joint. The fog was just rolling over the hill in the last of the light; a few advancing white tendrils fingered their way into the meadow. In the twilight, shadows deepened and the bushes seemed to hunch, taking on ominous shapes. The wind picked up, and something moving caught the corner of my eye. *Christ!* I'd swear I saw a wolf lurking in the bushes. *Don't be absurd,* I told myself, *the pot is making you paranoid! There are no wolves in California. Or are there?* I found myself creeping up to the bush in question, to reassure myself there was nothing there. Finally, I dove for the tent, seeking the enclosed space. Several times in the night, I woke with a start, alert from a cracking twig or wind whipping the tent flap, but then sleep would pull me back to the kaleidoscope of dreams.

On the fourth day, Kate returned. She arrived in the afternoon and found me sitting on the metal cooler, writing in my journal. We grinned wildly at each other. I closed my journal; we grabbed each other and kissed. How I had missed her, and now it felt good to have had enough separation to miss her. She seemed similarly renewed: more settled in herself, less tense and irritable, her love for me flowing again.

We spent two days on the land, telling each other of our experiences apart, making love, hiking in the woods and to the beach. After that, we hitched to the city to resume our political meetings and city life—dancing in lesbian bars, visiting with friends. For three weeks, we alternated three or four days in the city with the same on the land.

One day, just as we returned to the country, Frances's white Dodge Dart pulled around the bend and into the meadow, a dust trail pluming out behind it. She leaned her head out the window, not bothering to say hello. "The sheriff came by my place yesterday," she told us. "Asked if you had permission to be on my land. After I said, 'Yes, absolutely,' he told me no one had seen you two around for a while, so they got worried you were lost in the woods. So, he and a deputy came up to the land looking for you. I told him it was ridiculous that you were lost—where was there to go? Surely you had just gone to the city. And Karen, he said that he'd taken your wallet for identification purposes."

My mouth was open, stupefied. I reached in my pocket and felt the soft leather of my billfold, "That can't be because I have my wallet in my pocket. Wait, let me look in the tent." I ran to the tent and ducked inside. While we'd been gone in the city, they'd come and gone through my things. The clothes I'd left folded in a corner had been tossed around and lay in haphazard piles. Where was my journal? I tore through everything, searching, muttering, "God, it's not here, it's not here!" Dread was closing in on me. My journal was gone. And so was my address book.

All we wanted to do was to get away, get the hell out of there. Luckily, we'd been all out of pot, so there was nothing they could arrest us for, but that didn't quell our alarm. Frances offered to drive us back to San Francisco. We stuffed our packs with our clothes and took down the tent. On the drive to the city, Frances told us more. The sheriff and his deputy hadn't just come by themselves. They had brought two bloodhounds, search-and-rescue dogs, to sniff through our belongings.

I thought about the things I had written in my journal: sexual experiences with men, an acid trip, my evolving leftist and feminist consciousness, coming out with Kate—all my most private inner ramblings. All now being read by the Inverness police. I could imagine them smirking, reading parts out loud to each other, "Hey, listen to this . . ."

By now, my journal had probably been xeroxed and sent to FBI headquarters. It must have been the feds who had alerted the local sheriff to keep an eye on us. I figured it had all started with Bill. We must have been on a list ever since he had spied on us. And the jogger—was he one of them keeping tabs on us? It had been odd how he'd come by every day. I thought about Bill's scanning Donna's membership rolls, and it hit me: The Inverness police probably took my address book for the same reason, and now were comparing the names in my journal with names and phone numbers in my address book. I shuddered, horrified that I'd endangered others. That day, the budding writer in me got asphyxiated.

Later that week, when Frances went to the sheriff's office to retrieve my things, he changed his story. As the sheriff handed her my journal and address book, he laughed and said, "Oh, I saw them hitching out of town." He didn't seem worried that Frances would realize his previous story about our being lost in the woods was just a ruse. He knew there wasn't a damn thing we could do about it.

Chapter 30. Icebox Canyon

KATE AND I WERE ATTACKING the rusted iron bed frame with our paintbrushes. Bright blue paint spattered everywhere—on our clothes, on the parking lot gravel, and on our new puppy, Emma, who kept bringing us a stick to throw. We'd dragged the frame outside our one-room cabin into the parking area that ran along the row of Russian River cabins. Our new home, Pocket Canyon Cabins, was a group of flimsy wooden structures originally intended for summer vacationers from San Francisco. But the resort area's heyday had waned, and the cabins were now rented year-round to locals.

Even in its prime, the resort must have been a second-rate affair. Six one-room cabins, painted a stomach-wrenching mustard yellow, sat on the gravel lot cleared of all but a few redwoods. We'd spotted the cabins on our exploratory mission, when we'd driven up from the city in the used Datsun station wagon we'd bought.

The landlady, a stout woman in her fifties, had looked us over and asked, "Are you girls students?" When we said yes, we'd be going to SRJC in September, she nodded, brought us into the office, and pushed a rental agreement across the counter. "Okay, then. We don't allow any trash here. We run a respectable place." I wondered whether a couple of pot-smoking, radical lesbians fit her definition of trash. But we were getting desperate, so we both smiled politely and signed the papers.

Our new life: just the two of us, feeling lost and adrift, playing house. I worried about how we might be treated, knowing as I did how being "different" in a small town can be met with bigotry. Kate and I agreed to be in the closet unless we got a feel that someone was tolerant. Yet, strangely, we didn't think we were being obvious, painting the frame of our shared bed out in the middle of the yard for all to see. Later, when we became friendly with Valerie, she said our bed painting had clinched it among the cabin dwellers' gossip—they all knew we were gay. And according to Valerie, no one seemed to care.

IT WAS IFFY HOW WE WERE going to manage to pay the bills. In San Francisco, we'd gotten by on short-term odd jobs, food stamps, and savings. Now, Kate and I came up with a financial plan: keep getting food stamps, keep living as cheaply as possible, and beg our fathers for help.

How we were going to support ourselves long-term was a blurry unknown. Coming out as a lesbian had a disturbing consequence: It meant I could never rely on a man to support me, although our fathers were standing in for now. As independent and liberated as I felt myself to be, I'd grown up with the '50s paradigm that husbands support wives, and since I'd dropped out of school, I had no degree or training or any sense of a career path to sustain myself.

My school plan wasn't exactly academic. I wanted to explore art, and signed up at the free junior college for photography, pottery, and life drawing. Kate asked her dad for his old 35 mm Leica camera, using the lie that she was the one taking the photography class.

The shape of our lives changed. No more meetings of Radicalesbians, collective house dinners, or consciousness-raising groups. Kate and I drove together four days a week on the half-hour trip to Santa Rosa Junior College. On campus, we parted, heading to our separate classes. She was taking several English lit and composition classes in her quest to be a writer, while I was happy leaning into the clay on the potter's wheel, sketching nude models, watching the black-and-white images appear in the chemical tray in the red light of the darkroom.

Even though no one was hostile to us, I never felt at home at Pocket Canyon Cabins. In the pressure cooker of the tiny cabin, tension simmered between us. When Kate was mad, she became silent and withdrew. But there was nowhere to withdraw to, so she would immerse herself in an activity, ignoring me. This drove me wild. The more closed down and unexpressive she became, the more frantic and demanding I found myself.

ONE NIGHT, KATE WAS sitting on the floor, leaning back against the side of our bed while sewing a pant hem, not uttering a word. I could feel her anger—or was it mine? I went over to her and squatted, facing her. "Kate, what's going on?! What's wrong?!"

"Nothing. Nothing's going on." She didn't look at me, kept her head down, the needle moving in and out of the pant leg.

I reached for her, wanting to shake her out of her coldness, but instead of grabbing her, I pricked my finger on the needle. "Shit!" I was hopping around the little open space next to our bed, wagging my hand, feeling like a fool. But I couldn't stop myself. "Don't give me that cold-shoulder crap," I yelled. "Kate, I know you're upset about something!"

I stopped hopping and stared at Kate. Her small green eyes were narrowed beneath her tightly furrowed brow. Not a peep from her. She set the needle in the pincushion, folded the pants, put them next to her on the floor, and reached for a huge tome, *The Golden Notebook,* which she had planted on her other side. *Unbelievable!* There she sat, coolly skimming the pages. *She can't really be seeing the words, can she?* I grabbed the book and flung it across the room. "Stop it! Talk to me!"

Kate disappeared into the bathroom. She came out in her nightgown. "I'm going to bed," she told me. And she climbed into our bed, pulled up the covers, and became a silent lump.

Burning with fury, I grabbed my jacket and went out into the night, Emma at my heels. My breath came short and shallow in the cold air. I wanted to murder Kate. Yet the quiet, the glittering stars, the pine smell held me as my breath slowed. I bent over and petted Emma, stroking her long, soft fur as she leaned into me. I sighed and straightened up. "Come on, girl, let's go." I turned back, heading for bed.

In the spring, Kate and I enrolled in a women's jujitsu class on campus. We began to make some friends among our classmates, which eased the tension between us. Our teacher was a cop, and ran the class in a militaristic fashion. He had us do sit-ups and push-ups while yelling, "Come on, you sissies!" at our weak-armed, wobbly push-ups. Yet there was something amazing about facing the lineup of the entire class, grabbing the lapels of the white *gi* of the woman facing you, swiveling around to spoon into her while thrusting your hip just so, and flinging her over your shoulder, until you had thrown twenty women as if they were lightly stuffed duffel bags.

To *be* thrown was to feel your body fly in the air, to land with a resounding *smack* of your arm against the mat, body rolling with the momentum, not fighting it, and to rise to your feet in the exhilaration of being completely uninjured!

WHEN MY FATHER ANNOUNCED in early May that he was coming for a visit, my first thought was *He's gonna know.* I hadn't officially come out to him, although I figured that after our earlier, "I hope this phase won't last too long" conversation, he had his suspicions. I knew his first look at our one-room cabin with its double bed taking up most of the space, would settle any doubts he had.

I was determined to tell him on our drive north from the San Francisco airport. As I drove, my throat felt jammed and each choked minute ticked against my nerves. By the time I turned off the freeway in Santa Rosa ninety minutes later, I was still voiceless. When we entered the redwoods, Dad beat me to it, as I was focused on rounding a curve. "Ah, what sort of . . . " He paused, cleared his throat. "*Hrrrum*, what sort of relationship do you and Kate have?"

We now had a used VW van, since our Datsun had died. The boxy vans are lousy curve huggers, so we careened a bit rounding the bend. "If you mean are we lovers, the answer is yes." The edge in my voice startled me. My assertion came out more defiantly than I'd intended.

I glanced over at Dad. He had his face in his hands and was crying. I pulled over onto the weedy shoulder and shut off the engine. Silence. As a child, I'd seen my father cry before, often rushing to comfort him—"It's okay, Daddy, it's okay"—but now his crying made me angry. It felt like I had spent a lifetime feeling sorry for my father.

He lifted his face up, took a handkerchief from his back pocket, and blew his nose. "When your mother . . ." he began, faltered, tried again. " . . . Early in our marriage, your mother was involved with another woman . . ."

"With *Marian,* you mean," I interjected vehemently. I wanted him to know my mother had told me first. That I understood the story differently now. My mother had not been some pitiful, mysteriously depressed woman, but a woman with a grief-filled heart, a lesbian trapped in a marriage, a woman electroshocked and drugged and therapized by a homophobic psychiatric system.

"Well, I just knew something had happened between her and another woman. It wasn't until some years later that I found out it was Marian," Dad said.

My father, the scientist. He could be so literal at times, missing the point I was trying to make, the emotional implications. I couldn't find my breath.

"But what I'm trying to say," Dad continued, "is you have to understand: When I found out your mother was a lesbian, I thought about leaving her. But then I realized if she had tuberculosis, I wouldn't leave her, so I'd stay with her through this disease, too. That's how we thought of it then—as an illness. So, it's going to take me some time with you."

Dad and I stared at each other, eyes moist, torsos turned in our bucket seats.

With Dad, I had swallowed my own pain to bind him to me. I had been desperate to buoy him up as the strong parent. It had all been a sham. Now that my mother had told me the secret, I saw that homophobia had shattered us all.

My chest and throat ached with that familiar but unspeakable pairing: *How I love you; how I hate you.* He was admitting why it was hard for him, I had to give him that. "Okay, Dad, I can understand that" was all I could manage. I started the car, and we headed for Pocket Canyon.

When we got to the cabin, Kate had dinner ready: our standard cooked veggies with rice, a salad topped with sunflower seeds and tahini dressing, and freshly made carrot juice. Dad shook Kate's hand in the doorway, and we sat down at the dinette set. He raised his glass of juice as if to make a toast, but then simply took a sip, leaving his mustache tipped with orange foam. Dad gamely dug into his food, but both his and Kate's faces were a bit grim. I so wanted him to like her, and her to get to know him, but it was a competitive war from the beginning. When they started their verbal sparring, I felt caught in between, as I had at meals with my parents.

As their conversation veered through the women's movement, politics in general, and existential issues, whatever the subject, they took opposing stances. "Life is great! Things are changing, full of possibility! We're on the edge of a great revolution in sex roles and culture," Kate declared, while my father held to "Life is tough and terrible! Disaster is around the bend. It won't work out."

My father, with his sad eyes. It hit me then: My father was depressed, had been depressed my whole life. I had only thought of my mother that way, that my father's sadness was simply in reaction to his troubled wife, the sick one. But now I realized something in him was defeated, while Gloria had reclaimed herself.

And Kate. I looked at her face, hardened with its stubborn, tight jaw as she argued with my father. She was immersed in her argument, and never looked my way. I thought she might reach out more, for my sake. In that moment, her insistence bordered on meanness; I saw no kindness there. Sure, I agreed with her that there was lots of cause for hope, but did she get it at all how excruciating life could be? Did she have a clue how much pain my father and I had survived?

As soon as the meal ended, I burst out, "You must be tired, Abe, still on East Coast time. How 'bout I drive you to your motel?"

The next morning, I picked my father up at his motel in Guerneville. I had taken the day off from classes while Kate went to school. Sightseeing seemed the thing to occupy the time. We headed over to the Napa Valley.

Somewhere along the road, after stops for tastings at a couple of wineries, Dad blurted out, "Your mother—I hope she has made peace with her predilection."

Oh, Dad. Can't you even say the word? Silly that I hadn't expected this question. Something in me clenched, and I found I couldn't say the word either.

"She *has*," I replied, then went silent. I felt protective of my mother, didn't want to reveal the details of her life to my father, her wild year of sleeping with every woman in sight.

It was at the third winery's deli, where we bought French bread, cheese, and fruit, and were eating at an outside picnic table, that Dad said, "I'm glad your mother has come to peace with herself. Once, I met with her psychiatrist. He was a specialist they brought in just for Gloria. Um . . ." Dad hesitated, cleared his throat.

"Yes?" My stomach was knotting up.

"Well, what he specialized in was treating homosexuals. He told me to have faith, that there was hope for her. That he had helped other homosexual patients. He gave me an article about a gay man he had successfully treated to become heterosexual."

"Jesus, that bastard! They treated Mom as if she was sick and perverted and to be cured when she was brokenhearted for Marian.

And how twisted for you, to be given false hope. God, what an awful mess."

Dad sighed, "Yeah, what he said gave me a glimmer of hope, but it was a false hope. It was a terrible time."

I heaved a big sigh, too.

As I drove us back into the redwoods, Dad announced, "Karen, I've changed my plane reservation. I'm sorry, but I'm going to leave tomorrow. My flight leaves at noon."

"Oh. Okay." Relief mixed with a sudden sense of defeat. His five-day visit, shortened to two. My father just couldn't take it. But then, I was used to that—wasn't he always leaving me?

AT THE END OF MAY, Kate went all out for my twenty-first birthday. Our friends, Sally and Jennifer, let us use their cottage, as our space was too cramped. Kate invited women from the city and our new friends from our jujitsu and VW repair classes. Sally and Jennifer lived in a fairytale cottage: They were renting a former caretaker's home on a three-hundred-acre horse ranch in the Valley of the Moon. We gathered in their living room, with its stone fireplace and big picture window, looking out on a huge meadow with solitary live oak trees amid grazing horses. To me it was a beautiful, wondrous place: sheltered by pines, but facing light-filled open country, so unlike the frigid redwood forest.

Kate had festooned the living room with crepe paper garlands and balloons. We all donned paper party hats, passed joints around, ate a potluck meal, and succumbed to great gales of laughter. I was giddy with being loved by Kate and celebrated by my friends. It seemed to me we were commemorating more than this marker into adulthood. There was the triumph of our relationship. We'd come out together and been lovers a year and a half, bonded by our shared life in the women's movement; had suffered surveillance and disillusionment; and been through a hard winter in the woods. Now, we'd made it to the other side.

A month after my birthday party, Sally and Jennifer bought a house, and we snatched their fairytale cottage. We were moving there with two other women. It was the realization of a dream: not just a beautiful place, but a collective household with women friends. We knew Dotty from jujitsu and Martha from our VW repair class, and had a budding friendship with each of them. The house had three bedrooms, so Kate and I would share a room, and Dotty and Martha would each have their own. In our premove planning meeting, they both said they didn't mind living with a couple.

Our fourth weekend in the house, Kate and I began painting our bedroom. We'd agreed easily on the colors: cream-yellow walls, like afternoon light in autumn, and rust trim to warm the room. I hummed as I painted, my overalls and bandana splattered with the colors of fall leaves and golden light.

By the end of our first painting day, I went to bed completely beat, a contented exhaustion. I got under the covers before Kate and was asleep before she even made it to bed. In the morning, I woke to an empty bed.

I was at the kitchen counter, puttering around with breakfast things, when Kate emerged from the adjoining living room, looking sleepy, still in her nightgown. Her straight hair was so mussed, it was in a tangle. Dotty, also in her pajamas, followed her out of the living room and into the kitchen.

"Hi," I grinned toward them. "I'm having granola. Want some?"

Dotty mumbled something about going to the bathroom, and walked past me and down the hall.

Kate said, "I need to talk with you."

As we walked down the hall to our bedroom, my body felt strange; my midsection was closing in on itself, but my mind was thinking, *She's changed her mind about the paint colors.*

We each sat on the bed's edge, our bodies turned only partially toward each other. Kate began, "Last night, when you went to sleep early, I waited up for Dotty to come home. We stayed up talking, and, well, then we made love. We spent the night on the hide-a-bed in the living-room couch."

Now the contraction included my heart and my throat. I could barely breathe. My temples began to pound and my chest ached. "Kate . . . how could you!?" I burst out, and then managed to contain myself. I was on a knife's edge, knew I had to handle this right. My breathing shallow, I started over, exercising all my willpower, trying to sound calm. "So, do you want to continue being lovers with her?"

"Yes, this has been coming between Dotty and me for a while."

Memory flashed then—looks that had passed between Kate and Dotty, eyes holding each other across the dinner table, their dancing together at my birthday party. I tried to hold back my rising panic. "This is going to be really hard for me, Kate. I mean, jeez, we all *live* together. How do you think I'll feel, not knowing if you will be sleeping with me or Dotty each night?"

We'd talked about the idea of having other lovers. The ideology of nonmonogamy had dominated our Radicalesbians group. Kate and I had concluded that there might be room in our relationship for others, but we'd both asserted that doing so would not separate us or lessen our love for each other. But it had all been theory up until now.

"Actually, Karen," Kate went on, "I don't want to be lovers with you anymore."

I could not speak. I found myself rising, my body moving out of the bedroom, there was the blur of the hall, the *thud* of the front door closing behind me. Then I was running across the driveway and into the thicket. I hurled myself belly down onto the dried grass, sobbing into the earth until I was spent.

When I got back to the house, it was empty. Both Dotty's car and Martha's were gone. I figured the three of them had left for our karate class, the one we'd all joined because there was no jujitsu over the summer. But then, why had they taken two cars? My mind was swirling, and I couldn't think clearly. A chilling quiet now filled the house, and I found its emptiness unbearable, so I jumped in our VW van and drove the twenty miles to the martial arts studio.

No Kate or Dotty at class, just Martha. I joined the line of women moving into horse-stance position: wide legs, knees bent, pelvis tucked, elbows held into the ribs, fists hard and tight. We went through the moves in unison: jab, forward kick—*traitors*—backward kick—*cowards, deserters, where could they be?*—slash, upward block—*why? why doesn't she love me?*—punch, downward block.

Dotty's car was still gone when we got home after class. Inside the quiet house, Martha asked, "What's going on? Why are you so upset?" I told her what Kate had said to me, how now my chest wouldn't quit aching. She put her arm around me and let me cry.

The afternoon passed in a blur. Martha went off to visit a friend, and I alternated between sitting stuporously on the couch and wandering about the house.

When Martha got back, she took one look at me and said, "Let's go out to dinner. You need to get out of here." We drove to a local restaurant and bar, a popular place, one of the few restaurants on that strip of country highway, and on a Saturday night, there was an hour wait. No problem—we had nothing but time. We sat out on the wraparound porch with our drinks. My first was a Kahlua and cream, my favorite. After that, I switched to screwdrivers. I intended to drink.

When we finished our meal, we sat back out on the porch, where I nursed my sixth screwdriver. The place was owned by a famous San Francisco madam, now retired, who had a menagerie of exotic animals that she kept in pens on the front lawn. In the twilight, I could just make out the shapes of three llamas and an ostrich. I didn't know if I ever wanted to leave this surreal setting and return home. I dreaded facing either possibility: the deserted house or seeing Kate and Dotty there together. I ordered a seventh screwdriver.

As we made our way to Martha's VW bug in the parking lot, it was a miracle that I was still standing. After a winter of spartan eating alternating with cleansing fasts, I was the thinnest I would ever be in my adult life: 108 pounds of me, drenched in alcohol. My agitated nerves must have been keeping me erect.

The house was black when we arrived, the darkness of the mountain looming behind it, set off by stars. No car in Dotty's spot. The country quiet that just yesterday I had found so soothingly pastoral now grated: How horribly irritating, the buzz of crickets and the lusty croaking of frogs. After Martha went to sleep, I paced the hall that ran along the bedrooms, then through the kitchen and into the living room. Back and forth, like a zoo tiger in its cage. Finally, I took a bath to calm myself and got into bed. Sleep was impossible.

At 2:00 AM, I heard car wheels crunching on the gravel driveway. I got out of bed and walked down the hall toward the front door. I heard the porch door open and close, the creak of the porch boards, then two voices talking in whispers, giggling. As Kate and Dotty came through the front door off the porch, they stopped short, seeing me standing there, a shadow in the dark. Kate said,

"We've been out picking plums in the U-pick plum orchard today. We've got tons of them in the car . . ." She was smiling and talking, talking about inanities.

I leapt at Kate, fury catapulting me. I grabbed her by the shoulders, pinned her against the wall next to the door. I began to shake her as I yelled, "What are you talking about? Where were you? How could you tell me we are through and then just leave!"

Hands were on me, and I was pulled to the floor. Dotty had jumped me, little Dotty with her tiny, small-boned body. She was on top of me, but a jujitsu move came through me—just like our teacher had promised one day in a pinch it would—and now she was under me. I had her long black hair wrapped in my hand, and I was banging her head against the floor, using her hair to pull her head. My own blood raced through me with each satisfying *thud.*

Then I felt more hands on me, tugging. Martha and Kate pulled me off Dotty, who got up and moved close to Kate. They started to turn away, Kate taking Dotty's hand as they moved in the direction of the living room. Then Kate stopped and turned back toward me. I was dusting myself off, but straightened and looked at Kate. Those icy green eyes of hers were narrowed at me. That mean voice said, "You will not get me back this way, Karen."

OVER THE NEXT MONTH, I fled and returned several times. *Taking a break,* that's what I called it in my mind. When staying at the house became too unbearable, I would go visit friends in the city for a few days, then come back to the country.

I wasn't ready to let go. I kept hoping that Kate would come around, realize it was just the novelty that drew her, and resume as my lover. Each time I came back, my fantasy got more battered. Kate and Dotty would disappear together for hours on end. When Kate and I were both at the house, if I expressed any sadness or anger, she would give me a fierce look and then walk out of the room. I tried hard to hold my emotions in, because I didn't want to drive her further away, but that suppression ate at me, made me feel crazy and lonelier than ever.

But one day I did manage to make a request of her. "Kate, I need to spend some time with you, just the two of us," I stated. "It's too hard to go from our being together every day to this."

She surprised me by conceding, "Sure, let's go do something on Saturday."

We drove over to the Napa Valley and visited wineries, just like tourists, just as I had with my father. As Kate drove along the Valley, I found myself almost mute in the passenger seat.

After several wineries, the lump in my throat had only increased. It was too horribly familiar, this making myself invisible to hold the other's love. I had thought with Kate I could be myself, be loved for all of me. As we drove back toward the Valley of the Moon, my ability to be stoic weakened by wine, I started to cry quietly.

Kate glanced over at me. "There's no need to be sad," she said simply. She didn't stop the car. "I still love you. I want you to stay and live with us as my friend."

"I don't know if I can" was all I said, silencing my hurt.

But I didn't leave—although clinging against all odds was making me ill. It was shameful, part of me knew, to take such treatment. I lost my appetite, couldn't sleep, and took up a daily habit of smoking pot and drinking.

One night, just as the household was sitting down to dinner, the doorbell rang. It was a surprise visit from a couple from the city, Barbara and T.J. They had been up for my birthday party, but I hadn't seen them on my recent stays in the city. We made room for them at the table, brought out extra plates. T.J. pulled out a joint, which we passed around before eating. Just as we were about to dig into our food, T.J. asked, smiling broadly, "So, what's up with y'all?"

There was a silent pause. Kate started to say something, but the room was closing in on me, and I couldn't hear her properly. Noise heaved itself out of me in one great sob, and then I was tumbling sideways toward Barbara's shoulder. My head hit her and then rolled back, and my chair tipped and rocked as I slumped onto the floor. I could hear, but it all seemed muffled and far-away: the scraping of everyone's chairs, Barbara asking, "What's wrong with her?" as she put her hand against my face, then Martha's voice fading in and out, "*... they broke up ... not eating ... too much booze ... Let's get her some air...*"

Hands were holding my feet and shoulders, my body swung aloft, and I was deposited on the cool concrete patio outside the living room. "Karen?" A voice leaned over me, not Kate's. Something broke loose in me then: A keening wail echoed off the patio walls. When it ebbed away, sobs began, great gulps of air moving in and out of my lungs. My fingers curled tightly into my palms, and my body grew rigid. "She's hyperventilating," Barbara said. "Breathe slowly, Karen, it's all right, just slow down." After a while, the spasm lessened and I opened my eyes. T.J., Barbara, and Martha were gathered around me, crouching with their hands resting on me.

Kate and Dotty came outside then, standing at the far edge of the patio near the door. Kate peered over at me. For a moment, I thought she might be worried about me. "She's faking," she said. "She just wants attention." Then she and Dotty disappeared back inside the house.

Kate knew all my secrets; I had told her how I had exaggerated my injuries in childhood to get sympathy from my friends. In my

Chapter 31. Fire Escape

I'D ALMOST FORGOTTEN, AFTER two years in California, how humid New York could be. The sticky summer evening hit me as I stepped out of the air-conditioned JFK Airport to board the shuttle bus to Manhattan. Outside the Midtown bus station, I hailed a cab, and felt slightly nauseous as the cabby careened in and out of traffic heading downtown. I'd had a couple of cocktails on the plane.

Mom greeted me over the intercom at her apartment: "You'll have to walk up; the elevator's busted." As I lugged my two suitcases up the five flights to Mom's studio, I felt the sweat gathering in my armpits and the small of my back. Gloria's place was a home I'd never seen.

"Sweetie!" There Mom was, grinning at me as she held her door open. She ignored my sweating and panting from the stairs, and embraced me in a big hug as I dropped my suitcases in her narrow hall. I started crying. "I know, baby, it's tough, I know," Mom soothed. "Didn't get to tell you, Stella just broke up with me last week. Left me for my friend Joanna. Some goddamn friend! Hell with them. Come on in and see my place."

The tiny studio apartment was filled with the furniture I had grown up with, only pruned down to the essentials. The mahogany coffee table my father had built to Frank Lloyd Wright's design was covered with feminist magazines—*Ms., Off Our Backs*—an amethyst crystal, a conch shell, and two blue ceramic ashtrays. The old brown couch I used to lounge on while reading books and drinking Cokes faced the fireplace. Fire was my mother's element. She'd told me how ecstatic she was to have found a working fireplace in a New York City apartment.

Mom's recent black-and-white photographs lined the mantel: still-life patterns of sand dunes and fences, rows of battered New York garbage cans. I remembered the time Mom came home from the mental hospital, gathered all her cameras, and sold them. In the years since, I had often wondered why; now I understood that her passions had been a dangerous and forbidden territory.

"Come on, let me show you my porch," Mom took my hand with a gentle tug. I was a bit dizzy. I almost tripped over the two steps up to her raised sleeping area. "Careful," Mom warned as I stumbled. We circled the bed, and she opened the sliding glass door.

"Ta *da!*" Mom beamed proudly as we stepped outside.

"But, Gloria," I giggled, "this isn't a porch, it's a fire escape!"

"Yeah, but it's my bit of outdoors in New York City. And look how I fixed it up." Mom had put boards down over the open metal flooring. A row of brilliant red geraniums in individual pots circled the edge of the railing. A rocking canvas recliner took up all but the little standing space where Mom and I leaned close together, looking down. We could see below us the soot-blackened buildings with their ornate concrete scrollwork and the signs for the antique dealers who lined her street. The shops were closed, leaving her block quiet by Manhattan standards. For a moment, the Sonoma landscape I'd left gathered behind my eyelids: the meadow with its live oak trees, the woods around our cottage, Kate with her new lover. Pain seared my chest. And then I was back with Mom in Greenwich Village, Mom pulling me inside. "Come on, let's have a drink."

"I'm fixing you and me each a martini!" Mom declared. We were standing in her kitchenette, a corner of the studio space crammed with miniature kitchen appliances. I braced myself for the martini, in its own way an initiation into adulthood, or at least my mother's nod to my achieving that status. I watched Mom open a cabinet, put two cocktail glasses on the counter, take out gin and vermouth and a shaker, get ice and olives from the fridge, mix, shake, and pour our drinks.

We moved to the couch. I sank into its familiar softness. The martini burned my throat as I took a large gulp, but then I quickly felt the sharp edges of things softening, an inner tension releasing. "How are you, sweetie?" Mom asked, reaching her arm around my shoulder.

"It's been awful." My throat constricted and the words came out in a whisper. A few tears leaked. I imagined sobbing in my mother's arms, but I couldn't quite let go to this new mother who could now offer solace. My fierce longing was overpowered by the longtime reflex of pulling back. Besides, right now I wanted to forget, not remember. I brushed my tears with the back of my hand and changed the subject. "What happened with Stella? I thought you two were doing so well."

"After I moved from Jersey, we spent day and night together. It was great. Now that we could be at my place, we didn't have to worry about running into her husband in the elevator of her apartment."

"Her *husband?* She's got a *husband?* Gloria, can't you find a real dyke, not a married woman?"

"Don't get all righteous on me! They don't live together anymore. He lives one floor up in her apartment building, though, and he still pays her rent. She doesn't want a hassle from him."

"So, what happened?"

"I took Stella with me to my consciousness-raising group at Gay Older Women's Liberation. I thought she might really get into it. She got into it, all right, but not like I thought. We went out to a bar afterward with my friend Joanna and a few others. And then, the next thing I hear, a couple weeks later she tells me she and Joanna have started seeing each other, and it's over between us. So much for sisterhood! I could kill that Joanna!"

"Man, that's as bad as Kate sleeping with Dotty and then dumping me."

Mom shook her head, her round face pulled down in a frown, her eyes watery. "Damn! Hey, let's go to a café, have a bite to eat, and I'll show you some poems I've written about Stella."

Mom stuck a manila folder under her arm, and we went out into Greenwich Village. Her street, with its closed shops, had few pedestrians, but when we turned the corner onto Fifth Avenue, we joined a throng of walkers, swept along in the energy and pace of Manhattan. We walked through Washington Square as dusk gathered, its park benches filled with old people, teenagers, and couples of all ages, and found an outdoor café.

My mother bent her head over her poems as she read them to me. They were bitter, filled with longing and betrayal and regret. I stared at her. Although her short cut was curlier than my long hair, we looked alike. Those poems—how they made me sad for my mom, outraged for both of us—but I just took Mom's hand, squeezed it for a moment, and let go. She looked up at me, startled, as if she'd almost forgotten I was there. I knew Kate, my pain, was the furthest thing from her thoughts.

"These just poured out of me this last week, since Stella said it was over. She and Joanna took off to Provincetown. Fuck them!"

Mom grew silent and rested her head in her palms, eyes distant, not looking at me. Then she raised her head and slapped her hand on the table, "Hey, that's what you and I need—to get away. Provincetown's a big enough place. You know what, let's go take our own vacation there for a few days. Maybe a whole week. What do you say?"

THE SIDE STREETS OF Provincetown were narrow, lined with New England clapboard cottages, some weathered to a faded gray, others painted white with green or black shutters. We rented a second-story one-bedroom apartment from an old-style butch with short, slicked-back hair who lived downstairs. We'd found the listing in a New York gay weekly. She greeted us gruffly, and I wondered if that was just her style, or if she thought we were lovers and disapproved of our age difference.

We spent the first day at a beach outside of town. This was not the warm-watered Jersey shore of my childhood, but the frigid New England Atlantic, the beach buttressed by huge sand dunes sparsely covered with long, dry grass. We put down our towels and sat looking out at the waves. For me, moments of stillness brought an ache, Kate's absence pounding in my heart like the surf. It seemed inconceivable that I could go on without her.

Our second day in Cape Cod, we walked along the main street of Provincetown, filled with ambling lesbian couples and gay men, as well as straight tourists, until we found a lesbian bar called the Pied Piper in full swing, jammed with women on its dance floor. We ordered drinks at the bar and found a small table to sit at along one wall of the large dance floor.

"Come on, let's dance!" Mom declared. She grabbed my hand, and we found a spot amidst all the flailing elbows. Mom threw back her head as she danced and snapped her fingers, singing along with Aretha's "R-E-S-P-E-C-T, find out what it means to me!" Something in me loosened, a knot held in my chest and belly for the last month. I found myself stamping my feet as I danced and sang with Mom, " . . . Ooh, I want a little respect!"

As we left the dance floor, someone called out, "Hey, Gloria!" Mom turned and waved. "Hey, Arlene!" Mom introduced me to a group of six women she knew from the city. I was a novelty, their lesbian friend's lesbian daughter, and they welcomed me with enthusiasm.

In a pause between dances, I looked around the room at all the women: tanned from the beach, sweaty from dancing, many braless, their nipples showing through their T-shirts. The thought of starting over terrified me, but in that moment, my fear ebbed, and I was buoyed by the throng of women flirting, dancing, and laughing. They were sexy, yes, but reassuring, too. There was life beyond Kate, though I couldn't quite imagine it yet.

When we got hungry, Mom and I left the bar and found a seafood restaurant that overlooked the harbor. Sailboats rocked on the water. The rain had begun. It started lightly and then became one of those East Coast summer torrents, sheets of water hammering down from the blackened sky.

After dinner, we raced to the apartment, newspapers over our heads. There were two double beds, and we each lay on one, reading our paperbacks, inhaling the damp, salty air. We could hear the rain on the roof, and the thunder, which had earlier rumbled in the distance, got closer. I put down my book and counted the seconds between the lightning flash that momentarily lit the darkness outside and the loud clap of thunder. "One thousand one, one thousand two . . ." I was chanting softly. *Bang bang bang.* Then, it came again, its rhythm faster—*bang bang bang.* I realized the sound was not thunder, but a pounding on the front door of our rental. Mom and I looked at each other, puzzled. The banging repeated, louder and more insistent. "I'll go see, Mom," I offered as I got up. I went through the kitchen to the front door, which opened onto a landing. I flicked the porch light on. A woman was standing there, rain pouring down her long dark hair.

I opened the door. "Hello?"

Rain dripped off the woman's nose, her eyes red-rimmed. She smiled weakly. "Hi. You must be Karen. I'm Stella."

"Stella!" Mom exclaimed. I looked over my shoulder and saw Mom standing in the doorway between the bedroom and the kitchen. "Let her in, let her in . . ." she directed me. I stepped aside and Stella came into the kitchen, water pooling at her feet. She set down a small suitcase on the linoleum. My mother moved close to Stella to help her out of her raincoat, threw it over a kitchen chair, and stood facing Stella. I retreated to sit at the far side of the kitchen table.

They seemed to be rooted, facing each other in the middle of the room.

"Joanna and I have been at it, Glor. Fighting like cats and dogs the whole time we've been at the Cape. It was a big mistake."

"And a hell of a thing you did to me!"

"I'm so sorry, Glor." Stella began to cry softly, then choked out, "Can you forgive me?"

"Sweetheart, I've missed you terribly!" Mom stepped close to Stella, who flung her arms around Mom's neck. They both were crying now, holding each other close. Then they were kissing, as if they were alone. I was mesmerized, never having seen my mother's passion for anyone. Finally, Mom stepped back, as if coming to, and glanced over at me. "Stella, let's make you some coffee, get you warmed up."

That night, I moved my things out of the bedroom and slept curled on a daybed pushed against one wall in the kitchen. Gloria and Stella stayed in the bedroom until late the next morning, while I puttered around the kitchen and made myself breakfast. I was happy for my mother, determined not to let loneliness enfold me. Instead, I plunged into my mystery book while I waited for them. Reading diverted me from some feeling that prowled in me, something fierce and fanged. It was out of the question to be jealous of Stella.

They finally emerged, moving languidly. Gloria's round face glowed like a happy full moon. I stared at my mother over my buttered toast as I joined them at the table in a second breakfast, struck silent with amazement at her metamorphosis. Stella made up for my muteness, chattering about the beautiful morning, now that the storm was past, and what wonderful things she'd heard about me.

She seemed familiar, this Stella. She had a prominent nose, an easy smile, deep brown eyes, and a body with that lushness of full hips and thighs that the women of my family hated in themselves. Jewish, I figured. Her long wavy hair was parted in the middle, just like mine. In fact, she looked a bit like me, like an older sister or an aunt. She was somewhere in her late thirties, much younger than my fifty-year-old mother, as was most of the crowd Mom hung out with.

"Gloria told me what an awful time you've had of it." I realized Stella was speaking to me. She reached her hand across the table, grasped mine. "I'm so sorry," she said, looking right into my eyes.

She gave my hand a squeeze. "But the good thing is, this way, I get to meet you." Then she flashed me a radiant smile. In its warmth, I couldn't help but grin back.

At the end of breakfast, when Stella went off to the bathroom, Mom said, "I want to talk to you about something." I tensed.

"Listen, Stella and I would like to go back to the city. Today. But there are still three days left on our rental. It would be a shame to waste the money; you could stay here if you like, enjoy the Cape a while longer—it's easy to get back to Manhattan on the bus—or come back with us. What do you think?"

I knew what my mother was saying, could see the yearning in her eyes: She wanted some time alone with Stella to reconnect. I imagined her tiny studio, that one open space without privacy.

"No problem, Glor, I'll stay here. You know I love the beach."

"Are you sure, honey? We'll have lots of fun together when you get back in town." Her face looked troubled, like she wasn't certain whether she was asking too much.

"Sure, Mom. I'll be fine."

I helped them pack my mother's car, waved as she and Stella drove off down the narrow street. I wasn't too terribly bereft, knowing that in a few days, I would be with my mother again. Besides, it meant so much to see my mother's joy that I wanted to give her the chance to have more of that. Ironically, seeing her driving away with Stella gave me hope that for the first time, my mother could be there for me. Her happiness shored me up, created ground where there had been none.

Chapter 32. The Village

"HELLO, DARLING," Mom greeted me at the door of her apartment. She was dressed in a T-shirt and cotton drawstring pants; Stella, who stood right behind her in Mom's little foyer, was wearing a flowered Japanese kimono. They welcomed me in a relay of hugs, Mom passing me to Stella. They were both smiling in a dreamy-eyed way.

"Sorry if I interrupted," I mumbled, embarrassed. I hadn't called to warn them I was coming back a day early.

"Don't be silly," Mom replied. "You're just in time for dinner!"

I made a dash for the bathroom, and when I reappeared, Mom was tinkering at the stove, stir-frying vegetables in a wok. The table had already been set, but Stella was adding a place setting. On the stereo, Roberta Flack was singing her love ballads.

The first time ever I saw your face
I thought the sun rose in your eyes

Mom's studio twinkled with candlelight. Two white tapers burned in a pair of tall brass candlesticks set at one end of the Danish dining table. Votive candles in red glass holders were perched on the coffee table and the nightstand, and in a row along the ledge that divided her kitchenette from the rest of the room.

I sank onto the couch, held spellbound by the romantic atmosphere. The air seemed thick, the colors of the room vibrant, the music swirling.

"Dinner's ready," Mom called. Stella and I sat at the table while Mom brought in a salad topped with grated raw purple beets and pale green sunflower sprouts. I could see Mom had been catching up on health food cuisine amid her changes. I munched on my salad, wordless. It still stunned me, the novelty of witnessing my mother loving another adult.

THAT NIGHT, MOM MADE up the couch with sheets and a blanket, and I lay down on it a few feet from the raised platform where Mom and Stella slept. In the morning, I woke and glanced at the two of them entwined in sleep. Mom was on her back with her arms around Stella, who was snuggled onto her shoulder. I quietly opened my camera bag and got out my Leica. I was standing over them, readying my first shot, when Stella started yawning herself awake. Mom stirred and kissed her softly. *Snap*.

"Good morning. You don't mind, do you? It was a good shot," I chirped as they both looked up at me. Mom answered me by kissing Stella again, more deeply. *Click*. When they stopped, Stella looked a bit startled, but Mom soothed her. "She's a photographer, like me; needs the practice." Stella grinned up at me then, and snuggled closer to my mother, hooding her eyes. *Click*. Through the lens of my camera, I watched Mom close her eyes and tighten her arms around Stella. Her mouth clenched into a look of taut ecstasy, like she couldn't get enough of her, like she could squeeze her to death. *Snap.*

At breakfast, over our toasted bagels and peppermint tea, Stella offered, "Let me take pictures of you two." Something eased in me then: something that lay hidden, something feral. I couldn't name it, could only sense its taut crouch relaxing. *I like Stella*, I thought.

We were all still in nightgowns—thin summer ones. Mom and I sat close together on the couch. She put her arm around my shoulder, and we grinned toward Stella holding the camera, cheek to cheek. Then Mom pulled down the shoulder of my nightgown, and kissed my bare shoulder. "Now you two," Mom said, and took the camera. Stella smelled like talcum powder. She put her arm around my shoulder in a tight embrace. "Smile!" Mom commanded, but there was no need. We already were.

MOM AND STELLA alternated nights sleeping at each other's place. Sometimes I forced myself to stay at Mom's while they went over to Stella's, to give them some privacy, but most nights I followed them like a lost puppy. Stella lived in a studio on the sixteenth floor of a fancy high-rise with a white-gloved doorman, suited and capped. By Manhattan standards, her one-room modern apartment was spacious, with a couch facing a bank of windows, and a set of chrome and glass shelves along one wall with artfully arranged vases, sculptures, and a collection of owl totems.

When we stayed there, Stella hung a hammock for me from the metal hooks of her balcony. Unlike my mother's metal fire escape landing, this was a true balcony. I would clamber into the hammock, curling my body above Sixth Avenue and Twelfth Street in the warm summer night, trying to ignore the honking.

Those first weeks in Manhattan, I often had trouble sleeping, thinking of Kate. I would reach out to the balcony wall and push myself in the hammock, hoping to rock myself out of obsession. I often woke with a start, heart and throat tight. Always the same dream, with variations: Kate and Dotty, laughing and mocking me, as if I had no right to sorrow, while they walked away from me down the hall of our Sonoma cottage holding hands, disappearing into their newly shared bedroom.

One night, I couldn't bear lying outside in the hammock awake any longer. Stella sat up in bed and flicked on the bedside light when I slid open her balcony door and stumbled into the apartment around 3:00 AM. Mom was snoring loudly beside her.

Stella's face in the lamplight, round and soft as if her baby fat had never melted away, her brown hair curling to just below her shoulders. "Can't sleep?" she asked. I nodded. She pulled her side of the covers back, sat up, and swung her legs to the floor. "Sit, sit." She patted the bed next to her knees. I shook my head, standing near her.

"Afraid of bad dreams, *shayna maydeleh?*" Stella reached up and stroked my face.

I almost let myself cry. A person could learn to love Stella fast.

"Don't worry, sweetie. Here, have one of my Valiums." She reached for the bottle on the nightstand, then handed me a pill and the glass of water kept always at the ready for her own pill taking. I hated sleeping pills and sedatives, but I was desperate. I swallowed it.

"Thanks a lot, Stella," I mumbled.

I trundled back out to the balcony, hoping soon to be tranquilized into dreamless sleep.

DAYS WERE EASIER than nights. After I got back from Provincetown, Mom and I had a couple weeks to hang out before Labor Day marked the end of her summer vacation from her job teaching young adults at the Educational Guidance Center for the Retarded. Stella was working on an interior design project for a client, which kept her busy most weekdays. Mom and I wandered Greenwich Village together. So newly dispossessed, I drank in Mom's stomping grounds, this little square of Manhattan, even though I was uncertain whether I would claim it as my home. That Mom lived here made it home enough. Her companionship soothed, and the city distracted me.

We stopped for noshes in Greek restaurants, bagel joints, or delis, perused bookstores and record shops, lingered at a feminist coffeehouse on Seventh Avenue. As we tootled around, my mother seemed transformed, glowing with energy as if her new life sent a current through her. It both astonished me and made sense, now that I understood how she'd been forced to dampen herself, burying who she was.

A couple times, I vented to my mother about how awful the breakup had been—the shocking abruptness of Kate's declaration of shifted affection, the absolute blockade she erected to hearing my feelings. My mother's face took on a fierce look. "I'd like to kill her!" she declared.

On the weekends, Stella, my mother, and I would go dancing at lesbian bars—Bonnie and Clyde's or the Duchess—or to a private party at one of Mom's friends. The hostess's apartment would always be bursting with women drinking, dancing to the blasting stereo, and passing joints around a circle, amid political arguments, gossip, and roars of laughter. Mom knew lots of women and would introduce me with excited gusto—*my daughter Karen, back from California,* like that was the greatest thing on Earth: Persephone returned from the underworld to her mother, Demeter.

ONE SATURDAY AFTERNOON, Mom, Stella, and I went to see a feminist theater group perform in a church on West Fourth Street. They asked members of the audience to stand up and describe their dreams and fantasies, which the troupe then acted out. When it was announced after the performance that another theater improvisation group was open for members, I was jazzed. Something for me to do, to begin sinking into New York.

The next afternoon, Mom and I were sitting in the booth of a coffee shop, eating lunch. "Last night I remembered something," she announced.

"What?" I put my half-eaten sandwich down on the white ceramic plate.

"The one and only time I ever went to a lesbian bar before all this—and how afraid I was."

"Huh. You went to a *bar?* When was that?" Another startling detail. This had been happening on our journeys around town. I was getting bits and pieces of my mother's story. Even though I already knew the secret of Marian, other hidden events of my mother's life seemed to come in flashes of remembrance, as if she could only recall them one by one. Her memory of those days was blurry, from the electroshocks, the drugs, and the silence.

"When you were a child, but after the affair with Marian, and after having been in a lot of mental hospitals. I was with a woman psychiatrist. I'd always been with male doctors, and I thought maybe a woman would help more. But she had a man's head."

"No kidding—don't they all!" I chimed in. My stomach was edging toward sour as I wondered: What had this one done to her?

"She told me, 'Why don't you go to New York City and find out if you really are a homosexual?'"

"I told her I didn't know where to go in New York, so she found out the name of a bar for me, and I went. I was scared stiff. It was in the day of real butch-femme roles, and there were some tough-looking women in there, with their short hair slicked back into a duck's ass. I sat there a while, but I didn't say a word to a soul. I made one attempt, and it didn't work. So I went home and I just stayed very miserable, feeling very inadequate and sick, like there was something really wrong with me."

I reached for her hand across the table, saddened, the weight of my mother's failure, shame, and humiliation lumped in my chest.

Mom held my hand a moment, squeezed it, and let go. Her expression shifted from pensive into a half smile. "Lucky that I got into the women's movement. It did more for me than all the damn hospitals and psychiatrists, and all the damn medication, ever did! It's given me a whole new life!" Her grin broadened. She had elf eyes, twinkling, irrepressible.

"Yeah," I agreed, "we're both lucky, you and me, huh?" Oddly, a certain kind of joy was rising in me. I sat buoyed by my mother's reminder: I was part of this new era. Sure, I'd lost a lover, but I didn't have to face years of devastation, go an eternity without, my way barred to finding another love.

Chapter 33. Immigrants

WE WERE DOING A WARM-UP exercise when I noticed Natalie. It was my first time attending the lesbian theater improvisation group, which met on Sundays in a huge loft in SoHo. One at a time, each woman took a turn standing in the center of the room and saying "no." Some nos were whispered, some howls of anguish, others cries of defiance accompanied by a foot stomping the hardwood floor. When Natalie stood in the center, her dark eyes shimmered with intensity as she belted, "No!"

My turn. I stepped into the center of the studio, surrounded by the group of women. I closed my eyes and felt the "no" welling up in me. Arms at my sides, fists clenched, I was remembering the previous night. Kate and I had been discussing our shared belongings over the phone. We didn't have that much to divide, but we quibbled over who was to get Laura Nyro, who the copy of *Sisterhood Is Powerful.* As our bickering escalated, Kate suddenly screamed, "You penny-pinching Jew!" I held the phone away from my ear, stunned, knowing that Kate had just inherited over a hundred thousand dollars on her twenty-first birthday from a trust fund.

When I'd first arrived in New York, there'd been this crazy *never let go* part of me that, even after everything with Kate, had been clinging to the fantasy that I might go back and live with her. That kept hoping she'd love me again. But distance had helped me come to my senses. Distance, and being cocooned by my mother, being welcomed and loved by Stella, and finding a community to immerse myself in. Kate's spewing hateful words at me over the phone finalized my divorce from her. I hung up.

Eyes closed, breathing deeply, I felt a wind of fury swirling up my body. My mouth wide, my *"no!"* echoed off the walls of the SoHo studio. When I opened my eyes, I saw Natalie smiling and nodding her head, eyes alight.

I WAS SHY. What did I know about dating? Kate and I had just stumbled into being lovers. Thank God Natalie was bolder. She sauntered over to the studio corner, where I was gathering my things after my second meeting, and said, "Hey, would you be into going to see *La Dolce Vita* tonight?" The Fellini film was playing at a movie theatre that only showed foreign films. *A kindred spirit*, I thought.

Afterward, we went out for a late dinner at one of the Cuban Chinese restaurants that line Eighth Avenue in Hell's Kitchen. I was enthralled that Natalie was so city-savvy, turning me on to this exotic cuisine. When I told her about Kate's "penny-pinching Jew" epithet that had fueled my "no," she exclaimed, "Jeez! Stereotypes of us Jews—does it never end?"

We talked intensely for a couple hours while I savored the spicy, rich flavors of our dish of finely minced squid in black bean sauce with rice and fried sweet plantains. At the end of dinner, Natalie leaned toward me across the table. "Come to my place?"

Excitement and fear held me wordless. I nodded yes.

As we stepped out onto the street, I spotted a phone booth. "Gotta call my mother," I told her. "I don't want her to worry." I got Mom on the first ring. When I told her I'd be spending the night at Natalie's, she said, "Good for you, sweetie. That's great. Have fun!" I smiled . . . my new mother, cheering me on.

The entrance to Natalie's apartment building on Avenue A was a narrow door next to a pawn shop. The dim hallway was empty, and we couldn't wait until we'd climbed the stairs. We leaned against the wall, kissing furiously. I was learning the anxious thrill of the semi-public lesbian kiss: *My god, what if someone opens their door?*

She took my hand as we jogged up the four flights to her three-room railroad flat with its shared toilet in the hall, and made straight for her bedroom. Natalie was a student of modern dance, versed in the body. She showed me how two bodies can move together, two naked bodies, as we rolled from her mattress on the floor onto the carpet. We rose one over the other, limbs twining, torsos arching and contracting, our bodies connecting and separating. I had never imagined this pas de deux, never known such fluidity between two bodies.

Natalie's touch on my flesh was leisurely in its exploration, as if to say, *No hurry, all this for you.* Natalie showed me the savoring of the body, how a body can sing. Then her touch became insistent in its urging: *Open to me, open.* And I did.

The scary awkwardness I had anticipated became the wonder of learning a new lover's body, the sense of power in giving pleasure.

When I woke, darkness. The pitch black of a moonless night. I fell back to sleep and woke hours later to the same inky air. Natalie stirred beside me, reached over to her nightstand, and turned on a lamp. She scooted close and kissed me. "Time for breakfast!"

"It's still night," I mumbled, confused and woozy.

"No, it's ten AM, sleepyhead." She kissed me again. "I'll make us something to eat."

Natalie got up and headed for the kitchen, turning on lights as she went. As I fumbled into my pants and T-shirt, I noticed something I hadn't the night before, when my eyes had been only for Natalie: There were no windows in her bedroom. As I made my way through her rooms to the kitchen, I saw that the only window was in the middle room, her study, which looked out on an airshaft. Her desk was stationed in front of this window, with a view of a concrete wall. The faint smell of rotting garbage came in through the partially open window. The dimmest of light filtered down from the rooftop one story up. I had never known of such a thing: an apartment that never saw daylight.

In the kitchen, Natalie was pondering the contents of her refrigerator. She put two plates on the table, each holding two slices of whole wheat bread. A jar of peanut butter sat between the plates, its lid off, the end of a kitchen knife jutting out. The table itself was actually a claw-foot bathtub set against one wall of the kitchen, over which Natalie had a plywood board.

"Peppermint tea okay?" she asked, lifting a kettle from the stove.

"Uh-huh," I nodded, distracted by my surroundings. It had struck me, staring at that bathtub table: These were rooms where immigrants began life in this country. How odd to think of my grandparents' generation, the Jewish migrants, passing through this tenement. I could imagine the women, dress sleeves rolled up, wet arms glistening as they bathed their children amidst the hubbub of this kitchen, could almost smell the incense of rendered chickenfat, could almost see the jar of *shmalts* resting on the stove. Here we were, full circle, in the place where that generation had toiled, the majority laboring in the sweatshops of the garment district, in the hopes of moving to somewhere better. Years ago, they had gone on to the outer boroughs. The next generation had moved to the suburbs. Now, Natalie was back here, living alone—unthinkable for a woman in that culture. We were our own immigrants, women apart from families and men, journeying back to ourselves.

After breakfast, we performed our own unorthodox *mikvah*—the Jewish ritual bath. We piled our plates in the sink, leaned the plywood against a kitchen wall, and filled the tub. An immersion not to purify the body, but to go on celebrating it. Natalie got in first, and I leaned back against her. She soaped her hands and ran them over my neck, along the hollow of my clavicle, across my breasts and belly, thighs and vulva. I sank against her liquid skin, sighing, giving over to her stroking. My breath deepened into the moans of release. Then I turned my body around, kneeling, and kissed her, caressing her body, pressing my slippery front to hers, reaching my hand inside her. Natalie's cries echoed through the tenement apartment.

Chapter 34. Mother Courage

LIFE WAS DEVELOPING for me in Manhattan. Natalie and I saw each other a few times a week. Mom and Stella and I hung out together, cooking meals at one of their apartments or going out dancing or attending feminist events. In my theater improv group, I made some friends and started spending time with them. The pull to stay in New York was strong. Why return to a California bereft of love? But if I was going to stay, I couldn't keep crashing at my mother's tiny place, or depending on her to support me. I needed a place to live, and that meant I needed a job.

One afternoon, Natalie and I were strolling down Eighth Street toward her East Village apartment, when we ran into her friend Leslie. We clustered on the sidewalk, next to one of the boutiques that sold ratty antique mink coats and used bell-bottom jeans.

"Just quit my job at Mother Courage," Leslie told us. "Know anyone who wants it?"

Mother Courage was a lesbian-owned restaurant that was a hangout for the feminist community. Gloria and Stella and I had eaten there a couple times. "I'm looking," I piped up. "What's the job? I'd love to work at a place like that."

"I was one of the assistant chefs. Just call over there for Barbara or Dorothy, and you can tell them I recommend you."

"Yeah, but I don't know how to cook."

"Don't worry about it. That didn't stop me!" Leslie waved her hand in the air, as if to shoo away doubt. "Hey, I'm off, see ya." She turned and started down the street.

"Thanks!" I called after her.

After I got the job at Mother Courage, Gloria put out the word and found me a place to rent. It was a room in the apartment of a woman she knew from the old days of Women Strike for Peace. Camille had left her husband and two teenage sons in New Jersey and moved into Greenwich Village. At forty-five, she was among those middle-aged women who'd gone wild with the women's movement—the ones like my mother, who astonished us young, know-it-all feminists with their hipness and their radical politics.

Camille had two lovers, young men in the early twenties, not much older than her sons. I was mildly disgusted and a bit intrigued. She was out of town with one of them the weekend I moved in. Natalie and I took turns lugging my one suitcase from my mother's studio the few blocks over to Camille's. The apartment was on the ground floor of a three-story old brick townhouse, originally a single-family dwelling that was now divided up.

My apartment was at the juncture of Eleventh and Fourth—two streets that would never have met uptown. I loved that the Greenwich Village streets ran askew, eccentric like its inhabitants, in contrast with Manhattan's orderly grid up above Fourteenth Street. Eleventh Street became the main artery of my days: I would walk west of Camille's to Mother Courage, close to the Hudson River, or head east to Stella's apartment, just a block and a half away from Camille's, at Sixth Avenue, or to my mother's, a few blocks beyond Stella's. As I strolled along the mostly residential street with its neat townhouses, most of them divided up into apartments, I'd peek in windows, wondering if I'd spot any of the famous artists, musicians, or poets who lived in the Village. I'd cross the busy avenues, with their madly honking cars and yellow cabs, reveling that I was part of an urban quarter with such a bohemian legacy. A contentment filled me as I made my way, sometimes humming to myself, a sense that this neighborhood was the place where I belonged.

A couple of blocks from Camille's lay a gaping hole between two brownstones, all that was left of the townhouse that had blown up two years before, in 1970, when members of the Weathermen had been attempting to manufacture bombs. Walking past the site, Natalie and I had a heated discussion about feminism, the Left, what revolution meant. We both agreed that the Weather Underground had gone off the deep end, but she was still working within the Left, while I had abandoned it for the women's movement. Natalie was intensely committed to a Marxist group. The group sounded homophobic to me, and I worried that she had to suppress too much of herself to be in the group. "How can you work with people who don't respect all of who you are?!" I demanded. Really, I was fighting not to lose Natalie, because she was considering going off to work full-time with this group in their Chicago cadre. What I didn't say was, *Don't leave me!*

ONE SUNDAY, AT THE END of our improv group, several of us piled into one member's car. The driver, Florence, had offered to drop us all off on her way home. We got to my place first, and as I untwined myself from the mesh of limbs in the back seat and stepped onto the sidewalk, I noticed that Natalie was still in the car. Someone pulled the door shut, and I saw Natalie smile and wave as the car took off. I stood there stunned. In the two months that we'd been seeing each other, we had always been together after the group, spending the night at one of our places. My legs felt wobbly, my throat lumped with rejection, and as I turned away, I held back tears. What the hell? Was she sleeping with someone else? We had no agreement between us, no words to define what we were to each other.

As I stumbled home, I thought about how Natalie was an admirer of Emma Goldman, the radical anarchist who believed in an open sexuality. She loved that Goldman espoused both revolution and the free giving of love and pleasure, beyond the strictures of marriage. Natalie, my free-love girlfriend. As it was, my relationship with her was way more independent than what I'd had with Kate. I liked that we didn't spend every minute together, but I was still raw from having been left for another woman. The terror of abandonment hovered, and the idea of Natalie with someone else filled me with jaw-clenching agony.

A couple days later, I called Natalie and said I needed to talk. We met on a wooden bench outside a church on Second Avenue, not far from her apartment. I wasn't sure if I would be able to say what I needed to say if we got together at one of our places and started kissing. We faced each other for what seemed a long while in silence, her face softly expectant, letting me find the words. I couldn't bear to ask her if she was having sex with anyone else. Instead, I said that I understood she believed in a totally open relationship, but I had realized that because I was still healing from the hurt of Kate leaving me, it was too hard for me. She raised her hand to my cheek, touched my tears that were streaming down. "You're so open with your feelings, so beautiful." She smiled at me with her big eyes. I waited, silently, for more, but she made no argument to bind me to her, just stroked my hair as I wept.

LATE ONE NIGHT, a few weeks after I broke up with Natalie, I came back to Camille's after a shift at Mother Courage in my usual after-work state of feeling both hyper and exhausted. I was fairly drunk from sipping wine all shift, and clumsily slammed the apartment door. Camille called out, "Hey, Karen, that you? We're hanging out—come join us!"

"Hang on, be there in a sec," I called back.

Camille and one of the boyfriends were sitting on the couch. He was hunched over the coffee table, rolling a joint. She looked up and smiled, gesturing for me to sit in the overstuffed chair that faced the couch. Her two lovers looked so similar that I had trouble not mixing them up: Both had stringy, sandy brown hair tied back in a ponytail, placid faces, and gangly bodies. I believed this was Jim.

"You're just in time," Camille said to me. "We're gonna trip. We have two hits of acid; Jim wants a whole hit, but I only want to do half, so why don't you join us? It'll be a blast."

It *was* Jim, then. I was restless and bored, and the thought of just hanging out in my room didn't appeal. *What the hell.* "Sure, sounds great," I answered.

Camille got out a scissors and cut our shared blotter paper in half. After we'd each swallowed our scrap, Jim lit the joint and took a toke, and we passed it around.

I sat there stoned, waiting for the acid to come on, staring out the window at the backyard. The sumacs had lost most of their leaves, so I focused on the trunks, lit dimly by a spotlight that shone on them, waiting to see if they changed colors or started swirling around, as the bare earth had during my one other acid trip, back in Iowa.

This time, the effect didn't seem that intense. The tree trunk just wavered a bit and glowed a dull yellow. I was still staring at one of the sumacs, as if it would give me the secret of life, when Camille's voice called, "Let's go out." The three of us put on our jackets. It had drizzled earlier, and the late-night air seemed thick with the aromas of wet asphalt, car exhaust, dog droppings, and soot. We turned from Eleventh Street onto Seventh Avenue. Outside the bars, taxis were swerving to the curbs to pick up the gay boys who were flagging them down. Many twosomes got in cabs.

Constant honking jarred the night. My nerves twitched with each horn bleat. I noticed a skinny drag queen wearing a sleeveless minidress and heels standing on the sidewalk outside a bar. *He must be freezing,* I thought. His face was turned toward the exiting patrons, a middle-aged face, and his blond bouffant wig was slightly askew. *So pitiful, he can't get anyone to take him home.* Something about the way his eyes beseeched each patron made me think he was one of the most pathetic people I had ever seen. Then, it was as if his loneliness found a home in me and echoed throughout my chest cavity. I felt consumed by sadness, and suddenly, the Village that I had found so vibrant had become sordid and dismal. It was unbearable. I tore my eyes from his face and stared down at the filthy curb. "Let's go back! I need to go back to the apartment," I said.

When we got inside the front hall, I lagged behind Camille and Jim, fumbling in my jean pocket for my room key. I called to their backs, "You two go ahead; I'm gonna hang in my room."

Camille turned around, walked up close to me. "Come on," she said softly, "let's all hang out together."

Something in the intense way Camille was staring at me felt creepy and cloying. *Get away from me, leave me alone.* Camille reached her hand toward me, but I backed up. "No, really, just need to be by myself." I escaped into my room and locked the door.

I opened the wooden shutters on the two windows that faced the street, and pulled the room's one bentwood chair up close to the window nearest my bed. The street was deserted. I stared at the darkened windows of the small corner restaurant across the street, the only business on our residential block. The restaurant sat on the bottom floor of a nineteenth-century apartment building, five stories tall, with ornamental cornices, its brick facade painted white. I had thought the building beautiful, but now it loomed like an unfriendly hulk. Probably no one spoke to each other in its halls. The traffic light on the corner was turning the street shadows red, yellow, green, red, yellow, green—a silent urban metronome. Emptiness ticking.

The street colors beat in the rhythm of my loneliness. Alone, all alone; alone, all alone. Hadn't this forlornness gripping me lived in my body forever? For a brief time, it had crouched hidden in some crevice—abated by the camaraderie of Freedom School, the euphoria of coming out in a feminist community—but now it pounced, rising through my heart into my throat, spreading down my limbs. Paralyzed with its weight, I stayed in the chair, staring, leaden.

Camille was pounding on my door. "Karen, are you all right? Karen?"

I managed to get up, go to the door, but I kept it locked. I leaned against the wood, found words. *Focus on my mouth. Move the jaw, the lips.* "Yeah, Camille, I'm cool."

"Come on, Karen, you don't have to be alone! Come sleep with us."

For a moment, longing rushed through me. I imagined cuddling with Camille in her loft. Being held against her softness. But, of course, he would be there, too. Would Camille be in the middle, or would I have to sleep between them? Then hands were stroking, reaching for me, hands and a penis and lips . . . was that what she meant? It was arousing and repulsive at the same time. "No, just want to be alone!" I found myself shouting through the door. Did I? The biggest lie on Earth. I heard her footsteps fading in the hall.

Back in the chair, staring. Night had deepened to predawn, and the stoplight colors no longer seemed to fill the street. Coming down. The loneliness percussed its litany, but more slowly: *No Natalie, no Kate, no one loves you.* I was tearless, pupils dilated. At first light, I willed myself: Leave the chair. Go.

My wobbly legs knew their way along Eleventh. By now, the doorman at Stella's recognized me, and just nodded as I made my bleary-eyed way to the elevator.

It was Mom, wearing a long T-shirt and nothing else, who opened the door. "Shhh, Stella's asleep," she whispered. Then she looked at me, swaying in the doorway, reached out her arm, took my hand, brought her face close. "What happened?"

"I'm tripping on acid, been up all night, Mom." Mom—the name just slipped out. I hadn't called her that since the end of high school.

She pulled me closer, into the room, closed the door with one hand while holding on to me, then turned her body next to mine and guided me by the elbow to the couch, as if I were a disabled person, or a toddler. She helped me lower myself, then stood nearby, looking down at me. "I'm thirsty," I managed to croak in a whisper.

Mom went to the kitchenette in the corner of the studio and returned with a glass of orange juice. Cool, sweet acidity; I could feel its progress down my throat.

Mom sat down on the couch. She moved her body right up against mine and put her arm around my shoulder. The couch sat along a wall opposite a curtainless bank of windows that looked down Sixth Avenue. I could feel the warmth of Mom's arm on the back of my neck, the calming sensation of her hand stroking my shoulder, as we stared toward the apricot dawn lighting the skyscrapers. She sat with me in blessed quiet, no questions.

I leaned my head onto her shoulder, letting myself close my eyes. Mom was murmuring, "Shusssh, shussh," as she stroked my hair. My hair follicles were sending pings of current along my scalp. For a moment, my reflexes gathered themselves to fight her—*I don't need you*—and then something in me gave way, letting go to an exquisite consolation. I could have wept, but I simply rested there, as if it were forever.

Chapter 35. Unlearning to Not Speak

I HAD BEEN FOOLING MYSELF, I had to admit, wanting to be so urbane, so cool. Although I loved New York, it was too much for me. When I was growing up, nature had embedded itself as a primary solace, and I just couldn't go on in this absence of green. It wasn't that I wanted to return to the country; I needed urban, but softer. Time to go back to California, to the city by the bay.

I hated to leave my mother. It tore me up, but I believed if I stayed, my roots would grow too deep and I would be stuck in New York City for the rest of my life. Besides, it didn't seem fair that Kate should inherit California in our breakup. I'd be damned if I'd let her. My San Francisco friend Stephanie had called and offered to do the legwork to find us an apartment, since she'd just been dumped by her lover. Her offer made it easier to return—at least I'd have a companion.

I remembered that other leaving, the day I left Mom after high school. Then, I had fled, trying not to feel terrible about abandoning my depressed mother.

Now, she and Stella walked with me the block and a half from Mom's to Fifth Avenue to hail a cab. They flanked me, my two mothers. Standing waiting for a taxi, Mom gave me the fiercest hug, her eyes full and sad. As the taxi pulled to the curb, Stella and Mom added a flurry of kisses and hugs as the driver put my two suitcases in the trunk. There was the taxi door closing, the blur of movement. I glimpsed them, holding hands on the sidewalk as the taxi shot away, waving their free hands furiously. My mother—there was so much more life in her now. That helped me go, and gave me something to hold on to.

MY FRIEND STEPHANIE had found us an apartment in an Oakland neighborhood composed of stucco cottages and two-story wood-frame houses, their tiny front lawns varying from neat to disheveled. As I walked to the co-op supermarket on Telegraph Avenue and returned with my arms loaded with groceries, the nearly deserted streets seemed a suburban wasteland, devoid of the vibrancy of New York, the quirky Victorian urbaneness of San Francisco, just across the bay, or the beauty of my longed-for California countryside.

At night, I did not feel safe roaming the streets, as I had in Manhattan. The Big Apple rocked twenty-four hours a day, and I had felt relatively free to walk its avenues in the postmidnight hours. Now, Stephanie and I spent the evenings in our living room, drinking screwdrivers made from cheap vodka and frozen orange juice, and smoking pot when we had it, while we played Joni Mitchell's new album, *Blue,* over and over. The empty vodka bottles piled up in our trash.

The loss of Kate and our house in the Sonoma countryside haunted my dreams. Night after night, I dreamed of the cottage nestled in pines, with the scrub-covered hills I'd loved to hike rising behind it. Inside the cottage, Kate laughed with Dotty while their backs were turned to me. Nightly, my gut felt lanced with betrayal and rejection, and I woke with a pounding headache.

I got a part-time job working the lunch shift at the Red Barn hamburger chain. Workers had to wear hideous orange smocks and orange caps. Hungover, I could barely keep up with the frenetic pace, and I quit after a few weeks to avoid the embarrassment of being fired. My next job was running a luncheonette in an office building: restocking vending machines, making coffee, and ringing up purchases. In slow times, I sat doodling in a notebook and writing mournful poems. The hours blurred. One night, my boss called to say I was fired because I had left one of the vending machines with its door open, its cash accessible.

Being far away from my mother and Stella left me hollow and disoriented, as if there were no ground under my feet. Neither my mother nor I could afford frequent long-distance calls, so we wrote letters, both declaring how we missed each other terribly. I longed to run back to her comfort, but stubbornly refused to cede California to Kate. I sensed only vaguely that something in me needed to find myself outside the shelter of my mother.

In February, two months after I had left New York, my mother wrote that she'd broken up with Stella. Stella had plummeted into her chronic depression, something I hadn't witnessed during our jubilant days together in Manhattan. I felt sad for all of us, but in a dull, distanced way. I couldn't let myself feel how shattering it was, to lose this new family in which, for the first time, my mother had found love. It was an odd twist to have my mother be the one to leave a depressed person, but I thought I understood: Gloria had lost so many years to her own grief that she didn't want to be with someone trapped in despair. I wrote, "I'm so sorry it's worked out this way, but your sanity and strength are most important. If Stella's depression and need for you are sapping your energy, it's no good." I didn't see the irony in my advice: how my childhood had been sapped by my mother's depression, but I'd had no option to leave.

ONE EVENING IN EARLY summer, I went to a Gay Liberation Front meeting in San Francisco. Someone announced that KPFA, the local listener-supported Pacifica radio station, wanted to start two gay programs: one created by gay men, one by lesbians. Who wanted to work on it? I leapt to sign up. Two groups emerged from that meeting and began producing shows: the gay men started *Fruit Punch,* and we women initiated *Lesbian Air.*

Only one of our group of eight had any radio experience. I was excited but nervous that we had a weekly hour-long show to fill. But to my relief, when we arrived at KPFA, we were welcomed by straight feminists who, at this station, had fought for and pioneered a feminist radio program called *Unlearning to Not Speak,* named after the Marge Piercy poem taped to the door of their office.

> *. . . She must learn again to speak*
> *starting with I*
> *starting with We*
> *starting as the infant does*
> *with her own true hunger*
> *and pleasure*
> *and rage.*

The *Unlearning* programmers tutored us. We broke into two groups, with four of us per group clustered around one of the professional reel-to-reel tape recorders as our mentor demonstrated how to locate the exact spot on the tape to cut, how to lay it on the metal editing block, cut it on the diagonal with a razor blade, and splice two cuts together. The skill of these foremothers, and their *we can do this* stance, helped me overcome technology phobia. To discover I could do this was thrilling, better by far than learning to tune up my VW Bug.

One afternoon, I went into one of the tiny editing booths with an unedited tape of a coming-out story—one of several we were using for our first program—a notebook, and a fresh razor blade. The claustrophobic booth was lined with white soundproofing particleboard, and only just big enough for one Ampex reel-to-reel tape machine, a rickety rolling desk chair, and a tall garbage can. I began listening on headphones, pausing the tape to take notes on a pad, starring the parts of the story that seemed most vital. As I rewound the tape and went over the interview again, I became completely immersed in the woman's story and the creative process of paring it down—making an edit, listening to it, adding a tiny splice of a breath if the timing was too tight. I was so swept up, the closed-in space dropped away. Finally, a grumbling stomach roused me to glance at my watch—my God, hours had gone by!

During our early shows, I discovered something about myself: Live on the air, I was terribly shy, but during prerecorded off-air interviews, to be edited and broadcast later, I relaxed into a curiosity about the women I interviewed, engrossed in the details of their stories, and able to ask questions. I didn't know yet what I had stumbled on—something so fitting that I would spend the next ten years as a radio producer and recording engineer.

IN THE WINTER, Gloria visited me at the lesbian collective I'd moved into. She slept on our frigid, unheated back porch, chipper and uncomplaining. My housemates loved her: the hip lesbian mom, happily eating our vegetarian meals and sharing our feminist vision.

My mother had agreed to be interviewed for the radio show, so I took her to the recording studio. At the radio station, we faced each other across a long metal folding table, mikes on stands pointed at each of us. In the three years since we'd both come out, I'd heard bits and pieces of my mother's story, but had never really asked for details of what she'd experienced and what it had meant. Now, I asked my first question: "I'd like to know how you felt when you married my father."

Gloria leaned toward me, bringing herself closer to the microphone. "One of the reasons I married your father was that I wanted to get away from home. I wanted to have a home of my own, and I wanted to have children. I certainly don't think I was in love with your father; I liked him as a person—he was a nice man—but . . ."

"Did you ever tell yourself in your head that you loved him? Did you feel like you loved him?" I asked into my own mic.

"No. I thought I liked him, that he was a good man and we could be friends. But I never really was excited about him. I never felt that I really loved him."

This was no big surprise, given what I now understood as my mother's suppressed sexual identity. Yet her stating this lack of love was oddly comforting—it made sense of the deadness and silent tension between my parents. I went on without much pause, "Did it ever occur to you *not* to get married—that you had that option?"

"No, I was brought up to feel that that was what a woman did: get married. Work wasn't important; school wasn't important. You went to school to meet a man, and you went to college to meet an educated man."

"You went to college, but you didn't take it seriously?"

"No, I guess I didn't."

Once I began asking my mother questions, I stopped noticing the studio's microphone stands piled up in one corner, the white soundboard walls, or the tan wall-to-wall rug mottled with stains from years of recording sessions. My focus was on my mother's expressive face as she spoke. Finally, we could share this.

"So, when did you start having a relationship with a woman?"

"Marian. It was when you were a baby. She was my best friend. I really loved her as a person. We spent a lot of time together, just as friends, talking, going fishing, sharing our ideas and our thoughts. And then one day she told me how beautiful love could be between women. She meant love on every level—including the emotional, sexual, intellectual. She didn't have to convince me, because right away it felt natural. Because I really loved her as a person. When I say 'I loved her,' I know I didn't have those feelings for your father. I may have liked him a lot and thought he was a good person, but I wasn't thrilled by him, or excited by him. I was bored."

"Did you go through guilt feelings, or did you feel perverted or anything, when you started being lovers with her?" I wanted to know this, mostly to understand my mother, but also because my generation had no sense of lesbian history, no images of women before us loving each other without shame.

My mother's round face widened with her smile, as she shook her head a couple times in remembrance. "When I started being lovers with Marian, I never felt better in my life. I was excited and thrilled and all the things you read in the books. I felt so good that

I wanted to take you, leave your father, and just go off with her and live forever and ever together."

"Did you ever ask her if she'd do that?"

"No, because I knew that wasn't what she wanted. When I look back on it, it was very 'closet-y.' We were both married. We really cared for one another, but she wanted the security of her home. Anyway, I saw her every day, and you saw her every day, when you were very little."

I interviewed my mother for close to two hours. Knowing I would later edit it gave us the freedom to wander through her story. She elaborated on the despair of losing Marian, how electroshock therapy wiped out her memory, her experiences in the mental hospitals, going through withdrawal from psychiatric drugs when I went off to college, and having sex with many women during her first, wild year after coming out. We both spoke of the deep connection between us. There had been so much secrecy, shame, and unexplained grief, and now, we were giving voice publicly to the unspoken and taboo, to what it was like to reclaim a joyous, woman-loving life.

THE NIGHT THE INTERVIEW was broadcast, I sat in an alcove outside the on-air control booth, hunkered into a tweed wool love seat with frayed arms. It had sunk low over the years it had served as a way station for guests or programmers waiting to go on the air. Tonight, I couldn't bear the bright lights of the on-air booth, with all its electronic paraphernalia: the bank of shiny silver tape machines—one of which would have my tape whirling—the microphones, turntables, and control board fanned in a U surrounding the board operator. I needed a place that was dark and soft.

From the couch facing the closed control-room door, I watched the red light attached to the doorframe light up, the signal that someone was live on the air. Her voice came over the alcove speakers: "This is KPFA and KPFB in Berkeley. Up next: *Lesbian Air.*" The light went off as she started the tape. And a buzzing began in my chest.

A friend of mine sat next to me on the couch, but I barely felt her presence. I was conscious of being excited and proud of the final product, the first full hour-length show I had ever produced, edited, and mixed with music. But a state of agitation had taken over my body. I gripped the couch's arm as if it were the mane of a bucking bronco, in order to ride out the broadcast.

First there was the oddity of hearing my own voice as my introduction went out across Northern California, from the Pacific ocean to the Sierra mountains: "*My mother and I are both lesbians; she's fifty two and I'm twenty three. A lot of my friends have asked me what it's like to have a mother who's a dyke, and I tell them it's made an incredible bond between us . . .* "

Then, there was my mother's voice, telling her story, "*. . . I can't quite remember when I started getting so depressed that I wanted to kill myself, but it was sometime after the affair with Marian broke up . . . and I've been in so many hospitals, I can hardly remember how many. So many different kinds of places, some of them so expensive, and some of them very nice—you know, comfortable. But they were really just to keep you off the streets!*"

I had thought I was over the shame, now that I had a political analysis to explain what had happened in my childhood. When I read Phyllis Chesler's *Women and Madness*, with its in-depth critique of the psychiatric treatment of American women, I felt enraged and affirmed. I knew others would relate to my mother's story, that it had relevance beyond one woman's experience.

But as I listened to the broadcast, shaking came over me, rising in waves from my belly. The silence in my childhood was embedded deeply in my body, and each act of asking a forbidden question and voicing what had been taboo beat against my sinews. It left me raw, breathless, and pulsing with fear and exhilaration.

"YOU KAREN, THE RADIO PRODUCER?" A woman driving a VW van had pulled up to the airport curb and leaned across the passenger seat, yelling out the open window.

It was May 1975, a year after the broadcast of my interview with my mother had aired on KPFA. I'd emerged from Los Angeles International Airport into a hot, smoggy Friday afternoon. The organizers of the weekend conference, called Lesbian History Exploration, had told me to look for a blue van.

I grinned and nodded, and the driver leapt out, slamming her door and coming around to the sidewalk. She was wearing cutoff jeans and a handmade silk-screened T-shirt with AMAZON in purple letters. She slid open the van door and heaved my bag inside.

The van proceeded to the next terminal to pick up another passenger, a slender woman in her late seventies, whose head was wrapped with silver braids, giving her a kind of halo. She looked like someone from another time and place. When I saw her waiting on the curb, I thought of a French countrywoman stirring a big black pot over an open hearth, not a presenter at a lesbian conference. She turned out to be Elsa Gidlow, a lesbian poet. I'd never heard of her, but during the conference, I learned a surprising fact: This woman, born in 1898, had, in 1923, been the first in America to publish an openly lesbian book of poetry.

Elsa was given the deference of the front passenger seat, and as we roared off, I was left to my own thoughts, since it was impossible to hear much over the rev of the VW engine. I was nervously anticipating my own presentation. The conference organizers had discovered my interview in the catalog of the Feminist Radio Network and tracked me down.

The VW made its way north along the coast, heading for the Jewish summer camp that had been rented for the occasion. We pulled up in front of the main building, a large, rustic wood meeting hall. We were among the last of the 150 or so women to arrive. Most were milling around the hall, hugging old friends, gathering in clusters. Shyly, I stood there, uncertain what to do. It was a great relief when one of the organizers took me aside to look over the sound equipment they had arranged for my presentation.

The next morning, I found myself picking at my breakfast, my stomach queasy. I decided to go directly to the meeting hall to double-check the equipment. The large, vacant room echoed my footsteps as I walked over to the portable tape machine resting on a wood table. I threaded the tape and played a brief snippet, checking the volume.

I sat in the chair next to the table laden with equipment, and stared at the room, with its rough-hewn camp decor of unpainted wood walls and hardwood flooring, tension gripping my stomach. About ten minutes before the program time, women began wandering in. I smiled in their direction, and then bolted for the bathroom. When I got back, the room was nearly full. The chatter of one hundred or so women hummed through the meeting hall.

Finally, it was time. The room quieted as I stood on rubbery legs and cleared my throat to give a brief introduction. Then I leaned toward the tape recorder and hit the play button. Our voices, my mother's and mine, began reverberating through the room. This time, unlike radio, there was no hiding: I was in the same room with the listeners. A vibrating began in my body, and I lifted out of my skin, hovering over the crowd. I looked down at the women. I saw their faces—heads bent forward in absorbed concentration.

Reassured, I sank back into my body just as my mother was describing her electroshocks: " . . . *they sent me to this place, and they gave me an electric shock. And it was terrible! After the first shock, I called up my parents. 'Get me out of here!' I used up all my change, called up all my friends, and pleaded, "Get me out of here!' It wasn't until eighteen shocks later they let me out of that place. When I got home, I didn't remember where we lived or the streets of the town. People would come up to me and say, 'Hello, Gloria,' and some of them were probably old friends, but I wouldn't know who they were . . .* "

My mother's words hit me in a new way. The numbness I'd felt when first hearing her words left me, and the pain of what had happened made my chest ache. I found myself quietly weeping. I wished I could hide in the back of the room. Instead, I raised my face and looked out to see that other women were crying, too. It was all right, all right to feel this, and to let others see.

I stayed in this new state, connected and present, held there by the women in the audience, as my mother continued the story. By the time she got to quitting therapy, giving me her blessing, and her own coming out in the women's movement, we were all smiling. There were hoots of laughter as she described her sexual blossoming and wild promiscuity that first year.

Toward the end of the tape, I asked, "*I'd like to know how you feel, identifying as a dyke. A couple months ago, I called you, and you sounded like you felt so tough and so good!*"

"Yeah. I feel absolutely wonderful being a dyke. A fifty-two-year-old political dyke. I feel strong; I feel good within myself. I still have a lot of pain, but I'm dealing with it. You know, living isn't all fun. But I feel good about being a dyke—there's no doubt about that. So . . . what more can I tell you?"

"Well," I responded, *"all I can say is that we've been through a lot together, a lot of hard times, and pain and anger, and your being a lesbian is just so incredible for me. I mean, it's made this bond between us that will always be there. It's this bond—"*

My mother finished my thought: *"I know it makes me feel closer. Once I was able to accept you as a lesbian and myself as a lesbian, you know, there were no secrets anymore."*

After the tape ended, several women made their way up to me. They told me how moving the recording had been, how deeply it affected them. One woman said to me, "If you never do anything else in your life, you have done something by sharing this story."

Chapter 36. Woman Share

COMPLAINING ABOUT OUR lovers was a bond my mother and I shared, because Gloria, like me, chose women who drove us nuts with their wandering lust, the giddy push-pull of intimacy and then flight. They ran, we chased. One of those women was Giovanna, my neighbor on Clarke Street, whose ground-floor apartment faced mine across a narrow gap between our buildings. The Oakland block, with its cheap rent and fourplex apartments, had become a lesbian enclave, its own little bell jar of friendships, entanglements, and intrigues.

Giovanna was an artist and a pothead. We started as friends. One afternoon, we lay on my bed very stoned, and somehow ended up exploring each other's naked bodies and becoming lovers. Before our relationship, I had admired Giovanna's relentless devotion to her art. She spent hours at her easel, painting on canvas. But now, need rose up in me like warm dough, and I began to sulk, feeling like a sidekick to her work. There'd be moments when she was attentive to me, when we'd gab nonstop on our hikes with our dogs in the hills, during sex, or when she taught me her mother's recipe for calzone. Then I'd feel the sweetness of her attention, and be placated.

On Thanksgiving, after we'd been together about eight months, the flu kept me from going down the block to our friends' feast. Giovanna went alone. The next day, she brought me turkey left-overs and announced she was breaking up. She'd ended up taking a woman she'd met at the dinner party back to her apartment, and decided she was really into her. Later, through her thin curtains, I could see the shadows of her and her new girlfriend, and hear them making love. Furious, I wanted to hurl something across the gap. Instead, I called my mother and complained bitterly. She echoed my outrage, then added, "Darling, you're better off without that shithead!"

Several months later, Giovanna rang my bell. She told me how sorry she was, and began her love refrain: *What a fool I've been. How special and wonderful you are!* With that, some place inside me went warm and droopy. I wanted to believe. I forgave her.

AFTER BEING REUNITED a couple months, Giovanna and I went away for the weekend to visit a collective of women living on land in the country. Giovanna knew one of them. At the end of dinner with the group in their farmhouse kitchen, Giovanna disappeared, along with her friend. The two of them had been sitting at one end of the table, their heads close together in an animated conversation.

I tried to ignore my growing anxiety, but as sunset deepened into indigo, they still hadn't returned. I stepped outside, into the fading light, the first stars blinking dimly. The crickets had started up. "Gio—vaaaaa—nna?!" I yelled out into the darkening meadow.

Silence.

I stepped back inside, shaking my head as the screen door *thunked* behind me. I turned to the two women I'd met that day still at the table. I tried to sound casual, but my tone came out strained. "Do you have any idea where Giovanna and Michelle went? It's getting dark, and they're not back."

They looked at each other, then back at me. Linda shrugged. Rena, a woman with curly red hair, coughed, then said, "Giovanna went off with Michelle? Well, then they probably went over the hill to the tepee on the other side of the land. Michelle often spends the night there."

No, damn it to hell, this couldn't be happening. I must have had a stricken look, because Rena added, "Oh, I'm sorry."

I couldn't believe it. I stepped back outside. Surely, I'd see a flashlight and two bodies stumbling toward the house. Surely, Giovanna had just asked Michelle to show her around the land or get a peek at the tepee. There was no moon, just a black country sky thick with stars. A chorus of bullfrogs were croaking their low, forlorn refrain, "Ribbit. Ribbit."

That night, Linda and Rena were kind. They let me rant about how I couldn't believe Giovanna was doing this again.

"Come sleep with us," Rena offered. In their double bed, Linda and Rena spooned while I perched at the edge, too jumpy to accept their offer to cuddle. Soon, their breathing slowed, and one began snoring lightly. There wasn't much sleep in me. I lay there obsessing: *How could she? How could she?* I drifted between that state and anxious dreams.

At dawn, I stumbled outside and sank into a battered metal lawn chair with flaking paint, staring at the hill as if I could will Giovanna's return. I considered driving away. *But then, how will she get home?* I stared at the hill in the dim light, its weeds brittle and dry from the rainless California summer, my eyes burning.

In midmorning, I saw them: two figures coming down the hill. They were holding hands. My stomach lurched and I stood up. When they got close enough to notice me, they dropped hands. Giovanna came up to me, while Michelle stood back a ways.

"Hey," she said, smiling.

"What the hell, Giovanna?" I yelled. "How could you just go off, not a word?"

When she shrugged and gave me another smile, I leapt. Grabbing her T-shirt collar with both hands, I intended to shake her, but the force of my leap knocked us both to the ground. I was partly on top of her, her face near mine. Michelle was yelling, "Goddamn it, knock it off!" Giovanna's breath was heavy with the scent of marijuana. *She's stoned,* I thought. *There's no talking to her.* We untangled, got up, and dusted ourselves off.

On the ride home, we were silent. My fury steamed around me, fueling my foot on the gas pedal. *Go, go, get home.* Giovanna sat in the passenger seat with her sketchbook in her lap, doodling furiously. When I pulled up on our block, we each unloaded our bags from the car, carried them into our separate apartments, and closed our doors without a goodbye.

All my friends said, "Don't let her back! She's never going to change." I concurred, "Never again with that shithead!" My mother sent me a note: "Hi, love, I just put another hex on Giovanna and her house—I hope you will not be too troubled by her being next door."

And for a while, I held out. But then, she began her Siren song—*you are so beautiful; you are so wonderful*—and I did not stop up my ears with wax. I clung to the driftwood of our relationship, terrified of drowning if I let go. The only thing that saved me was Giovanna's move to New Mexico, to paint in that high desert light.

AT FIRST, MY MOTHER dated women her age who had been only with men—single or divorced older women now active in Women's Liberation. She was supported by the prevailing belief in feminist circles: Any woman can be a lesbian, and should be, instead of being oppressed in a relationship with a man.

One summer when I was between jobs, I went East for two months. Gloria was living with Sarah, a woman also in her fifties. It was Sarah's first lesbian relationship. My mother had found them an apartment within milliseconds of their becoming lovers, but now Sarah had backpedaled to a rarely sexual, almost-roommates stance. Sarah and I made small talk over meals, but there was little room to ease into knowing each other. My mother simmered with disappointment and resentment, and the tension between them was palpable.

We all suffocated through July in the reduced oxygen of the humid, tense apartment. In August, my mother and I headed for the Jersey shore. She had the summer off from her teaching job, but Sarah had to remain in the city and work. We stayed in a bungalow that Sarah and her brother had inherited when their father died. Gloria had bought out the brother's half, which I thought was a disastrous mistake. But there was no stopping Gloria when she had an impulse; she was a leaper.

During the week, my mother and I lay on beach towels on the white sand, slathering ourselves with Coppertone, reading junky paperbacks, jumping in the gentle Atlantic surf. The salty air felt like home, like the best part of home. I sunbathed in the proximity of my mother's love, trying to bake out my hurt from my latest busted relationship. With my mother, I was not just loved, but adored.

Toward the end of each week, I could feel my mother disappearing into anxiety. She always hoped for a good weekend with Sarah, but feared otherwise. Friday night, we'd go to pick Sarah up at the bus station, and she'd descend the bus stairs, smiling somewhat grimly. *Oh, shit, here we go!* I'd sigh to myself. We'd go back to the cottage and have the dinner Gloria had prepared, but conversation soon lagged. I tried to fill in the gaps, telling them tales from my California life, as desperate as I had been as a child trying to entertain my parents to distract them from their bitterness.

I WAS BACK IN CALIFORNIA in early fall when my mother called to tell me she and Sarah had broken up.

After that, my mother switched to younger lovers. While she was recovering from her breakup, she told me, "You know, I dig young women; we're in sync. I can't relate to those old-style butch-femme women, those bar dykes who aren't political. And the other women my age, those divorcées into women's lib—they can be uptight bloody bores!"

On my visit the following summer, I discovered my mother had a lover who, at twenty-five, not only was a year younger than I was, but also shared my name. When I met her, something in me went cold and hard, a feeling that I did not want to examine. Instead, I covered it over with a strained warmth. Luckily, the year before I'd started using Chana, my Hebrew name. Nonetheless, it was eerie to hear my mother saying "Karen" to her lover. Weird and a bit creepy. I actually liked Karen, and we got along well, but in my body there was a tidal undercurrent—crash: *I'm jealous, I hate you;* whoosh:

mustn't feel that. Around the two of them, I would find myself with a tightened throat, queasy stomach, or tearing eyes. That was the price of pretending everything was cool.

Again in the fall, back in California, I heard from my mother that things weren't going well. Karen had gotten involved with someone else, but wanted to keep seeing my mother. Gloria wavered, and they were on and off. Then, one night she saw Karen and her other lover dancing at the Duchess. "I was a bit drunk," Gloria told me over the phone, "and something came over me and I just went up and socked Karen's girlfriend. I got thrown out of the bar. Of course, I feel bad, but I must say, in the moment it sure the hell felt satisfying."

Six months later, Karen called me. "Hey, how are you?" She didn't pause for an answer. "I'm gonna to be in the Bay Area. I met this woman from L.A. when she was visiting the Big Apple, so I'm flying out, and we're planning to drive up the coast. Can we crash with you?"

"Sure, no problem." I had not yet learned that word for boundaries, "n-o."

Karen and her new sweetie arrived a week later in the evening. As soon as I showed them into my place, the girlfriend took one look at my shabby futon that I'd opened as a bed for them in the living room, and started screaming, "I'm not staying in this rat hole! We have to leave, now!" When Karen shook her head, the lover said, "That's it, I'm going back to L.A.!" and stormed out.

"Aren't you going after her?" I asked.

"Nah, I'm staying here. She's been bugging me the whole drive up. A real pain in the ass."

"Ah . . . okay." *Gulp*—alone with Karen. Left to play hostess, I asked, "What do you want to do?"

"Let's go dancing!" And for three nights, we did. At a lesbian bar complete with a disco ball, the air thick with cigarette smoke and sweat, we lubricated ourselves with Black Russians. We moved to the thump of the bass, the disco lights pulsing to the music. Our bodies slanted toward and away from each other as Donna Summer sang, "*Oooh, love to love you baby*" for sixteen minutes, the relentless beat and the colored lights inducing trance. In the sway of our movement, I could feel the pull of Karen's body, its enticement. She threw her head back as she danced, raised her arms as she snapped her fingers, which accentuated her large breasts, the curve of her waist, the flare of her hips. I resisted by sitting out the slow dances.

Each night, Karen slept on the living-room futon. The third night, we came back to the apartment half-smashed. I had already crawled into bed when Karen appeared and sat down, her body close to me. She was leaving the next morning. "I just wanted to tell you what a wonderful time I've had."

She reached over and stroked my hair, leaning forward for a dark hug. I was starting to reach up and pull her toward me when Gloria's face flashed in my mind. My mother was my rock, outlasting all the lovers who had come and gone.

Stone sober now, I said, "Good night, Karen." It almost sounded like I was talking to myself.

ONE VISIT WHEN GLORIA was coming West, I drove my battered blue VW Bug to the San Francisco airport to pick her up. The car had a broken heater and a hole in the floorboard, but it was summer, so the drive across the bay to Oakland wasn't so bad. It was hard to talk over the loud *click-click* of the engine, and I had to focus on holding the stick shift in a vice grip to keep it from popping out of fourth gear.

Back on my block, Gloria suggested, "Let's see if we can go to the country. I'm dying for nature. Whadda ya say?"

There were feminist groups living on communes in the country, so we called around and found WomanShare in southern Oregon. They were a collective who gave five-day workshops to support themselves. By luck, they had a workshop coming up in a couple of days. The topic was lesbian sexuality. "Sign us up!" I said over the phone.

We got a ride from a local woman who had a decent car. It wasn't until we had arrived and unloaded the car, been greeted by the five collective members and several attendees, been fed soup and homemade bread, and were sitting in the living room as a group, beginning the first evening's check-in, that it hit me: *I'm at a sexuality workshop with my* mother. *Oh shit!*

Gloria and I prided ourselves on not being uptight with each other about our sexuality. Our lives had blossomed in the women's movement culture, whose heart was the belief that sharing intimate truths was liberating. We had—separately on East and West Coasts—participated in group self-help gynecological exams with warmed speculums, flashlights, and mirrors.

But this—to be at a small sexuality retreat together—was a bit close to the edge. *Thank God,* I thought, when I heard an organizer explain that each day there would be two workshop times to choose from, and some all-group activities: swimming in the river, folk dancing, and softball. I planned to head for whatever meeting my mother didn't.

It took maybe half a day for me to fixate on a woman in the group. I had been single for two years—my longest period ever. Over this time, my longing and libido had landed on one woman after another. Unable to restrain myself, I would declare my feelings to the woman in question as if I were making a commencement address: topic, argument, conclusion, usually ending not in thunderous applause, but in a panicked stare or a firm "Sorry, I like you, but only as a friend."

This time, I tried to be subtler. I just gazed ardently at Lucinda when we spoke, and managed to eat lunch next to her. She chatted with me, and laughed with great guffaws, so I felt encouraged.

Much of the day, my mother and I went our separate ways. At night, we shared a little wood structure with twin beds. It was called the Coop, after the chicken coop it had once been. Lying in our beds, we would recount to each other details of our day. I bemoaned not knowing if Lucinda reciprocated my attraction, and how when I was near her there was buzzing in my chest, tightness in my stomach, and a brain filled with molasses.

The next-to-last afternoon, the entire group met outdoors around an unlit campfire circle. Women from a neighboring collective called Cabbage Lane were giving a guest lecture. Calling themselves the Radical Singles, they explained how they had spent the summer in an experiment to learn how not to be possessive with their love. The goal was to open up to loving more than one; exclusive coupledom was discouraged as proprietary and limiting. In the quest to live their principles, each night they put their names in a hat, shook it up, and picked one. The agreement was that you would spend the night with your hat-picked partner, and together explore whatever level of intimacy and sexuality you wanted to share. "So," the Cabbage Lane women said, "want to try it tonight?"

That night after dinner, one of the Cabbage Lane women passed around slips of paper for us to write our names on. Someone produced a straw hat.

The hat started its round on the side of the room opposite me. I watched as Lucinda's paper scrap fluttered into the hat. *Yes,* I whispered to myself. When it came to my mother, she held the hat in her lap for a moment, then shook her head and passed it on.

Half of those participating put in their names; the other half would draw names, until everyone had a partner. My turn: Close my eyes, reach my hand in, feel the thin paper slips against my finger pads, lift one out. Resting in my palm in simple blue ink, but leaping at me as if neon: Lucinda. I announced her name and grinned at her across the room. I couldn't tell her reaction—was that weak smile an attempt at covering disappointment, or was she suddenly shy?

I raced to the Coop to grab my toiletries and headed for the bathroom, where I took a quick shower, brushed my teeth, and changed my underwear. When I went back to toss my dirty things on the bed, my mother was on her cot, reading a paperback. She looked up. "Nervous?" she asked.

I nodded.

"Try to relax and enjoy yourself," she said. "After all, it's only for one night."

Lucinda was waiting for me, sitting on one of the log seats that surrounded the campfire circle. I sat down next to her, clutching my sleeping bag. She had said something, but it hadn't penetrated.

"What?" I asked.

"I've changed my mind," she repeated. "I'm sorry, but I realize I just don't want to do this."

"But we don't have to *do* anything," I said, trying not to plead, but my voice came out in a high-pitched squeak. I took a breath and tried logic. "The agreement was to spend the night with the person, no matter what."

"I know, and I'm sorry, but I changed my mind." She reached out and squeezed my arm as she rose, and then she was gone.

Back in the Coop, my mother sat on my bed with me while I leaned into her and cried, but she could comfort me only so much. It seemed obvious to me this rejection was personal. Hadn't Lucinda put her name in, willing to spend the night with whomever—except, apparently, me?

The next morning, I joined the other name-in-the-hatters at the fire ring. We were supposed to report back on how it had gone. Two of the Cabbage Lane women were facilitating. Lucinda had shown up, but sat away from me. As soon as we began, I blurted out the story, then broke down crying. The woman next to me put her arm around me. The Cabbage Lane women lit into Lucinda—very bad show, to step up to such an agreement and not carry through! The others made murmurs of sympathy for me. Lucinda looked like she might cry.

My satisfaction was immense. I could almost feel these women lambasting all the past lovers who had done me wrong.

Chapter 37. Identity House

WHEN PATTI HEARST WAS kidnapped from her Berkeley apartment in 1974, the Symbionese Liberation Army sent her ID to KPFA to prove they were the ones who had her. I was at the station, working on a *Lesbian Air* program, when Randolph Hearst came by to pick up his daughter's ID. In his wake, there was excited buzz throughout the station. We could look out across Shattuck Avenue and see the great telephoto lenses the FBI had set up, pointing at us from the suite they were occupying on the seventh floor of the Great Western Bank building. Over the next weeks, the drama intensified: The SLA sent several recorded communiqués to the station to be broadcast, the FBI kept trying to get its hands on those tapes, and station staff and volunteers figured all our phones were tapped.

In the midst of it all, our Lesbian Air group was in crisis, split over ideology: the lesbian separatists versus the socialists. I straddled both camps. In daily life, I was a separatist, having friendships exclusively with other lesbians. By inhabiting feminist, often women-only spaces—bookstores, music festivals, and lesbian bars—we developed a feeling of kinship, a shared vision in which we mixed erotic charge with radical rebellion against patriarchy and a thrilling sense of empowerment. But as an ideology, separatism seemed to me to be a dead end: Since men wouldn't disappear from the earth, if they were hopeless to change, then we were doomed. I hadn't abandoned caring about racism or class inequities, or the belief that economic justice meant a socialist system where wealth and resources were shared, but I was swept up in lesbian feminism's focus on sexism as the root base of the oppression pyramid, and it obscured those connections. I was confused about how it all fit together.

Then Erica joined the radio group. A Jewish girl from Hoboken, she had a New Jersey accent that reminded me of home. She was a firebrand, her lips pursed in passionate monologues, and I went gaga. She worked for a separatist newspaper, *Dykes and Gorgons,* and painted large canvases, abstracts with vulva-shaped triangles. We became instant friends, and once, sitting on her couch together, I leaned close and stammered, "Um, I, um, I'd like to kiss you . . ." She looked alarmed and wouldn't let me touch her, arousing an aching longing in me. I never tried again, but I kept half hoping for something more, the unrequited ache so familiar it was almost a comfort—didn't love always involve suffering?

With Erica present, *Lesbian Air* meetings became even more fraught with diatribes and verbal warfare. At one meeting, altogether too much like the others, Erica proclaimed, "Lesbians have *got* to band together. It's for our own survival to fight off the male supremacist society. They're raping our world!"

Helen shouted, "What about capitalism? Working-class men are oppressed, too! How in the hell can we have a just society if we don't all work together?!"

I hated conflict. "Can we get back to talking about our next show on self-defense? Who wants to interview that jujitsu teacher?" I ventured.

It wasn't long afterward that the socialists announced that we separatists were kicked out of the group. Despite my ambivalent politics, I was presumed separatist because of my association with Erica.

The world was spinning upside down. Patti Hearst, after weeks kept blindfolded in a closet, emerged with a new identity: "Tania," proud revolutionary. The SLA photographed her holding a submachine gun, standing in front of the SLA logo of a seven-headed cobra.

I'd changed my look a bit, too. My friend Sonia had agreed to trim my midback-length hair, but she cut it crooked, and with each attempt to straighten it, it got shorter and more crooked. I loved my long hair, but long hair did not fit the prevailing dyke look. I stared mournfully in the mirror at Sonia's latest disastrous attempt to even it out, now chin-length. "Oh, just cut it the fuck off," I told her, going for razor short, finally jumping off the hippie-femme high wire. Or was I pushed?

The irony was that we separatists had to go to the Man for justice. We sat in station manager Larry Bensky's office and told him our tale of expulsion. His decision was swift and Solomonic: In Free speech radio, no group would be allowed to censor its members, so our baby would be split in two, *Lesbian Air* now alternating shows with our newly formed *Radio Free Lesbian.*

ONE BY ONE OVER the next year, all my sister programmers dropped out, either too busy, losing interest, or embittered by our squabbling. Even Erica left. I was the sole survivor of both radio programs. My love of radio and my stubbornness kept me hosting the show for a community I now felt torn up by. It felt altogether *too* much like family. But I still believed in the power of women sharing stories, and in that basic tenet of feminism: *The personal is political.* That women taking action, through art or politics, create change.

A year later, I stood in the hallway of the radio station, staring at a notice thumb-tacked to the wall: "KPFA is currently accepting applications for a two-year grant position of full-time production engineer." I'd never wanted a job so badly.

In the realm of career, I was lost. Producing the radio show involved lots of work—hours of absorbing, exciting work—but no pay. Since I'd dropped out of Grinnell in 1970, I'd spent seven years scraping along in my counterculture lifestyle with odd jobs and occasional help from one or the other parent. I had worked as a telephone operator and an assistant chef, stuffed envelopes in an art museum, done housecleaning and childcare, been hired to promote a self-published book I didn't like, run an office coffee shop, sold filigree jewelry on the street outside Macy's, and flipped hamburgers. I was currently working overnight shifts in a battered-women's shelter, where I watched the women come in with their children in tow, hauling their own beleaguered bodies as well.

The classes I'd been taking for several years at Laney junior college were getting me nowhere. My father had called me a dilettante, and though I had protested, I feared he was right.

I was elated to get the KPFA production job, and I plunged full-time into a world of progressive media. My world had been a world of lesbians, but now I was working with a great diversity of men and women: musicians, political activists and analysts, writers, actors, and community groups.

The bulk of my time was spent in the control room of the recording studio, with its four-track reel-to-reel Ampex machines, equalizers, turntables, cassettes, mixing board, and adjacent studio large enough to mike a band. We did both live music broadcasts and recorded sessions with musicians, taped interviews, and mixed radio shows. KPFA was that rare place in the media that was a home to the Left, and its luminaries lumbered up the stairs to our second-floor offices: Angela Davis, Malvina Reynolds, Joan Baez, and many others. Enthralled, I recorded them or acted as their live on-air engineer. But shyness made me hold back; I did my job, but hardly introduced myself. And among my coworkers, I stayed withdrawn. I didn't socialize or share much about myself.

One weekend, I was invited by two women who produced *Living on Indian Time* to go with them to a Native American powwow. I had been Barbara and Pamela's on-air control board operator for several months. Before the show, we'd gab a bit, but it was mostly idle chatter, so I was surprised and touched when they invited me. On the drive home on Sunday, we were in the midst of telling each other stories from our lives, when Barbara said to me, "Chana, you don't have to make yourself such an outsider."

I was offended. What did she, a straight woman, know about being a lesbian? How on the outside of society we were! Then I felt embarrassed: What had she seen, how had I acted, that had revealed how withdrawn I could be? Within my indignation, some part of me knew she'd touched on something, but I couldn't yet see that I was living as if I carried Millstone with me, as if I was still the girl with the crazy mom, the Jew amid the descendents of the Dutch Reformed, marking me forever as an outsider.

But then the irony hit me: Here was an urban Indian, someone from the most marginalized and oppressed group in the country, as outsider as you can get, telling me not to be an outsider. Her words lodged in me, buried a glimmer of hope that there might be more of a place for me, if only I would let myself have it.

I HAD MY DREAM JOB, but discontent rumbled in me, and I was becoming more and more irritable. I was assisting everyone else with their radio projects, but not doing creative work of my own. I'd given up producing *Radio Free Lesbian,* in part because of the demands of the job, in part because it was a relief to let go of something with such painful associations.

One day I was given a shift as control-board operator for a brand-new music program. This meant I would be the technical disc jockey, spinning the records selected by the host while she introduced them. But when showtime arrived, the host hadn't appeared. I played some public service announcements to kill time, then threw on a record and ran to the record library, furiously grabbed an assortment, and raced back to the on-air room. The programmer never arrived, and I winged the show. The next week, the same thing happened, but this time I had prepared my backup show. Listeners called the station: great new show!

As a result, the program director asked me to take on being host of the show. That was the beginning of the program I named *A World Wind.* At first, it was exclusively a music show, featuring recordings from around the world, with an emphasis on female musicians. Over time, I expanded the program to include women guests reading poetry and prose, and interviews with local and international women artists, musicians, and activists.

During the six years I hosted *A World Wind,* my sense of myself shifted. Good interviews require engagement, curiosity, and a willingness to have empathy. I discovered an aptitude for listening, for drawing people out. Letters arrived at the station, thanking me for this show or that, for something that touched someone. I gained confidence. I was still shy, but not so guarded. Some part of me always felt like an outsider, but over time there were moments where it felt as if the world had opened to me, widened to include me more.

IN 1973, ABOUT the same time I started with the *Lesbian Air* radio collective, Gloria began volunteering as a peer counselor at Identity House, located in a church basement not far from her Greenwich Village apartment. Identity House was founded in 1971—two years after the Stonewall riots—with the radical idea of gay people offering support and affirmative counseling to other gay people.

From across the continent, I imagined a young woman approaching the door to Identity House's basement office, and hesitating. Dare she go in? Inside, in a tiny room, two dilapidated padded armchairs face each other. The door opens, and Gloria is bringing in the young woman. They sit opposite each other, and my mother encourages the young woman to speak. My mother's face is soft and welcoming; she understands how much fear there can be in exploring sexual identity. She listens intently. There is such triumph in her helping other gay people, supporting them so they will never have to endure the psychiatric horrors she had survived.

Each of us, my mother and I, was in therapy, but not the old Freudian, hierarchical style. I was seeing a feminist therapist. Gloria was seeing a Gestalt therapist, participating in a group doing primal therapy, and went on weeklong encounter groups at the Jersey shore.

At Identity House, she began training as a Gestalt therapist. She wrote me that she was coleading groups, as well as counseling clients one on one. Once, she called me, almost breathless. "I met Laura Perls at this meeting of therapists. People think it's just Fritz Perls, but they *cocreated* Gestalt. She asked if I'd like to be in her advanced training group. My God, the mother of Gestalt therapy is asking *me!*"

I'd never heard her so happy.

Chapter 38. Promised Land

GLORIA AND I ARRIVED AT Kennedy International in the thick of New York's summer humidity, already stinking with sweat, and dragged our bags into the muggy airport, whose air-conditioning had been shut off in one of the metropolitan area's energy brownouts. But we were both too excited to be bothered much: We were embarking on a monthlong trip to Israel, our first adventure in a foreign land.

In the El Al terminal, we took the escalator up to the departures level, and as we rose we were greeted by a huge silver Jewish star. My eyes teared up at the sight. I was slightly embarrassed—I was by far no Zionist, and such a reaction seemed corny. And yet the star felt like a marker for the trip, for some longing to experience a place where, for the first time in my life, I would not be a minority, at least as a Jew.

My friend Eliana, an American Jew who had lived for years in Israel, had encouraged this visit, saying she could connect us with plenty of Israeli feminists who would give us an insider experience.

We were planning a big trip to mark transitions for both of us: By the upcoming summer, Gloria would have completed her master's in social work, and I would be at the end of the two-year grant that had funded my job at KPFA.

At the gate, we were surrounded by Jews of all sorts: Israelis returning home, speaking to each other emphatically in Hebrew, American Jewish tourists, Hasidic men in their long black wool coats and hats, even though it was broiling hot. Looking over at a group of Hasids, Gloria muttered, "Patriarchal bastards!"

Before we could board the plane, a uniformed security agent took us together into an enclosed booth. He stared at our tickets and then asked a long list of questions, beginning with the inevitable "Were you given any packages on the way to the airport?" and ending with "Are you Jewish?" When we nodded yes, he let us go. *What if we weren't Jewish?* I wondered, *What then—a body search?*

It was evening when we landed. We took the bus into Tel Aviv in a jet-lagged daze, past concrete apartment buildings with solar panels on their roofs. We registered at our hotel, dropped off our luggage, and staggered out to a restaurant.

I stared at the menu, not knowing what to ask for. My stomach clenched with anxiety at feeling not in control. I looked up at my mother, head down in her menu. "Glor, would you make up your goddamn mind; otherwise we'll be here all night!" She didn't defend herself, and that made me even crabbier. I was embarrassed that I had regressed into a ten-year-old brat who was yelling at her mother for no good reason. But I couldn't stop myself.

The next morning, we went downstairs in the hotel to an Israeli breakfast buffet, a spread of olives, tomatoes, yogurt, hard-boiled eggs, herring, challah, and fruit. When Gloria finished eating, she got herself more coffee, returned to our table, lit up a cigarette, and inhaled deeply. I had hated her chain-smoking my whole life. I hated the smell, and the way the smoke choked me.

A waiter rushed over to our table and exclaimed, "No smoking in public on Shabbat!" Gloria rolled her eyes at me, smashed out the cigarette, and muttered, "You finish eating. I'll take my coffee to the room."

Before leaving, she breezed by the buffet table, grabbed some hard-boiled eggs, and wrapped them in a napkin—provisions for our lunch. The same waiter intercepted her and yelled, "All food must be eaten here! You *cannot* take food!" Other patrons turned their heads to stare. Mortified, I wanted to sink under the table. My skin flared, hot and burning, as the old shame of my mom swept over my body, so familiar.

Later that day, back in our hotel room after we ventured to the beach, I complained, "I *hate* Tel Aviv! It's ugly! It's so hot! So muggy! And crowded! Jeez, the rest of Israel better not be like this!"

My mother soothed, "It'll be all right, sweetheart, you'll see. Let's make our calls so we can move on."

We called the women on our list, the friends of friends we had sent notes to in advance, hoping to be invited to stay, although no one had answered. Our primary contact, Sonia in Haifa, offered to rent us her ex-husband's apartment on the cheap, but it wouldn't be available for a few days yet. In the meantime, we discovered there were campgrounds throughout Israel that had cabins with cots, but only one had any openings.

Gloria and I arrived at Camp Lehman, just a few miles from the border of Lebanon, in the afternoon, patting ourselves on the back that we had navigated the local buses. The farther north we went, the more soldiers got on the bus, wearing their army green uniforms and berets, Uzi submachine guns slung over their shoulders.

We ate at the campground restaurant, a screened-in bare-bones room. Schnitzel again. How sick I was already becoming of this bland, breaded, overcooked chicken. As we left, Gloria "borrowed" two glasses from the table by sticking them in her purse. There were none in our cabin, since most Israelis arrived at camp in cars loaded with food, plates, and utensils. As we sauntered away, we were followed outside by the maître d', who yelled at us in Hebrew. We kept walking, as if deaf. Then he repeated, even louder, in French, "*Madame! Ou sont les tasses d'eau?*"

Once again, I was mortified by my mother. Shame overshadowed my pleasure that he took us for French, not Americans. Our pursuer was now right next to my mother, holding out his hand. She turned around, faced him, and emptied her purse of the glasses, which he reached for as he glowered at us.

As we made our way back to our little wood bungalow, neither of us said a word about the incident. The heat had drained us. We rested on our canvas cots, each glued to our paperback. A tense, resigned silence vibrated in the tiny space between our cots. During the night, we heard the *boom* of gunfire in the distance.

THE SHRILL RING OF the phone startled me awake. It was early morning, and as I sat up in bed, it took me a moment to orient: *Haifa, I'm in Haifa*. After I hung up, my mother called out, "Who is it?"

"Just someone calling Sonia's ex."

Neither of us could get back to sleep. Instead, we lounged together in my mother's bed. She told me about a new therapy group she was in that was an experiential training group. "The group lets the person express her upset, grief, and anger as the group witnesses it." She gave me an example, "Like for me with your grandma," she said. "You know how cold she can be. Always complaining about Grandpa. She never even held or kissed me. She made me feel so unlovable."

Anger rose in my throat and was held there, suspended. The feeling was the knot of taboo. I was now sharply, fully awake. I sat up in the bed. I hesitated, then I croaked, "Um . . . Mom . . ." the anger clotting my throat. "Look, Glor, I've got anger, too, anger toward you from childhood."

Here we were, perched on the Haifa hillside, and I could not look at her. And then I did. She had sat up and turned toward me. Her soft face greeted me, her skin browned from the sun, her silver hair curling over her forehead. "Yes?" she encouraged.

"I've just felt terrible on this trip. I know I've been snapping at you. I feel so guilty. It's like I'm a sullen twelve-year-old again, and I just can't seem to stop myself."

My mother said, "I can take it. Why don't you express your anger now? I mean, the real anger." She looked me in the eye, solemn-faced.

I clamped down. "I can't. I feel guilty."

"If you change 'I feel guilty' to 'I resent,' you will get to your anger," Mom said.

My stomach contracted. I wanted to, but I was terrified. The guilt rose, riding the old beliefs: *It's not her fault. What right do I have to get angry at someone who's sick? She can't handle it. This could kill her.*

"You really can take it?" I asked in a half whisper.

She nodded.

I gathered my breath and tried to say, "I resented . . ." and sputtered to a stop.

My mother just sat there, looking at me.

This time, I managed, "I resented being ashamed to bring friends home." I stopped, my breath so shallow that I felt a bit faint.

"Yes, what else?"

I glanced over at my mother, then looked away. *Take a breath. Begin again.* "I resented putting you to bed at night, picking you up off the floor, putting out cigarette fires, helping you to the bathroom." Once I started, it kept coming. "I resented being scared you would die. I resented dealing with your suicide attempts. I resented being left alone."

Gloria listened, nodding. Then she said, "You're just speaking. You don't sound angry."

My stomach was a fist, held and clenched. I could not say it louder, angrier. The old terror gripped me, its singsong voice chanting—*If you get angry, your mother will die. You'll kill her. She'll die she'll die.* I was jolted to realize that, of course, my mother knew all these things; she'd been there, after all. It was just that no one had ever once asked me how I felt.

I could do no more, but I felt an opening, a loosening of the hard knot inside me.

My mother reached for my hand.

"It was terrible for you," she said. "I'm so sorry. So, so sorry."

AFTER HAIFA, WE TOOK a *sherut,* an eight-person van, to Jerusalem, where we'd been invited to stay with Dinah and Gretta. The couple were my age, in their late twenties; Dinah was American, Gretta Dutch. They lived in a rambling old house made of golden Jerusalem stone with Gretta's two young boys, a rabbit, and a puppy. They welcomed us warmly into their messy, chaotic household.

My mother and I visited the Old City of Jerusalem, with its carless cobblestone streets. In the souk, Yemenite and Bedouin dresses—black with red embroidery—hung from high hooks along the narrow alley walls. Spice stores filled the air with sweet, tangy scents. Light shafts poured through openings in the overhead arches, making the stone walls glow golden, lighting the street goods in their riot of colors: crimson, orange, saffron, black. It amazed me, to be in a place so alive and so ancient.

Before we were admitted to the Western Wall, we passed a guard station, where our bags were searched. Then we entered a huge open square with Israeli flags flapping, and on one side, there it was: the Wailing Wall. We approached the women's section, a much smaller section than the men's. I found a spot and pressed my face and arms against the warm limestone. My mother was right next to me, her hands raised with palms flat against the wall, her body leaning into it. I closed my eyes and was filled with the smell of stone, the sounds of women praying and—was it crying?—yes, crying all around us. And then I found myself crying, too. I hadn't expected this, hadn't expected to feel anything. My hands felt something in the stone, a memory, a whisper: *diaspora.* The point of exile.

Something was vibrating in me, shaking itself awake. Grief swept through me, a wordless mix of the communal, my own family's history, and what I had so recently expressed to my mother. Stories swirled in me: Grandma Katie, Dad's mom, crying for her lost family. *I was sixteen when I told my parents I was going out. I wore only my one set of clothes when I left Ukraine with your grandfather. They would never have let me leave. Oy gotenu, I never saw them again!* She was weeping for her grandparents, beaten to death during the Russian Revolution.

Grandma Katie and I cried together over the mass grave of Babi Yar outside of Kiev, where, we guessed, the Nazis had slaughtered the rest of her family. I thought of Grandma Miriam, churning with unhappiness at being stuck marrying a greenhorn in America, her hatred leaving her hard and bitter, depriving my mother of love. Isidor, my mother's dad, voicing his shame: *I was an ignorant Jew from the shtetl, an uneducated peasant—we knew nothing, there is nothing to tell you.* The stones accepted my grief, warm in their enduring.

Around me, women mumbled prayers and children giggled. I opened my eyes and looked around. Women, mostly old, were sitting on plastic chairs with prayer books, rocking their bodies as their lips moved, whispering the text. Others of various ages were writing their longings, wishes, and prayers on slips of paper to stick in the wall's cracks. I thought of our oppression as women in this segregated part of the wall—the unequally small portion allotted to us women. A fantasy came to me: a group of us, heads covered with shawls, bodies pressed against the wall, wailing and rocking until the power of our keening pushed down the divider.

MY IRRITATION WITH MY mother had, for the most part, left me. There was enjoyment now, at sharing an adventure together. We spent our days in Jerusalem wandering the Old City, and our evenings hanging out with the women who congregated at Gretta and Dinah's over long informal dinners, talking about the Israeli women's movement, clitorectomies of Arab women, and the Egyptian women the feminists were beginning to make connections with. Gloria and I told our stories of coming out to each other, to laughter and whoops from our listeners. I loved her like this: expressive, passionate. The Israelis shared how hard it still was to be out as gay in such a small country, where everyone knows each other's business. Gossip, they told us, is the lifeblood of Israel.

One afternoon, my mother and I were alone in the Jerusalem house. Our trip was nearing its end, and we were both feeling melancholy. We were sitting on the couch in the living room, talking. Gloria suggested we take turns doing peer counseling to help us get through our doldrums.

My mother went first. "Would you hold me?" she asked. "I feel like I need to be babied." I scooted closer and reached my arms around her, but as soon as I did, my stomach clenched with nausea. Rage nibbled at my throat. "I just can't do it!" I said, and dropped my arms. I couldn't keep from blurting out, "I mothered you too many years when I shouldn't have had to!" I was sweating, and my face felt hot.

"Oh!" My mother pulled away from me, averting her eyes, her mouth pursed. I thought she was about to cry. Silence ticked between us.

When she looked up, there was sadness and something else in her eyes: a look of recognition. "I'm glad you can say it. Of course. I understand," she said.

I gazed at her, amazed. She did, she understood.

My mother moved close, took me in her arms, and began recounting her memories of mothering me: sitting in a rocking chair, singing me lullabies, building sand castles together at low tide in Atlantic City.

A painful pressure gathered in my throat. I remembered the sand castles clearly. The other images—of being rocked and sung to—floated as sensations in my body.

My mother began rocking me. The swaying loosed a sob in me that ripped itself upward from my chest. One sob followed another. We rocked and I wept. I felt the firm wrap of my mother's arms around my back, and smelled the salt of my own tears on her neck where my head rested.

"But then," Gloria said, "your mother got sick. I felt very guilty that I couldn't take care of you. I wish I could make it up. I couldn't help it. I was very sick."

"I know, I know." I grew quiet. On this, we agreed: Her grief and madness were not her fault. Her heart had been bludgeoned by a sexist society and homophobic psychiatry. This analysis relieved us; there was truth in it, although simplified. I could feel my mother's sorrow over our mutual loss. I felt suspended, there in my mother's arms, something akin to forgiveness hovering between us.

Chapter 39. T-Bone

IN THE YEAR SINCE OUR TRIP to Israel, my mother decided to move to the West Coast, to my town, finally resolving the dilemma that had been tugging on us for ten years: Were we going to spend our lives three thousand miles apart? She was coming now for her August vacation right into the whirlwind of my life.

I was bursting with excitement to see Gloria, but a bit dizzy from the previous week's adventures. I'd slept with Emily for the first time, but it hadn't gone that well. I'd actually fallen asleep in the middle of having sex with her. I blamed it on the fact that I was exhausted from my predawn shift working as an engineer at a San Francisco television station, but it seemed a bad omen.

The next day, I'd gone on a camping trip with my friend Dee. I was friends with her lover Julie, but when Dee began to stroke my back as we sat staring at the full moon over the Russian River, I let myself slip into the reassuring thought that they were on the verge of breaking up. Back in the tent, we made love. This was new—for me to be the one with multiple lovers.

Now, I was flying with the thrill of being desired by two women. It gave me a sense of power. I'd slept with Emily on Thursday, and with Dee on Friday, Saturday, and Sunday. Gloria arrived on Monday. I ran to hug her as she came out of the jetway with her tabby, Sean, in a carrying case. We drove to my apartment, piled her things in the living room, and watched Sean sniff around his new environment. "Let's eat; you must be starved," I said. "I'll make you something you've *never* had." I got out the bag of tortillas.

In between flipping the tortillas in the frying pan, I gesticulated with the spatula, telling her about my romantic adventures. Gloria was sitting at my yellow Formica kitchen table. Her head was cocked to the side, and her shoulders bounced to the rhythm of her chuckling. It was a look that made me feel adored, that she took delight in my screwy life. I grinned proudly as I set our plates laden with tortillas, refried beans, avocado, tomato, and salsa onto the table. Gloria dug in, always game for something new.

BY FALL, I WAS DOWN to one lover. The high of being desired had turned into the strain of juggling. I'd made a mess of it, keeping each lover a secret from the other for too long, until circumstances pushed me into telling. One night, Emily and I went to a concert at La Peña, a leftist Latin American community center. We were sitting in the audience before the house had quieted, when I heard a hiss behind me. It grew louder. *What the hell?* I turned around to face—*oh God, Julie*—Dee's longtime girlfriend, whom Dee was in the midst of breaking up with in part because of me. Between clenched teeth, Julie spat, "How could *you*—a Jewish woman—*do* such a thing to me, another Jew? Shame, shame on you!" I blanched and turned back around, stiff with guilt. I knew I had done her wrong when I slept with Dee; she'd been my friend, too, after all, although I didn't agree with the Jewish part. What did clan loyalties have to do with this? Emily leaned over and whispered, "What the hell was that about?"

"I'll tell you later," I whispered back.

Neither girlfriend was happy, and I knew I had to choose. For a few weeks, I waffled. Weighing things rationally, it seemed I had more commonality with Emily, a middle-class, politically active Jewish woman, but I kept feeling sleepy around her. Bored, really. And my mother's comments about Emily—"That woman talks *a lot*. I mean, she doesn't *listen*"—had stuck with me and given me pause. And it wasn't simply Dee's difference as a working-class, butch, Catholic girl that intrigued me. There was something exciting in how she admired me, touched me, wanted me, and something intangible beyond that. That intangibility should have been a red flag, but I went with its pull, my Taurean bull head down, charging after my matador.

MY MOTHER DIDN'T JUST move to my city, she moved onto my block, three houses away. It was my doing. She had asked me to find her an apartment to rent, so when I noticed that a place was open on my block, I figured it would be a good starter apartment. Then I started to worry about my mother's need of me, how she wouldn't have any local friends and might cling. I started to panic: *My God, what have I done?*

What I didn't consciously acknowledge was my need of my mother. But I soon found myself leaning into her. After a decade apart, our new routine became daily visits, popping back and forth between apartments. With her on the block, I stopped spending as much time with friends, and withdrew into the ease of hanging out with my mother.

She cooked me meals, which I ate with relish. Since the strict vegetarian days of my early twenties, I'd started eating chicken and fish again. Gloria reintroduced me to a forbidden delight: thick, juicy, bloody steak. I didn't tell my friends that she grilled me huge T-bones, served with a baked potato slathered with butter, chives, and sour cream. Our secret, carnivorous gluttony. This was food from my childhood. I even reverted to ketchup, pounding an upended Heinz bottle with the heel of my hand, listening for the *glug* of the red blob dropping onto my plate, mixing with the steak blood.

Gloria was more resilient than I'd imagined. She had given up a full-time therapy practice in Manhattan, but not long after her arrival, she began volunteering as a therapist at San Francisco's gay counseling center, Operation Concern. The staff gave her referrals, and within a year she established a practice. She made friends close to her age by joining an older lesbian organization. She found like-minded women, spiritual seekers who got together to listen to Ram Dass tapes and meditate. Soon, I was hanging out with her friends as well as my own.

I saw more of my mother than I did of Dee. Dee worked the night shift delivering the *San Francisco Chronicle* to newsstands around the city—a job for which she carried a handgun—and took classes at San Francisco State during the day. We got together mostly on the weekends, which kept our time together datelike for the first year of our relationship.

In our second year, Dee asked if I would live with her. I hesitated, uncertain. I had never lived with a lover since so long ago with Kate. I'd lived alone for eight years and was used to my own rhythms, having a space to withdraw into. "I don't know," I told her. "I need to think about it."

"You're afraid of intimacy!" she declared emphatically.

Was I? Was that it? I decided to see a therapist. In my first session, I told the therapist, Laura, that I wanted help deciding whether or not to live with Dee. I figured four weeks would do it. "Okay," she nodded, not contesting my absurd claim.

After three months, I decided: *Leap, take a chance on love, but stay in therapy.*

When I told Dee, she said, "Wonderful, I'm so glad!" Then she added, "When we live together, I need to be nonmonogamous."

My stomach lurched.

"I need this," Dee went on, "because as an incest survivor I need to be free to pursue my own desire and not feel owned by another."

I felt ill. She'd started her own therapy. I guess this was what she'd figured out. What could I say to that?

I went to my mother for sympathy. Kvetching about our lovers continued to be a pastime of ours. This time, though, when I told her my shock at Dee's declaration, she didn't start yelling about how rotten Dee was. "You two need help sorting this out," she said. It was my mother who found us a couples' therapist.

Dee and I struggled along in couples' therapy, at a stalemate. I put living together on hold. In my own therapy I was beginning to understand that over and over I had chosen terribly wounded partners whom I would try to heal with my love, hoping for a miraculous transformation, as if—voilà!—they would become stable and deeply attentive to me. Of course, it never worked, and just left me resentful and martyred. I started to get how linked love and hatred and suffering were for me, embedded from childhood. My new mantra became: *I have a choice.* I still clung frantically to Dee, but some part of me was gathering strength.

ONE FALL EVENING, I went over to Dee's for our Saturday date. "I've got something to tell you," she said, as soon as I was in the door. I could feel my chest tightening. I just stared at her, not wanting to hear whatever was coming. "Last night, I was over at Renee's, and we kissed."

Now I had a sharp pain in my chest. "Kissed as friends?" I asked dumbly, hoping I misunderstood.

"No, we made out. And I want, I need, to be lovers with her. And to be with you. Will you agree to that?"

My limbs had gone numb, and it felt as if I would float off the ground. My throat ached. It was a body state that reminded me of those times after my mother's attempted suicides. *Don't leave me, no, this isn't happening*. I breathed slowly, summoning myself back. I wasn't a child. Perhaps I could handle this. I was down to two choices: leave her, or see if I could tolerate nonmonogamy. "Okay," I said. "I don't like it, I don't want it, but I will try it because I'm not ready to end this relationship with you."

In couples' therapy, we tried to make rules to create some sanity. But rules couldn't keep me from sleepless nights of obsession, rage, and agitation. It was ugly, and I couldn't bear it. But I did, for a couple months.

In one therapy session, Laura said to me, "You seem to have a limitless ability for suffering." The truth of this jolted me. Was that how I wanted to keep living? I began to see that with Dee, abandonment was the same red cape that lover after lover had waved in my face, and I charged at it, despite the spears in my back.

I started to grasp how profound the abandonments were that I'd suffered as a child, and how I'd learned to abdicate my needs to keep my mother alive. But now my mother was with me, her house and body just feet away. She was finally able to be the grown-up whose steady presence provided a resting ground. And because I was mothered at last, my frantic need for a lover had a counterpoint, a place were I was held. Something tight in me was loosening.

Two weeks later, Dee called me, crying. Renee had broken up with her. Little cartwheels of joy spun inside me.

"I need you to support my grieving," Dee said.

"I'm sorry you're hurting," I answered, "but don't you have a friend you could call? I don't think I'm the person for this." The firmness in my answer surprised even me.

Not long afterward, we went on a three-day cross-country ski trip. Back in our cabin after a day gliding on snowy trails, I ventured, "So, now that you and Renee have broken up, you're into being monogamous, right?"

Dee squinted at me and frowned. "That hasn't changed anything. I still need to be free."

I stared at her bleakly. "I have to go for a walk." Outside, the snow was blue in the evening light. I stumbled along a trail, now and then crunching through the top crust of snow up to my knees. I didn't get very far. Instead, I leaned against a pine tree and let loose, my tears an avalanche rumbling down the mountainside of my denial. *It's over, it's over* rang in my head.

When I returned to the cabin, it didn't occur to me to say, "I have to go home." Instead, we skied for two more days. Dee seemed oblivious, taking my silence for acquiescence, while I simmered with silent fury.

After Dee dropped me off on Clarke Street, I went right over to my mother's. As soon as Gloria let me in, I told her what had happened, not bothering to sit down. We were standing in her living room, and when I paused, she held out her arms. "Come here, *bubbala.*" I walked into them, and wept. When there were no more sobs left, she tucked me into bed.

Three days later, I broke up with Dee in couples' therapy. I needed the formal setting where there was no danger of succumbing to sex, and the third person as witness to ensure I didn't backslide. In our session, Dee accused me of giving up on her because I couldn't handle her incest story. "I hope one day you'll accept me as I am and be lovers again," she said.

There was a long pause as I searched for the strength to say, "That's not going to happen, Dee."

The therapist hugged us each farewell.

When it was my turn, she whispered in my ear, "Good job."

Chapter 40. Wilderness

AS I THUMBED THROUGH the listings in the *Bay Times,* the local gay rag, I was drawn to a notice for a monthly Jewish lesbian discussion group. It was three months since I'd broken up with Dee; surely I'd ached long enough. Time to reach out and meet new women.

I joined the group with an ulterior motive: I was on the hunt for a girlfriend. At first, I wasn't especially attracted to anyone in the group. One meeting, two members announced they'd gotten involved with each other. Lucky them. I'd met Dana, one of the couple, two years previously. She and I had been part of a women's anti-nuclear protest group Solar Spinsters, sitting in the road with arms linked in civil disobedience at the gates of Lawrence Livermore Labs, developer of nuclear weapons. After that group disbanded, Dana and I lost touch, until one day about a year later, when I saw her across a city street. She was distinctive enough that I recognized her from a distance: short like me, but with a wild mop of long, curly, dark brown hair. Now she had a bright pink streak in her hair. *Jeez,* I thought, *she really* is *of a different generation.* Dana was only seven years younger, but I came from the flannel-shirt age of lesbian fashion. Not one of my other friends had a pink streak.

At the next Jewish group meeting I announced I was planning to go to a singles social, something I'd never done. "God, I'm nervous. Anyone want to join me?"

"I'll go," Dana said, smiling at me.

I stared at her. "Huh? I thought you two were together." It turned out that she and her girlfriend had broken up.

The mixer was in a private house. Dana and I stood around the living room, paper name tags pasted on our chests, clutching soft drinks and making uneasy small talk with the occasional stranger who wandered by. It was a nightmare. But at some point during that evening, I looked over at Dana, and my mind made one of those shifts from *she's a good buddy* to wondering *hey, what about Dana?*

SOON AFTERWARD, Dana called. She had a pair of comp tickets to a Berkeley Rep production of *Medea,* done Kabuki style. Did I want to go? I restrained myself from ululating, from retorting, *Is the sky blue?*

The play was primal, tragic, intense. Afterward, we went to a coffeehouse. We talked nonstop, discussing the play, energetically batting ideas back and forth. I hadn't clicked like this with someone since I didn't know when—forever? After several hours and lots of herbal tea, I drove her home. Pulling into her driveway, I was faced with the dilemma of lesbian outings: Was this a date or just two female friends going out? It wasn't clear to me what Dana had in mind, but I was vibrating with excitement. I turned off the engine. Glancing at her sideways, I blurted, "I feel just like a teenager!" I reached over to put my hand on her leg, but it landed on empty air.

She had opened the door and was sliding out lickety-split. Or was it like a bat out of hell?

"Good night," I heard her say, amid my humiliation.

"Good night," I managed to choke out, my face aflame. And then she was gone.

A few weeks later, our Jewish group planned a weekend camping trip at the Russian River. As it turned out, Dana and I were the only ones free on Friday night, so we drove up together. The rest were arriving on Saturday.

The campsite was right next to the river, flowing a muddy green. The July day had been hot, so even though Dana and I arrived in the evening, we were sweaty and up for a swim. We stripped off our clothes and flung them on a nearby picnic table. I held back for a minute, and watched Dana walk down to the water and stand at the shoreline, dipping her feet in. God, she was curvaceous, luscious. I joined her, and we swam in the darkening waters to the sound of crickets and bullfrogs. After our swim, we decided to sleep outside, so we simply set our pads out and plopped our sleeping bags on top. We wiggled into our bags. "Good night," Dana said, and turned away from me.

What torture. I wanted her, but clearly that wasn't happening. I slept badly. The gang arrived the next day, relieving me of the possibility of making a bumbling move. That evening, as we all sat around the crackling campfire, Dana told the group that she loved to backpack but had no one to go with.

"*I'll* go with you," I offered, trying to sound nonchalant.

THREE WEEKS LATER, Dana and I pulled into the parking area at the Carson Pass trailhead at nine thousand feet in the Sierras, the entrance point for the Mokelumne Wilderness. We helped each other hoist on our backpacks and started up the steep incline.

Just before sunset, we arrived at the lake. There were granite peaks all around us, their mica flakes catching the last light and glowing golden, melting snow forming rivulets down their sides. We set up camp next to a pine tree, and, after a cold dinner of cheese, crackers, and dried fruit, tied a rope around a small rock. The plan was to throw this over a tree limb and attach our food sack to it to keep it away from the bears.

Dana tried to throw, and then I did. Pathetic, girlie throws, nowhere near making it over the limb. We started laughing, light-headed and woozy in the thin air, and a bit hysterical.

"Oh no, two femmes on a camping trip!" Dana said.

"Where are those butches when you need them?" I howled. Dee had always had a great pitch. By now, we were doubled over with laughter, clutching our stomachs, tears rolling down our faces.

We spent the next day lounging naked at the far side of Frog Lake, baking in the sun on the rocky shore, and then racing into the icy water. We'd whoop and come out tingling. My eyes feasted on Dana's body, her full breasts, the curve of her hips against the backdrop of the mountains.

In the afternoon, we disassembled camp and loaded our backpacks to hike to another lake. As we hiked, the footpath was surrounded by a riot of wildflowers: blue larkspur, yellow and violet columbine, orange Indian paintbrush, Mariposa lily. Around each bend, there were new vistas of mountain peaks. We paused now and then to gaze into the distance, exclaiming over such beauty.

For dinner, we made backpacker pesto over pasta. We had carried in a stick of butter, carefully wrapped in aluminum foil, which we melted with garlic, dried basil, and parmesan. We were both ravenous, but we ate slowly, savoring the meal's intense, explosive flavors. It felt like my taste buds were newly awakened, as if the fresh mountain air had heightened them.

After our meal, the sun began to set. We hiked up to the top of the ridge and sat facing west, looking out onto a broad panorama of the Sierras. The peaks all around glowed orange and gold. Behind us, the full moon was rising, and the high mountain air was rapidly turning chill.

"My hands are cold," Dana said.

I reached over and took her hand in both of mine. "Here, let me warm you."

She put her other hand on top of mine. We turned toward each other and I leaned forward. Dana's mouth met mine, our kiss soft and wet. We moved closer, twining our arms around each other, our tongues kissing harder and deeper.

As we made our way back to the tent, Dana said, "Uh, I don't think our sleeping bags will zip together, but maybe we could open one out flat. Put the other one on top. What do you think?"

I did not dance a jig, but silently thanked whatever gods a pagan atheist can revel in. "Yes," I simply answered, "yes."

FOR OUR FIRST SIX MONTHS, we dated and enjoyed ourselves. Dana traveled on business quite a bit, so we often met on weekends for sensuous reunions. But as delighted as I was, I was also fearful of ending up in another disastrous relationship.

There was certain sanity in my self-protection; it kept me from my usual diving in as soon as I'd slept with someone. For the first time, with Dana, there was the wonder of getting to know each other slowly in a way that felt real.

By seven months, the deepening of my feelings for her couldn't be denied. One evening when we were at my apartment, I nervously brought up the question I'd been scared to ask. Did she want to be monogamous?

"That's funny," she said, "I've been meaning to bring this up myself. On my business trip to Boston next week, there's this old college friend I'm planning to visit. There was always some sexual energy between us, but we never did anything about it in college. So I thought maybe it would happen this time. Would that be okay with you?"

My stomach lurched and my heart started banging. Then numbness overcame me, and I heard myself say, "Hmmm . . . well, I guess that would be pretty safe."

But my vision went blurry and I couldn't look at Dana. I imagined how I would feel seeing her right after she'd slept with someone else; rather than open and sexy, I'd be wary and angry. *Say it. Say the truth.* I looked up. "I'm sitting here trying to make it okay, but my stomach's in a knot, and, well, it just isn't." My heart was pounding hard.

She already knew my history with Dee and my previous lovers, but what she said stunned me. "Chana, you have an absolute right to your feelings about this. You don't have to try to change how you feel. I'm probably okay with nixing the Boston thing, but let me think about it. I don't want to agree for the sole reason of taking care of you."

We spent the night apart. I went and talked with my mother about the situation. "Even if she *says* she'll be monogamous, can I really believe her?" I was anxious. "I don't want to repeat my mistakes."

"I can tell Dana has a good heart. She seems steady. I think you can trust her, Chana," Gloria said.

The next morning, I took a walk with my sheltie dog, Naomi. As she sniffed the neighborhood yards, I was thinking hard. I was coming to love Dana. She was by far the most wonderful person I had ever been with. But if it came down to an open relationship, I knew in my bones I just couldn't do it. I'd have to leave. There was something oddly comforting in that.

That evening, we had our talk in Dana's bedroom, wanting privacy from her two housemates. Dana faced me on the bed. I could see her take a breath. I held mine.

"I've thought about it," she said, slowly, as if she was pondering it right then. She gathered speed. "But having an affair seems so superficial, so trivial next to what I have with you. I want to be with you, Chana. I think of your being a monogamous person as a trait, like having brown hair. It's a part of you, and it's not up for change. I accept that."

I sat perfectly still, taking in what Dana had just said. Then I reached for her, taking her face between my hands.

Inside me, everything was taut and quivering, just beneath my skin. We moved closer, and I kissed her cheeks, her neck. We tumbled down onto the bed and held each other. I stroked her face, unbuttoned her shirt. To be respected and cherished—that was the hottest aphrodisiac on Earth.

Chapter 41. Leaving Clarke Street

JUST A FEW WEEKS after we first became lovers, Dana and I were on a night out at Mama Bear's, a feminist bookstore and coffeehouse. We were munching on cookies and sipping herbal tea at a table in the room lined with bookshelves. The string of Indian bells hanging from the front door jingled, and I looked up to see Gloria. She spotted us, waved, and came up to our table. With a simple "hi," she plopped in an empty chair, nodded at Dana, and launched into a conversation about her day.

Later that evening when we were alone, Dana asked, "Does your mother always do that, just assume she can join you wherever you are?"

"What do you mean?" It hadn't seemed that out of the ordinary to me.

"We were on a *date,*" Dana said. "And she pretty much ignored me, and just gabbed with you."

"Yeah, I guess that was pretty rude." Actually, I hadn't really noticed my mother's exclusive focus on me until Dana pointed it out. Now I felt pulled in two directions: toward the familiar intensity of my connection with Gloria mixed with guilt at the thought of excluding her, and at the same time intrigued by this new possibility of carving out some private space.

I continued spending time with my mother, eating meals, watching TV, taking walks together in the park, but we'd lost one bonding activity: kvetching about my current rotten girlfriend. Sometimes Dana joined us after work for dinner at my mom's, and the three of us came to an easy camaraderie. Once, over a meal, my mother said, "That's terrible, Dana, how your boss didn't tell you about the big meeting!"

Later, Dana asked, "Do you tell your mother *everything?*"

"Well, yeah, I suppose I do! Does that bother you?"

"I guess it's okay, but it just feels a bit funny."

"It's just how it is between us." My tell-all habit had deepened since my mother had moved to the West Coast. She adored me, was always willing to listen to my anxious complaints and worries, and was my biggest booster. Why would I give that up?

"Listen, I'll try to rein in talking about you, but you know Glor loves you. Nosing in is just her way of caring."

TOWARD THE END of our first year together, Dana and I decided that I would move in with her.

I was buzzing with excitement and some apprehension as I walked over to my mother's to tell her my news. We sat in her living room. Gloria was stretched out lengthwise on her couch, with her cat, Sean, on her lap. She was crazy about that cat.

I sat in an armchair, facing the couch. I plunged in, "Guess what! I'm going to be moving into Dana's place in a couple months."

For a moment, a look crossed my mother's face, almost a wince. "Are you sure? That's a big decision."

"Well, it's kinda scary, but yes, I really want to try this." I felt a bit queasy. Was she really upset?

My mother looked down, petting Sean. When she looked up, she smiled at me. I could see she was trying. "Well, you know how I feel about Dana. I think she's marvelous. But it's not so easy, living together. You remember what a disaster it was with me and Sarah?"

"That was different. You two never seemed able to talk things through. Dana and I really talk to each other."

She clutched Sean as he was about to jump off her lap. "Settle down," she scolded him. He curled back against her.

"You know, I haven't lived with a lover since Kate. It feels like time to take a risk. And it's so different with Dana. For one, I'm older, and two, I've had a hell of a lot of therapy."

Gloria raised an eyebrow. "Okay, darling, maybe you're right."

But the unspoken hovered between us, the tectonic shift in our relationship. All these years, no matter whom I had been with, what lovers either of us had had, my mother and I had been each other's mainstay.

I took a small, inadequate stab at soothing her. "I know it'll be different, not living on the same block, but I'll still be over a lot. And you can come hang with us, too."

"Of course, sweetheart."

The day the moving van came, Gloria came down the block to see me off. I deposited the cardboard carrying case with my outraged gray cat in the back of my Toyota station wagon. Machick was meowing nonstop. Naomi waited on the curb, wagging her tail furiously, ready to leap in.

In addition to the full van, boxes with fragile items filled every free space in the car, crowding the passenger seat and the back seat. I started up the car, rolled down the window, and waved at my mother. She stood on the curb, smiling and waving, but her mouth was a brave, tight line, as if clamped against the outburst of a cry.

WHAT SCARED ME MOST about living with Dana was the thought that up close my foibles would be revealed, that she'd realize what a terrible mistake she'd made. Instead, she loved me anyway, bumping up against me with equal force when I got controlling, not letting me push her around. When I flung up my posters on the walls, decorating without consulting her, she came home, looked around, and said, "What're you doing? This is something we have to agree on."

At first, Dana's protestations startled me—often I barely noticed how I was acting until she confronted me. My mother had let me be irritable and crabby around her for years. Now, hard and embarrassing as it was, I experienced an odd relief in knowing Dana would stand up for herself. Little by little, we became amused by our head-butting, and by our equally fierce need to be right.

Since we had both returned to school, Dana and I shared a room with two desks, where we studied companionably. Dana was doing prerequisites for a master's in computer science, while I was finishing my undergraduate credits before attending grad school in clinical psychology. It had come to me that what I'd so loved about my radio program was eliciting people's stories, and that I wanted to go deeper into those stories by becoming a psychotherapist. It would be a long haul: one year to finish up my bachelor's degree, three years of graduate school, three thousand hours as an intern seeing clients under supervision before I could sit for my written exam and then stand for my orals, but I was determined.

ABOUT SIX MONTHS after I moved, my mother enrolled in a beginners' tennis class. "It's terrific fun!" she exclaimed to me.

"Wonderful, Glor!" I was delighted that she had a new interest. It eased my guilt at being less involved with her.

A few weeks into her class, she was swinging her racket when she felt a sharp stab in her shoulder. If only her pain had stopped there, but soon all of her joints were inflamed and aching: her knees, wrists, elbows, and hips. She was diagnosed with rheumatoid arthritis. Its onset was swift and relentless.

One night, the ringing telephone pierced my dreams. When I opened my eyes, the radio alarm glowed a red 2:47. Terror froze me a moment, and then I mobilized, bolting upright, rushing from the bedroom into the kitchen, where the phone rested on the table.

My heart beat hard. "Yes?" I asked, breathless.

The sound of sobbing. My mother's sobs.

"What is it?!" By now, my stomach was clenched.

"It just . . ." She stopped to gasp for air. "Goddamn it!" Another sob. "It just hurts so damn much. I can't stand it!"

"Oh, Mom, I'm so sorry. It's awful."

"I can't sleep! It hurts so much."

"I don't know what to do, Gloria."

"There's nothing. Nothing to do. I don't know what to do!"

"Oh, Gloria, I'm so sorry. I'm so sorry, I wish I could help."

As I hung up the phone, I looked up. Dana had trailed after me and was standing near me in her pajamas, but I hadn't noticed her. She held out her arms, and I walked in, weeping.

The calls came once or twice a week, ripping me from sleep, my breath quick and shallow, fear constricting my chest. Dana and I talked about it: These middle-of-the-night calls couldn't go on like this. It was too traumatic, too reminiscent of my childhood. I had to set a limit, even though it tore me up. It seemed easier to do over the phone.

"Glor, I gotta talk to you about these midnight calls."

"Yes, what is it?"

"Listen, being woken up like that scares the hell out of me. If there's something you need, like being driven to the emergency room, of course, call and I'll be there. But, if you just need to talk, I can't do it. I hate that you're in pain, but there's nothing I can do. If you have to talk to someone, call suicide prevention. Please, just don't call me before eight AM."

"Okay. I get it." She sounded glum but resigned.

The next morning, I had just gotten out of the shower, when the phone rang. I wrapped a towel around me and made it to the phone, which was ringing insistently.

"Hello?" My hair was dripping into the handset.

"Chana." My mother's voice quavered. "I hurt all over. I barely slept. This is horrible!"

I glanced over at the wall clock above the kitchen table. It was 8:01 AM.

OVER THE NEXT YEAR, my mother tried all kinds of treatments: a diet with no nightshades, acupuncture, Chinese herbs, and then the stronger guns, steroids and painkillers, but nothing stopped the disease's relentless progression. She honored my request not to call at night, and the morning calls eased up after she found other support from a disabled-women's group. She stayed as active as she could by swimming in a city pool kept extra warm for seniors, but pain and disability plagued her.

Once, I drove my mother down the coast to one of my favorite beaches. When we arrived, we parked the car, got out, and stood together staring at the steep path sloping down to it. "I can't," Gloria said, shaking her head, and burst into tears. I felt awful. "Don't worry," I tried to comfort her, "we'll find another beach." Sorrow hung between us.

AS OUR THIRD ANNIVERSARY approached, Dana and I played with the idea of having some kind of commitment ceremony, but were uncertain we'd go through with it. In 1987, among our friends, we knew of only one other lesbian couple who'd done such a thing.

One day, we went up to Redwood Park to take a hike and happened on the brochure at a park kiosk: "Oakland Parks and Recreation Department Wedding Sites."

"Let's just drive from site to site and look," I suggested.

We stood in the small outdoor amphitheater staring at the rough halfcircle of wooden benches, looking out at our invisible audience, imagining standing before them and speaking our vows. It gave us the willies, a thrill down the spine that whispered, *Yes, it's scary. Do it.*

When I told Gloria about our ceremony plans, she was unusually terse. "When is it?" she asked. "I'll write it on my calendar." She didn't ask much about it, or jump for joy. I felt awkward to be too jubilant around her, so I didn't go on about it either. We both knew it was another marker of my shift of primacy. I felt sad that she had no lover of her own, that she had never found someone to settle in with.

In a cabin on a cliff overlooking the Pacific, Dana and I planned our ritual. The ocean arced vast and fluid outside our windows. We asked ourselves the question—what were we committing to? We discussed, meditated, each wrote vows, and reconvened. *Let us nourish each other, in our togetherness and in our separateness. Let us grow old together.*

We decided we wanted a circle of intimates, only those who could wholeheartedly support us. That meant I didn't invite my father. For several years now, our relationship had thinned to once-a-year visits and occasional phone calls. He was still only nominally accepting of my being a lesbian, and hadn't grappled with his own history or opened his heart to Dana.

Dana invited her mother and father, telling them that they should come only if they could be truly supportive. Her mother came, her father didn't.

THIRTY FOLDING CHAIRS circled around an open space ringed by redwood trees, gigantic and solemn. Live flute music began a song of greeting. My mother was one of the four women who stood to cast the circle as sacred space, each in turn calling on the four directions and their associated elements of earth, air, fire, and water.

As my mother raised her arms to call the west, the element of water, I could see she had put whatever ambivalences she had aside and was giving it her all. Her voice rang out; her face was radiant. I'd never imagined my mother like this: a priestess showering us with her blessing.

Dana and I stood, turned to face each other, and read our vows. Then Dana's brother David and my friend Lorraine wrapped us in a white-and-blue *tallit,* a Jewish prayer shawl, while they each said a blessing. We listened, joined by the shawl, as around the circle our friends voiced their wishes for us. We fed each other challah—braided Sabbath bread—and wine, and passed both around the circle. Then our whooping friends hoisted us in chairs to the blast of klezmer music from a battery-powered boom box, dancing us in the air. Lowered back down, we joined hands with everyone to dance the hora, kicking with joy.

Back home a few hours later, Dana and I were sprawled on our two living-room couches. The floor was littered with wrapping paper and open boxes holding our presents.

I staggered up. "Where're ya going?" Dana asked.

"To call my mother," I replied.

Even my mother was surprised when I rang her on Clarke Street. "You're calling me on the night of your wedding?" she chortled. "I thought you'd be occupied with other things!"

The habit of narrating my life to and with my mother ran deep. I may have moved, I may have gotten married, but I couldn't stop myself from checking in. "Are you kidding?" I laughed. "We're beat. No action here but lying on the couch! But wasn't it amazing?"

"Yes, amazing," she echoed.

After I hung up, I went back to Dana. "Let's go to bed," I suggested. What I meant was that now that I'd talked to my mom, her voice my lullaby, I'd be able to sleep.

PART THREE: SINAI

Chapter 42. Rheumatoid

ONE MORNING, ABOUT a year after the commitment ceremony, I pulled up in front of Gloria's apartment on Clarke Street. We were getting together for a late breakfast.

Her car was parked on the street right in front of her place, so I was puzzled when I rang her bell and there was no answer. *Must be in the bathroom,* I thought. I rang a second time, and when she still didn't answer, I used my key.

I called out, and sure enough, I heard a muffled sound from the bathroom. The door was ajar, and I pushed it in. Gloria was sprawled on the floor, wearing a pale blue nightgown.

"Mom, what happened? Are you okay?"

"I'm fine, tripped on the bath mat, juz b'fore you came in." Her eyes looked puffy and watery.

"Let me help you up," I said, reaching my hand toward her.

"Nah, it's fine down here." She giggled.

"What?" I frowned, looking down at her.

"I mean, I can do it." She chortled, then tried to pull herself up, clutching on to the edge of the bathtub as she rocked forward, then sank back down, landing with a *plop* on her bottom. "Oops! Give me a lift, would ya? My joints are shot."

I grabbed her under the armpits. "Okay, one, two, three," and heaved as she lurched up. I helped her back to bed.

"Listen, could we take a rain check? I want to go back to sleep."

I stared at her. She did look exhausted and groggy. "Sure, no problem."

At home, my thoughts pushed against something that my body knew, but I didn't want to know. I wanted my mother's simple explanation: "I tripped and fell." But my bones ached with the familiarity of my mother's slurred speech, her watery eyes.

The next day, I called Gloria. "What happened yesterday when you fell? You seemed kinda out of it."

"Oh," she said. There was a long pause.

"Yeah, what happened?"

"I took an extra pill."

"What kind of pill?" A sudden heaviness gripped my body, my chest tight and sinking.

There was no point in her denying it anymore; she told me that her doctor had prescribed sleeping pills. "Halcion," she said. "My pain was so bad that night, I still couldn't sleep, so I took one extra."

Not this, not again.

Silence crackled between us, my mother's secret exposed.

It had been almost twenty years since I'd left for college and she'd detoxed from prescription pills. At the hospital, they'd had to shoot her with muscle relaxants to keep convulsions from choking her. Ever since then, she'd had terrible insomnia, but now, with severe arthritic pain, she needed help to sleep. How could I blame her? Still, anger flared in me.

"Jesus, Glor! Promise me you won't take extra anymore. It's dangerous! Promise!"

"Okay, sweetheart, I won't."

It was too glib, too easy, but for now, what could I do?

After I hung up, I leaned over the kitchen table, gripping my face in my hands. *My God, here we are again, full circle; I'm picking my mother up from the bathroom floor.*

OVER THE NEXT YEAR and a half, Gloria had one knee replacement, then a second. With each surgery, there were my visits to the hospital, and then her recovery at home and my rounds of bringing her food and books and videos, and then my driving her to rehab and back. But it wasn't these chores that ached in me; it was what they meant: the horror of her body's deterioration, and the claim it placed on me—*take care of me, help me, I need you.*

My mother bought an electric scooter and had a hydraulic lift for it welded onto her Honda hatchback. Her moments of greatest relief were when she was put on massive doses of steroids, creating temporary euphoria before the mood crash, while as a side effect her face grew round as the moon. But the dose was always gradually reduced because of the drug's dire side effects, and the pain returned.

One day she said to me, "If I get so bad I can't take care of myself, don't ever put me in a nursing home. That would kill me. Promise me you won't do that."

I looked at her, dismayed. She was single, had never found a lover since she'd moved, and even though she had good friends, it was me she relied on. Would I have to take her in, care for her until the end of her life? I wasn't sure that I'd be willing to, but her ending up in an institution *was* an appalling idea.

"No, of course not; we'd work something out," I said.

But as it turned out, it was not a problem we would have to worry about. There was no time.

Chapter 43. Diagnosis

IT'S ODD HOW THINGS happen: how that night I did something I almost never did—I turned on the ringer of my office phone after my last session with a therapy client. By now I'd completed my internship hours and was in private practice under a supervisor's license until I passed my orals. The ringing phone startled me at 9:00 PM, as I was sitting at my desk writing notes. Dana launched right in: "I'm at the hospital with your mother, in the emergency room. We've been here for hours. I didn't want to call until we knew something. It's her belly—filled with fluid."

Dana's words wavered and pulsed, some assaulting my ear, others whispering away.

"The emergency room doc says it might be . . . blankety-blank . . . or . . . garble garble . . . or cancer."

Cancer. The word hovered in the air.

My mother and I had gone lap swimming the day before at an outdoor city pool. It was a beautiful pool, set in the middle of a park, with live oak trees bordering its aqua waters. When we got out, she told me she was short of breath. "You better go see the doctor tomorrow," I said. She'd been complaining to me that despite all her efforts at dieting, her waist just kept expanding, and her pants were strained to bursting.

I put down the phone. The drive across the Bay Bridge was a blur of gray steel girders and red taillights.

In my mother's room, I found Dana standing next to Gloria's bed, holding her hand. They both looked up as I entered. Dana stepped back, and I went to my mother's side, leaned over, and kissed her. Her eyes skittered around, then met mine, piercing me with her fear.

"Sweetheart," I said, taking her hand and squeezing it, "we'll get through this. Tell me what's happened so far."

She took a ragged breath. "Well, first thing I went to see Dvora. She examined me, then sent me off for a chest X-ray."

Dvora was our family doctor.

"I was home waiting for the results, and when Dvora called, she said, 'Go to the emergency room, right now.' I was so scared. You were off in the city seeing clients, so I called Dana."

Dana took up the thread: "The doctor said there's fluid in her belly. He said she'll have scans tomorrow."

"I'll cancel my clients for tomorrow, and just be with you?" I realized it had come across more as a question than a statement.

"Whatever you think, darling," she answered. She was lying very still, as if drawn into herself.

"You matter more than anything," I said. "More than any clients." I saw the relief on her face, but I hadn't quite heard the plea underneath her words. I vacillated: How many of my clients to cancel? In part, it was magical thinking: *If I don't have to cancel my clients, that means this is not serious. It'll be okay.* I clung to an illusion of control. Part of me wanted to flee and pretend it was just a regular day, to be distracted by other people's problems. In the end, I kept a couple morning clients and canceled the rest.

When I returned the next day, Gloria was back from her scans. Dvora was staring intently at a chart in her hand. She was petite, with short brown hair, wearing corduroy pants and a jean jacket. Before I could speak, a thin man in a white coat entered the room, scowled at Dvora, and barked, "You have no hospital privileges here! I'm in charge of this case!"

I stood there, immobile. Didn't we already have enough stress? Dvora stood up abruptly, chart in hand. "Let's discuss this elsewhere," she said. They both exited. We could hear their muffled voices through the door.

"Jesus, what a jerk! Who is that guy?" I asked.

"He examined me yesterday in the emergency room, so I guess he's assigned to my case," Gloria answered. "He's a jerk, all right, but he's the jerk we got."

We smiled at each other, the grins of trapped people.

After a short while, Dvora came back in and pulled a chair close to my mother, reached over, and took her hand. "Gloria, I'm going for now, but I'll be back tomorrow. The Alta Bates team is going over the scans and will talk to you about the results. You're in good hands."

AN HOUR OR SO LATER, the thin man in white was back. Dana had left work early, and we were sitting in chairs next to Gloria, chatting. The doctor started speaking as soon as he entered the room. I was watching his mouth move, and I found my hearing had gone intermittent again, as if someone was fiddling with a radio dial. "A large mass . . . ascites, fluid in the peritoneal cavity . . . indicates ovarian carcinoma . . . until a biopsy of the tumor."

Everything crashed around me. There was thunder in my ears, my mouth tasted sour, the room had dimmed

"A gynecologist will be visiting you in a while, to discuss your treatment," the doctor mumbled.

He had barely left—perhaps we three were stunned into a stupor—before the door opened again and a woman in a white coat entered. A skirt with red and yellow flowers peeked out beneath her lab coat. She stood at the foot of my mother's bed and introduced herself; her eyes were warm and making direct contact with Gloria. She explained about the mass—that it was most likely cancer, but in any case, it had to come out. "You need the surgery, Gloria. The surgery will prolong your life," she stated.

My mother smiled, this time a genuine smile of relief and gratitude. "Oh, thank you!" she said. I could tell she was hearing this differently than I was. My mother clutched at hope. But I heard "prolong" as a death knell, a bell tolling *sooner or later, sooner or later*.

DANA AND I WERE sitting on a couch in the hospital lobby, holding hands. We'd just left Gloria's room but had needed to stop, rest, and breathe before stumbling out the entrance. I saw movement out of the corner of my eye, and glanced over to see the emergency room doctor hovering near me. He came around and stood in front of the couch. "You two are just terrific!" he said. "Real troopers!"

"What?" I said, looking up at him. There was a strange brightness to his eyes.

"You know, to be so calm and collected for such a grave diagnosis. Ninety-seven percent of cases like this are fatal. You two are really something!"

My stomach recoiled as if punched.

"Take care, you two!" He was grinning at us, almost gloating.

"Let's get the hell out of here," I said to Dana.

We'd been on our way out to dinner, and so we went, stuporous and without appetite, but it seemed the thing to do. We walked to Petroushka's, a Russian restaurant a couple of blocks from the hospital, and asked for a private corner table. Dana and I sat there, quiet and windless. The rage that had flared in me toward the doctor was supplanted with a lump of fear and anguish: Would my mother die soon? Spasms gripped my belly and throat, my hands and feet were numb, and my vision and hearing closed in.

The next day I went back to the hospital in the morning. Dana had gone to work. "How are you?" I asked my mother, after leaning in to kiss her.

"Much better. I can get my breath, now that the diuretics have kicked in."

"And how are you doing emotionally, I mean?"

"Up and down. One moment I'm really scared; the next I just feel in the end this will be okay." She looked at me with her moist doe eyes.

I sucked on my lower lip as I nodded acknowledgment. Then I started to tear up. "Anything on?" I asked, bobbing my head toward the wall-mounted TV. A few minutes of this kind of talk were all I could bear right now.

We were watching Vanna White spin the wheel on *Wheel of Fortune* when Dvora showed up as promised, regardless of the fact that she lacked hospital privileges. Gloria clicked off the tube. Dvora asked how she was. Gloria beamed at her, all sun. She adored her doctor.

Dvora told us she'd gone over the test results and talked to the hospital gynecologist. She explained about the tumor, that it was large and possibly wrapped around Gloria's intestines. She had a referral to an excellent surgeon who specialized in gynecological oncology.

"Gloria, we'll just take this one step at a time," Dvora said. "They're going to send you home soon, and then the next step will be a consultation with the surgeon."

"Yes, of course, one step at a time," my mother echoed.

Dvora patted Gloria's arm. "Good," she said. "I'm going now, but I'll be seeing you soon."

"Be right back," I said to my mother as I followed Dvora out the door. We stood in the hall. I told her what the emergency room doctor had said.

Dvora inhaled sharply and exhaled a quiet sigh. "Well . . ." she hesitated, " . . . in all likelihood, your mother will die from this. But no one can say the time line. I had a patient with ovarian cancer who lived several years."

She must have seen the collapse in my face. "I'm so sorry," she said, "This is so hard. Come here."

Dvora's arms were around me, and I was crying against her shoulder. She patted my back. After I quieted, we stepped apart. I blew my nose and gathered myself to say the next bit. "There's something else: My mother believes in honesty, and so do I. She has a right to know."

Dvora waited while a nurse wheeled a rattling cart loaded with medicines past us. "Of course, but truth is tricky, and not absolute. There's a negative impact to such a statistic, and it's not necessarily helpful, or of use to a patient. For Gloria, I think it makes sense to wait until after the tumor has been biopsied, the diagnosis confirmed, and her cancer staged. We'll have more information. Then she can be informed of the findings. Right now, she needs her strength to get through surgery."

"Okay, I can see that. Thanks."

I rearranged my face and stepped back in the room. Gloria looked at me. "You've been crying."

I could never really hide anything from her. "Yeah, this is scary."

"I know, darling, but here's what I've decided: I'm going to lick this thing," She nodded her head emphatically, her silver curls ringing her face. "I'm going to lick this thing, and I am going to live to write a book about my life."

I stood there a moment, uncertain what to say. Who could deflate the glory of her insistent vow? Not me. I stepped in close, took her hand and kissed it, then stroked her arm.

"That will be one hell of a story," I said.

Chapter 44. Intensive Care

ON THE DAY BEFORE my mother's surgery, Dana and I were helping her settle into her hospital room, when her surgeon arrived. In the month since her emergency room visit, my mother and I had met with him for a consultation, so we knew his manner was brisk. Now, Gloria sat up in bed, listening while he explained that he would remove as much of the tumor tissue as he could without damaging any organs it might be adhered to. Since some of the tumor had invaded her intestines, he would not know until the actual surgery how much intestine would have to be removed. At worst, she would end up fitted with a colostomy bag. "Any questions?" he asked.

"No," my mother said. She smiled then, a jaunty, defiant smile. "As I've said, there is no cancer in my family."

I stared at her, flabbergasted. Although it was true that the cancer diagnosis couldn't be absolutely confirmed until after surgery and biopsy results, no medical person along the way had suggested that there was any other explanation for the size of her tumor and her symptoms. *This is crazy,* I thought, *but then again, she needs hope.*

On the morning of surgery, just after dawn, Dana and I accompanied Gloria as she was wheeled on a gurney down the elevator, through the halls, and to the pre-op room. We sat with her while she was prepped, and then gave her a flurry of kisses and pats before she was wheeled away. As I watched her go, my heart started *ka-thump*ing fast.

We'd been told it would be a long surgery. We went back to my mother's room, luckily private, and Dana lay on Gloria's bed. I tried to read a paperback, but found myself unable to focus and gave up.

The surgeon's visit, six hours or so later, was brief but heartening. The tumor had been wrapped around various organs, and it had taken a long time to get it all out, but overall it had gone well. Best of all, he had been able to reconnect her intestines, so she didn't need a colostomy bag.

IT WAS EVENING, HOURS past my mother's surgery, when we were finally allowed ten minutes to visit her in the intensive care unit. Dana and I pushed through the double doors into a place so brightly lit it felt like a stage set. Machines beeped, bags of fluid hung from poles, monitor screens glowed with moving green lines, ventilators pumped and hissed, nurses in scrubs were everywhere.

We'd been forewarned that my mother was on a ventilator. Still, I wasn't prepared. As we neared her bed with its metal rails, I could see her eyes roaming frantically. A plastic tube filled my mother's mouth, pushing her jaw open, while a band of white adhesive covered her cheeks, holding the tube in place. Her hands were tied to the sides of the bed.

For a moment, the horror of her imprisonment so stunned me that I halted several feet from her bed. Perhaps my alarm showed on my face, because the nearest nurse said, "It's okay. Her hands are strapped to keep her from pulling the tube out. Patients who are still groggy from anesthesia try to do that."

I nodded, "Yes, I understand," and took a step closer to the bed, threading my way past the IV pole.

Leaning over my mother, I forced cheerfulness. "Hi, schnookie." Her eyes focused on me. I offered my good news: "We talked to the doctor. He says your surgery went well, really well—and you have no colostomy bag." Her eyes widened. I wasn't sure how woozy she still was, if her understanding might be blurry, so I repeated, "You didn't end up needing a shit bag."

Two nurses near me giggled. My mother raised her eyebrows, looking exclamatory.

Gloria began flapping her right hand against the restraint. I turned to the nearest nurse and asked if she could untie one hand. "Only if you hold it the entire time. Don't let go for a second," she said.

"Certainly, of course." I watched the nurse untie the strap. As I held my mother's hand, she scratched her nails against my palm.

"I know this is hard," I tried to soothe her. "This is just until you recover from surgery enough."

She kept at it, scratching my palm over and over, relentless. At first, I thought she was just expressing her anxiety. Then it hit me, what she was trying to convey. "Do you want to write something?" I asked. She scratched faster.

"Do you have a pad of paper and a pen?" I asked a nurse.

"I think so." She went away. When she returned with a pencil and a small pad, she said, "But I can't untie her other hand. It's not safe."

"That's okay. I'll hold the pad for my mother." I reached for the paper while I flashed the nurse a smile, dependent on her goodwill.

I gave my mother the pencil, letting go of her hand, and held the pad above her, where she could reach it.

In wobbly, primary-school block lettering, she began to write letter by letter, "W-h-a-t . . . " As she wrote, I read each word out loud: "What . . . did . . . I . . . do . . . to . . . deserve . . . this?"

As I read the last words, I let out a choked sound, followed by a hollow "ha ha." The embarrassed laugh jumped out of me as I imagined the nurses taking offense.

I said hurriedly, as much for the nurses as for my mother, "No, no. This isn't punishment. You're on the breathing machine because you're still weak. I swear, they'll take you off as soon as you're stronger."

Just as suddenly, my face began burning and my chest contracted with shame that I had laughed, as if making light of my mother's terror. These strangers didn't know the context of her fear: this reminder of psychiatric confinement. I imagined her memories of being tied down for electroshocks, administered over and over against her will, of being locked in a padded cell. The powerlessness of no escape.

I took the pencil from her and held her hand. "It'll be okay, Mom. This will be over in a while. I know it's awful. Hang in there, sweetheart." Her eyes brimmed, liquid with distress.

One nurse came close. "Mrs. Wilson, you did nothing wrong; we just want to help you. People need oxygen after surgery, but they might pull the respirator out, and that would be dangerous."

I squeezed my mother's hand and repeated, "As soon as you're stronger, you'll be off the ventilator."

The nurse motioned us to leave. "We'll see you soon," Dana added. I turned away quickly, not wanting to watch the nurse retie my mother's wrist.

WHEN I RETURNED THE next morning, she was still hooked up. For her, it must have been an eternity. Dana had to go back to work, so I was alone in the hospital that day. I was allowed to visit the ICU once an hour for ten minutes. Each visit was wrenching, filling me with anguish at my mother's distress. I tried to reassure and soothe her, but she remained frantic. As I held her hand, I could barely breathe myself. The *whoosh* and *hiss* of the ventilator, those inexorable bellows, ticked the seconds. It scared me that she was so weak she couldn't breathe on her own. She was sixty-eight, and more frail than I'd realized.

At last, late in the day, she was wheeled into her room. IVs and morphine drips were attached. There'd been a lot of cutting, and managing her pain turned out to be tricky. She would sleep awhile and then wake, whimpering, and I would call the nurse in and tell her, "She's still in a lot of pain."

One afternoon four days postsurgery, Mom was dozing. I sat nearby, my head nodding toward stupor, when the surgeon came in briskly. My head shot up and I called out, "Glor, Dr. Klein is here."

She startled awake. "Hello, doctor." She smiled in his direction.

"Good afternoon, Mrs. Wilson. I've received the biopsy results," he announced with little preamble. "As we suspected, they confirm ovarian carcinoma. Because the tumors have spread through your abdomen, I stage it as Stage Three." He offered no prognosis. "Any questions?"

Sorrow gripped me as I looked toward my mother. Her face had gone flat, almost expressionless. Her mouth hung open, as if it was hard to catch her breath.

"No, Dr. Klein," she said faintly.

When Dana arrived after work, she went off to the nearby medical students' bookstore and looked up statistics. "Do you want to know?" she asked me when we got home that night. "No, don't tell me." I knew Stage Three was one short of the worst. I was hoping the chemotherapy would at least extend her life several years, if not provide a miracle, and I wasn't ready to hear anything contradictory.

There's something repetitive and almost timeless about sitting in a hospital room: sounds emanating from multiple televisions—yours and those across the hall—the sterile walls, the clanking in and out of trays with food or medicine, the rounds of nurses checking vital signs. I floated along in exhaustion, witness to my mother's suffering and the rhythms of her care, struggling with when to advocate for her, when to remain politely quiet.

Sometimes my mother would wake from her morphine dozing and say, "I'm being kept here against my will. I want to leave! Why won't they let me go?"

I would remind her, "You had surgery. You're in the hospital—a medical hospital—and you're not healed enough yet to go home. Just a few more days."

"Oh," she'd say, with a resigned sigh.

The weekend arrived. Not just any weekend, but the last weekend in June: Gay Pride. Lunchtime on Sunday, I left my mother's hospital room and stepped into the crowded elevator on my way to the cafeteria. I knew that across town, rainbow flags lined the Market Street parade route. By now, Dykes on Bikes would have led off the marchers, the roar of their motorcycles echoing off the skyscrapers.

In previous years, my mother, Dana, and I had gone to the Gay Pride March together, cheering and waving as the marchers went by. Now, at the hospital cafeteria, I gathered lunch for Dana and me on a tray and made my way back to my mother's room, aching with an ineffable sadness.

Chapter 45. Halcion Daze

SIX DAYS AFTER MY mother's surgery, Dana and I brought her back to her apartment, helping her up the front stairs, pausing stair by stair, each holding an arm. "Made it!" Gloria said, smiling with triumph when we got to the front-porch landing. Although she was weak and fatigued, she'd regained some of her spunkiness.

"Once we get you inside and in bed, that's your big adventure for today," I teased.

Until her wound healed more and she regained some strength, she was confined to her apartment. The aftercare coordinator had set up a nurse to come by every day to change her dressing. We could hear my mother's cat, Sean, meowing when we got inside her front hall. "Coming, Sean!" she called out. I was glad she had him for companionship, especially now.

Dana went off to buy groceries while I walked to the pharmacy, a block away, to fill my mother's prescriptions. When Dana returned, she told Gloria, "I'm going to make you a big pot of chicken soup. It's my grandmother's recipe. It'll heal you for sure."

"How did I get such a daughter-in-law—and Jewish yet!" my mother joked. I could smell the aroma of the soup cooking while I arranged the pills on my mother's nightstand.

Gloria had been home a few days when I told her Dana and I were reconsidering going away over the Fourth of July weekend, plans we'd made before her diagnosis. "Go ahead," she said.

"Are you sure?"

"Yeah, you could use a break."

She was being generous, but I was torn. I felt guilty about leaving, but exhausted, and so in need of a break. In the end, we went, leaving my mother with a full refrigerator, daily visits from the nurse, and commitments from friends to drop by.

The morning of my return, I used my key to come into her apartment house, not wanting to make her get up. I noticed something as I approached her apartment door: One pane of its opaque glass had been replaced with a piece of plywood. *That's odd,* I thought. *It wasn't like that before we left town.* Worry gathered in my belly.

I found my mother in bed with the TV on. She clicked it off when I came in and gave me a broad smile. "Hi, darling."

"Hi, what happened to your door?"

"Oh, that," she said, still grinning. She waved her hand, as if waving away a fly. "Pfhhh, the police were here. They broke the glass to get in, but it's okay. The landlord sent someone to fix it."

"Huh?" This cryptic answer was heightening the bad feeling I already had. There was something loopy in her smile, and her speech was slurry. Her eyes looked glassy. Alarms were going off in my head, echoes from childhood. I felt short of breath. I gulped, gathering air. "What do you *mean,* the police were here? What the hell happened? Are you okay?"

"Well, I fell out of bed."

"You *what?*"

"I didn't get hurt, but I couldn't get back up, so I got hold of the phone next to the bed and dialed 911. They said they'd send help; then I changed my mind. I told them, 'That's okay, there's a bunch of us in bed here, and they'll help me up.'"

I was staring at her, momentarily speechless. Something had clamped down in my brain, and it was hard to think—as if the air around me were congealed and thick. In mental slow motion, I was trying to sort out the insanity of her story—*people in bed with her?* Had she been hallucinating, or just made up some wacked-out tale? But I didn't have to prompt her to go on.

"But the next thing I knew, two policemen were here. They broke the damn door. Can you believe it? They were going to take me off to the hospital—the loony bin, that is! Jesus, just because I made a joke! But just then my neighbor Tricia came home. She saw the door open and came to check on me, and told the police I had cancer and was on pills, that she'd take care of me, so they left."

The word "pills" rang in the air, reverberating to my bones. *Something's wrong here.* "You're not making any sense," I said. "What pills are you taking?"

My mother clamped her mouth into a fierce line and glared at me.

I looked over at the bunch of prescription bottles gathered on the nightstand next to her bed. I picked up the bottle of Halcion, her sleep medication. I had filled it the week before: ninety pills, a month's supply. As it was, her nightly dose of three was more than was generally prescribed, but she had built up a tolerance over the years. I held up the bottle and stared at it. There were far too few in there.

"Jesus, I just filled this for you, and now you've used up more than half?" Rage flamed in me. *Not again, goddamn it! Not again with the drugs.* Then I looked over at my mother. She'd put her hands over her face and was weeping.

I sat down on the bed, my own body heavy. I put my arms around my mother and pulled her to me. After a while, she whispered, "I'm just so scared. Day and night. So scared. So I take a pill."

My body softened then. I hadn't let myself fully see the terror that lay underneath her optimism and bravado. I unwrapped my arms from around her back and moved apart enough so I could look into her face, resting my hands on her upper arms. "Of course, I understand this is incredibly scary," I said. "But you just can't use the sleeping pills this way. We have to get you something for the daytime anxiety."

I called Dvora, who called in a prescription for an anti-anxiety medication. After I came back from the pharmacy, I brought my mother a glass of water and gave her one of the pills. "Here you go—Ativan," I said. "This should help you relax." Just then, the doorbell rang. It was the visiting nurse to change the bandage over the wound. That was a sight I couldn't bear to witness, so I said my goodbyes.

THREE DAYS LATER, my mother told me she was out of Halcion. She was staring at the TV as she said, "Call the pharmacy, would you, and get a refill?" She said this as casually as if she were requesting cold medicine.

I didn't have to do the math to know it was too soon. I got the feeling I was supposed to just go along and not notice. I was in a chair next to her bed. I leaned over, grabbed the remote resting on her lap, shut off the TV, and yelled into the silence, "Goddamn, Glor, you're still overdoing it, aren't you! That's why I got you the other pills for anxiety! I told you, you're only supposed to take Halcion at night."

Her face in profile had gone dogged and stubborn. "That Ativan, I hate it; it just makes me more nervous!"

"Well, then, we need to get you something else. Dvora told me the Halcion could give you terrible side effects if you take too much. It can even make you psychotic."

She turned her face to me. "Okay, okay, I'll stop taking extra, but *come on,* you know I can't sleep without the Halcion."

She was begging. It made me ill, but I knew it was true; between her pain, terror, and chronic insomnia, she'd never sleep. My anger was mixed with an ache for her desperation, for the look on her stricken face.

I called the pharmacy, but they wouldn't refill. "Too soon," the pharmacist said. So I called Dvora and we devised a plan: She would call in a new prescription for Halcion, and try a different anti-anxiety medication, but only if I or someone else held on to the pills.

When I asked the visiting nurse if she could dole out my mother's pills, she said no, so I resigned myself to the task.

That evening, my mother watched as I put the Halcion bottle back in my pocket, after counting out three. She said nothing, her face closed. A memory hovered between us: *Our next-door neighbor, small, blond Mrs. Jansen, walks across her lawn, through the fenceless border of pine trees between our houses, bringing over that day's pills. Mom has returned from two months in the mental hospital, after I found her almost dead, overdosed on sleeping pills. What shame and relief I feel, watching Mrs. Jansen count out Mom's pills.*

"It has to be like this," I said. "I'm going to hold on to the medications. On your own, you're gonna kill yourself with these. And I know how much you want to live."

During the week, I saw my therapy clients in the afternoons and evenings, so I gave Gloria her pills before I went off to work. It went okay for a couple of days, until my mother called me late one evening. "I dropped one of the sleeping pills behind the bed," she stated. "There's no way I can get to it there. You have to give me another."

My mind was in a tumult: *Oh my God, she's lying to me to get more pills. But can I accuse her of that?* Some part of me wanted to believe the truth of her tale. And, true or not, her desperation pulled on me; I just couldn't stand to deny her in the midst of such fear. Her suffering filled me with anguish. "Okay, I'll be right over," I found myself saying.

A few days later, the scene repeated itself. Gloria called; this time she'd dropped the pill in the shag rug, couldn't find it for the life of her. *Please bring me another.* This time, it made me both sad and angry. Dana and I had talked about what to do if this happened again.

Now, on the phone with my mother, I looked across the living room at Dana. She could tell what was happening, and she shook her head. I gathered myself. "No," I told my mother. "I'm sorry, but no, I don't believe you. You're going to have to get through the night without another pill."

I hung up, a cannonball lodged in my chest. Dana came and put her arms around me.

The next day, Dana and I went to see Gloria. She'd become more mobile and was sitting at the kitchen table, reading the newspaper. We sat down with her, but at first she just kept reading. Then she folded the paper and glared at me.

"I had a hellish night."

"I'm sorry, Glor. But if you keep taking extra pills, your body's gonna to be in more of a mess. I can't let you do that. It's not safe."

"Like hell," she said. "You know what it really is? You're just doing this to get back at me for your childhood, aren't you!"

Chapter 46. Spreading

WHEN MY MOTHER began chemotherapy in August, a friend of hers, a cancer survivor who had been treated at the same hospital, offered to go with her. I had dreaded accompanying her and was relieved to be let off the hook. Besides, I had an excuse.

"I need to immerse myself in studying for my orals," I told Gloria, "so I'm not going to be very available." In truth, I was trying to create some distance now that we were in for the long haul. I was hoping the chemo would extend her life for several years, and I needed to reclaim my own.

"I understand," she said. "Just study hard and pass."

As Gloria healed enough from surgery to drive and resume a semiactive life, she rallied. Her drugs became less of a struggle between us. Once she was prevented from taking extra pills, she became lucid again and stopped asking for more. Her fear seemed to ebb now that she had a treatment focus with the chemotherapy. She once again proclaimed, "I'm going to lick this thing."

One day, when we were hanging out in her living room, Sean purring in her lap, she said, "I've been thinking. You know what I'd like?"

"What?"

"To go to Hawaii with you. After your exam. Let's rent a place right on the beach, with its own lanai where we can sit out in lounge chairs and listen to the ocean. Just you and me."

I imagined it: just my mother and me, no distractions, the Hawaiian air sweetly scented with plumeria blossoms, the bitter sweetness of what would most likely be a last time. "Yes, that would be wonderful. I'll look into it and find us something," I promised.

IN EARLY OCTOBER—a few weeks before my exam—my mother called me. "I'm not sure, but I think the doctor said the cancer has spread to my liver." Her voice was tight with worry.

"We have to sort this out," I said, hoping my mother had somehow got it wrong. *Please, God, not so soon.* It had been only four months since that first day she had gone to the emergency room. A chill made my body tense. "I'm going to call her." I'd noticed a change in my mother: a certain hesitancy when she spoke, as if she were confused. She seemed vague and forgetful.

I called the doctor's office and left a message. When Dr. Donner called back at 10:15 PM, for a minute I almost felt sorry for her, at the intensity of her workload. But it made me angry, too. Something was wrong with the system.

"My mother is confused as to whether you said the cancer had spread to her liver," I explained.

"Yes," she replied, "she now has liver cancer. Confusion is part of that, because when the liver has trouble metabolizing toxins, patients can get very disoriented."

Somehow, I kept talking, but my voice had taken on a tinny pitch. "What does it mean that she has liver cancer?"

"Well, unfortunately, the chemotherapy is not proving effective."

I marched on. "What does it mean in terms of prognosis?"

"It's likely she won't live more than a few months—three or four."

My whole body had gone into a numb altered state, and I found myself repeating in a monotone: "You're saying she has just a few months to live—three or so?"

"Yes. I'm sorry."

In a wooden voice, I said, "I will be coming with my mother to her appointment tomorrow. She has told me she wants to know the truth of her condition. So, you need to inform her. It's not something I can do. Will you do that?"

"All right," she said. I thought I detected a sigh.

THE EXAMINATION ROOM was a small, narrow space with an examination table, one chair, a sink, and white cabinets. I sat in the chair while the doctor performed a brief physical exam on my mother, who was in her street clothes. "All right, Gloria, I will see you at your next appointment," she said. And then the doctor's hand was on the door. Before she turned the knob, I managed to gasp out, "Dr. Donner, wasn't there something else you had to discuss with my mother?" She paused there as if suspended, neither leaving nor turning back. I raced on, my voice loud with alarm. "Gloria, if there was some information about your condition, would you want to know it?"

"Yes, I want to know," she affirmed.

Dr. Donner lowered her hand from the doorknob, turned, and came back. She stuck to the facts. "Gloria, the chemotherapy has not stopped the spread of your cancer. It is now in your liver," she said succinctly. "I would say you have just a few months to live."

There was no crying, not then. After the news, my mother said she was too dizzy to walk to the car. We borrowed a hospital wheelchair. She stumbled into it, head bent, chest caved in like she'd just been sucker punched. While I pushed her through the halls to the hospital entrance, she said, "You're not going to keep studying, are you?"

I looked down at her head, at her soft silver curls, the lobes of her ears. The Silver Fox. It was a nickname I sometimes called her, teasing her that she was still a wild, sexy woman. "No, I'm not. I want to have time to be with you." I meant it. The orals, the rest of my life, were rapidly receding in importance. Nothing mattered more than these last days with my mother.

"Good," she said.

"What shall we do now?" I asked, once I'd pulled up to the hospital entrance, where she'd waited in the wheelchair, and we were both in the car.

"Let's go to lunch," she said.

Over the couple months of her chemotherapy, we'd taken to going to Saul's Deli. Her treatments left her nauseous, and she had trouble eating. Oddly enough, at Saul's, we'd share the huge family-size platter of smoked whitefish with bagels and cream cheese and a side of coleslaw, and Gloria never failed to eat. It was the same food her parents used to bring us on weekends from Tabachnick's Deli. *She's feeding herself Jewish soul food,* I'd think as I watched her eat.

Now we didn't have it in us to drive across town to Saul's. Instead, we stopped en route to Gloria's at the Claremont Diner. We sat across from each other in a small two-person booth and both ordered the blue-plate special: hot turkey slices with mashed potatoes, gravy, dressing, and cranberry sauce. I could barely feel my body, and after a few bites I looked down at the plate and pushed it away. My eyes had gone unfocused. My body was traveling in the land of the bereft, as I tried to imagine a life without my mother.

"Chana," my mother called me back. "Let's go to Hawaii—soon."

I looked up. "Okay." I paused, worried. What if she got so sick in Hawaii she couldn't fly back home? What if we were stuck there until she died? What a horrifying thought, to have to go through that without community, without any of our friends.

"I think I should give my clients a week's notice, so how about we make it the week after next?"

"All right." She sounded disappointed, her voice heavy. She picked at her food a bit longer and then gave up, too.

And then I noticed something I hadn't before, or, more correctly, something I'd noticed without taking it in: The whites of my mother's eyes had turned yellow.

Chapter 47. Devil's Slide

MY MOTHER PLUMMETED into her final days like a car careening off a cliff at Devil's Slide and plunging toward the gleaming Pacific. There was no turning back from the descent. And I dove with her, bound in the passenger's seat.

In the three days since her doctor's visit, my mother had had no bowel movements, and by the third day she was moaning with pain. I called the doctor's service. The weekend on-call doctor listened to my description of the symptoms and explained that she might have a blockage, which would be very serious. He said he would admit her right away.

"We're going to the hospital," I told Gloria. She was lying on the couch. "I'll get your shoes."

"Can't wear them," she gasped, short of breath. "My feet are too swollen. Just bring my slippers." She struggled up. She was wearing navy sweat pants, and I noticed the elastic waistband was straining against her bulging belly. It had grown huge in just a few days. I knew what this was, and knowing made me want to cry. I'd finally done some medical reading and learned a new word with both Greek and Latin derivations: *ascites*—fluid buildup in the abdominal cavity from liquid that seeps out of the bloodstream when the liver isn't functioning. A very bad sign.

At the hospital, my mother got wheeled off in a gurney, and I waited, paging absentmindedly through a *People* magazine while they performed tests. After her scans, the good news was that she had no cancer growth blocking her intestines. But she was much too ill to go home. I followed as she was wheeled to a room in the oncology ward. She'd just settled in bed and was saying hello to her roommate, an eighty-four-year-old woman with metastasized breast cancer, when a nurse came in and closed the curtains between the beds. "We're going to be performing ascitic drainage," she informed us.

A doctor arrived with a big needle. I held my mother's hand and turned my head away, trying not to look, but I kept sneaking glances, tugged by a mesmerizing horror. She gasped and clenched my hand while the doctor shot her with anesthetic, cut a small incision in her belly flesh, and inserted a thin tube into her abdomen. She was left with a larger tube coming out of her, and a drainage bag hanging from the tube, as if she had sprouted a leak.

Those first days of her hospital stay, I spent my free time with my mother but kept meeting with my clients. Even though it was clear she was extremely ill, I was holding in mind the doctor's three-to-four-month prognosis, which meant it was too soon to stop working. There were moments when I did some of my finest, most connected work, able to be truly present with my clients' suffering. I felt ripped open, and told myself, *There is no place too dark for you to go*. In other sessions, I felt the cold weight of the seconds ticking, the unbearable waste of time lost with my mother. I could barely stay in the room.

Much of the time I was swallowed up into an enclosed bubble, immersed in a world that was just Mom and me. Dana had a back injury that had gotten much worse since the day she'd spent hours with Gloria in the emergency room. But I had little focus for her suffering. In the face of my overwhelming grief, Dana put her needs aside to be there for me. Much later, we'd have to deal with the deep hurt and resentment that built up in her.

ONE DAY, I STEPPED out of my mother's room and went to find the nurse who'd been caring for her. She was sitting at the nurses' station.

"I wanted to ask you something," I started awkwardly. How to ask this?

"Yes?" She looked at me encouragingly, her face soft.

I liked this nurse, thought she was a real *mensch,* because when my mother had said to her, "Do you know I'm gay?" as she was taking Gloria's blood pressure, she'd simply smiled and said, "Great. Thanks for telling me." At first I'd felt a bit embarrassed—why did my mother need to make a point of that?—followed by an admiring, *of course,* a recognition that it mattered deeply to Gloria to be accepted as herself, especially her gay self. Now, at the end, she wanted no more hiding.

"Well . . . well," I struggled to find the words, "it's just that I've never seen anyone die, so I don't have a sense of a time line, of where my mother is in the process. I was wondering—I thought since you're an oncology nurse and you've seen so much, you might have an impression. Do you have a guess about how long she's got?"

"Hmmm," she answered, "people can surprise you, living longer than you'd ever guess. So . . . I could be wrong . . . but I don't think your mother's got real long. Maybe a few weeks."

I managed a whispered "Thanks," and turned to go back to Gloria's bedside.

My mother dozed on and off. When awake, she cycled between confused, foggy consciousness and clarity. I sat next to her bed, my body leaden, my senses dazed, half listening to the husband talking with his dying wife on the other side of the curtain.

Once, she awoke with a start and stared at me.

"Chana!" she called, sounding alarmed.

"Right here, Momushka." I'd taken to calling her every endearment and nickname I'd ever used. I reached over and took her hand.

She exhaled slowly. "Hard dream, intense," she said. She didn't tell me her dream. She squeezed my hand and let go, her eyes looking off to the right, her face pondering. "Yes, that's it, that's what it means," she whispered to herself.

She looked at me then and said quietly, "I'm dying, aren't I?"

Our eyes held. I inhaled, long and deep, and then let the air rush out of me. Another breath. "Yes," I answered. "You are."

We sat in a timeless moment, looking at each other, suspended by the truth.

Then she said, "I didn't want this; I wanted to live. I'd hoped at least for a long remission. But here it is."

"Yes," I concurred.

We hovered in the silence.

I cleared my throat. "There's something I want to tell you, something I've been thinking about. I hope this doesn't sound too weird. You know, all my life, whenever I've wanted to freak myself out, I'd imagine you dead, and I couldn't see how I'd go on, how I could have a life without you. But now, with Dana—even though I will miss you *terribly*—I can see how I'll go on."

"That's marvelous, darling. Knowing that makes me so happy." Her eyelids drooped, and she dozed.

When Gloria woke, a half hour later, she continued as if we hadn't paused in our conversation. She reminded me that she had made plans several years before with the Neptune Society to be cremated for a prearranged price. She told me where in her desk to find the Neptune Society paperwork and her will. I was impressed, and grateful, that she'd had the foresight to deal with this in advance; I couldn't imagine ever getting around to such a thing myself.

"Now, there's something I need you to do," she said. "Let's not prolong this thing. If I start to go, I don't want them bringing me back. I need you to do whatever it takes—whatever paperwork—so they don't try to jump-start me back with those damn electric shock paddles. I absolutely don't want that."

"I understand. I agree that makes sense. I'll take care of it," I assured her.

The process of getting the "do not resuscitate" form put in my mother's chart happened in a blur. My body marched on remote control from point A to point B, doing what was needed. My mother must have signed the form, and perhaps her doctor had to as well, but all I remember is standing in front of the counter of the nurses' station, handing them the completed piece of paper. Sure, in theory I supported the idea of no heroic measures for a terminal illness—why prolong my mother's suffering? Underneath that belief, a part of me wailed: *Stop! Don't take my mother! You want me to just let her go?*

FRIENDS OF GLORIA'S came by throughout each day, and sometimes while they sat with her, I'd go eat or take a walk in the neighborhood. Once, when I was off doing an errand, Gloria called Dana at work and asked her to come see her.

Later, Dana told me how she had stroked my mother's hair, sitting close. Gloria had looked at her and said, "I know you'll take good care of Chana."

One night, in the dark of 4:00 AM, the phone rang. It was a nurse calling from the hospital. "Your mother won't let us do any procedures on her, not even take her temperature. She's gotten paranoid; she says we're trying to kill her."

"I'll be right there." I'd been awake when the phone rang, sitting in a rocking chair in the spare bedroom, rocking and crying. A nightmare had woken me—I had them all the time now. I was too agitated to fall back to sleep, and I'd tiptoed out of bed, not wanting to wake Dana.

My mother was alone in her room with the lights on. Her roommate's bed had been stripped; she'd left the prior afternoon after refusing any further treatments. "Enough is enough. I'm too old for that," she'd said.

I found Gloria with her arms gripping the bedrails, her nostrils flared, her mouth in a deep frown. I moved up close. It took calling her name several times for her to focus on me. "Sweetheart . . . Gloria . . . Gloria . . . Momushka . . ." Her head turned toward me; then one hand reached for me, and I grasped it. I tried for a soothing tone. "The nurses tell me you're frightened that they're trying to hurt you, but it's okay, it's really okay. No one here wants to hurt you."

She released my hand, groped for the bed control, and held the button down while the bed whirred as she rose to sitting. Her eyes were wide with alarm and bright yellow-orange. "It's this feeling—this feeling I can't get over, even if it's not real—this horrible feeling that they're trying to kill me."

I saw the terror in her face.

"Yes, that feeling—something *is* trying to kill you," I said, "but it's not the nurses." I shook my head. "It's your own body that's trying to kill you. It's the cancer that's out of control."

"Oh, yes, it's my body." Her face eased with that simple, brutal truth.

"I'm right here, I'll stay with you," I said.

"Yes, stay . . ." she said, her voice dropping off. The next moment, she slept.

Later that morning, breakfast arrived, and she picked at some scrambled eggs and nibbled on toast. I ate her leftovers. It was one of those bits of time when she was both relaxed and lucid. *Maybe this would be a good moment to ask her,* I thought. It wouldn't be that odd, as now our conversations were laced with non sequiturs.

"Hey, Glor, do you remember that trip to the Big Island that Dana and I signed up for next spring?" I asked.

"Sure, I remember." Her head lowered, and she looked unspeakably sad. Then she looked up at me, her eyes brimming with tears. "Hawaii—you and I—we never made it, did we?"

"No." An ache gripped my chest. "God, I wish we'd gotten to." *What was I thinking? Maybe this is too weird to ask.*

"I was wondering, how would you feel if, um—only if you want, of course—would you like me to take your ashes with me and put them in the volcano?"

She laughed then, the only true belly laugh I'd heard from her in weeks. "Wonderful, yes, that would be wonderful," she beamed, eyes alight. "Throw me into the fire, into the volcano. Throw me back to the Mother!"

Chapter 48. Hospice

THE HOSPICE SOCIAL worker and I were seated in my mother's living room. The young woman had lowered herself daintily onto the couch after I'd let her in, which left me to sit in the chair facing her, with my back to the windows that looked out onto the street. I'd rolled up the shades, hoping to keep an eye out for the ambulance that was bringing Gloria.

I was struggling to focus on the woman's queries. It seemed as if I had grown long deer ears pointed toward the street, acutely alert and quivering, nerves poised for the slamming of a door.

Brenda, the home health aide, was in my mother's bedroom, making up the hospital bed that had been delivered the day before. The deliverymen helped to drag her queen bed down to the basement storage space. Another medical supply company brought a huge green metal oxygen canister that now waited in the corner of the bedroom. Brenda rejected the roll of egg carton foam I'd gotten from the hospital dispensary to help avoid bedsores. "Too hard to turn them with that," she declared. She was a heavy-boned woman, and her broad face took on a bulldog expression with her pronouncement. Since she would be doing the turning, I couldn't argue with her.

"Do you have any siblings?" the social worker asked.

Why so many questions, why now? Did she have *any* idea what it was like to be waiting for the ambulance to bring a mother home to die?

And then I heard it: an engine, a door, the sound of men's voices. I leapt up and went to the windows. "They're here!"

"Don't worry, they'll take care of bringing her in. Now . . ." the social worker was asking me another question, and her voice trailed after me as I bolted out the door of Gloria's flat and down the hall to the front doorway.

I watched two men go around to the back of the ambulance, open the doors, lift my mother out in a stretcher, and lower its stainless-steel wheels onto the street. She looked like a prone Humpty Dumpty; in spite of the ascitic drainage, her belly was terribly swollen, and the sheet arced in a curve over it. My legs felt shaky, and I steadied myself by leaning on the door frame. I glanced over toward my mother again. Even though I couldn't hear their words, I saw that the two men standing next to her were bantering with each other, and one was laughing.

The driver came up the front stairs. "I need to see the route we'll be taking."

I turned and led him to the apartment. There was a hall between the living room and the bedroom, made narrow by teak bookshelves my mother had installed. They held a mix of books and stacks of my grandmother's Limoges china, inherited a few years prior.

"Too narrow here," the driver said, surveying the hall. "We'll have to bring her in a sling."

I waited in the bedroom, wanting to greet her there. After a time, I heard voices, grunts, footsteps muffled by the wall-to-wall shag carpet. Then a crash, a male voice yelling, "Damn! Watch it!"

and the sound of shattering china. They brought her headfirst into the bedroom, swaying like a baby in a huge canvas cradle, and deposited her on the bed, with its pulled-back covers.

"Sorry about the breakage," the driver told me. He handed me a card. "Call this number, and my supervisor will help you declare an insurance claim." I said nothing and turned to Gloria in bed.

"Welcome home, sweetheart," I greeted her.

She smiled up at me drowsily, sedated on morphine. "Hi, darling. Thank God I'm home."

We sat together for a brief while; then I introduced her to Brenda and went out to the living room to finish the social worker's questions.

WHEN I ARRIVED AT the apartment the next morning, my mother had a complaint about Brenda, although she couldn't remember her name. "I asked that woman to help me out of bed, and she told me, 'You can't. You'll never get out of bed again!'"

"Jeez, I'm sorry. I'll have a talk with her." The statement was true, but much too brutal coming from a stranger.

I hated that we were dependent on Brenda, that she could hurt my mother. My first impulse was to fire her, but she'd been the only health worker available on the list that hospice kept. Instead, I admonished her. "Don't ever talk like that to my mother again! You have to be gentler." As if I could change her personality, as if I could control her.

AT THE HOSPITAL, Gloria had asked if she could come live with us. "I don't want to die here," she'd said.

She understood she couldn't manage on her own. How to honor her wish? I didn't want her to die in that hospital, either.

Dana and I had talked it over. We needed our home to be a refuge in the midst of all this. I didn't want it to be the place where my mother had died.

I had told Gloria that we were going to bring her back to her apartment but I'd be there a lot—most of the time—and we were hiring a woman to help take care of her. She'd asked, "How much will this cost?" She was worried that she would use all her money and leave me nothing. I didn't want to tell her there was no need to worry, because we wouldn't have to pay for help for very long. Her confusion had deepened, and the next day when I arrived at the hospital, I found her asleep holding a pen. A piece of paper rested on her chest. I picked it up. A jagged line of numbers spilled down the page, erratic multiplication with dollar signs, the numbers trailing off when they reached the millions.

AS FRANK AS MY mother was, she needed an emissary to ask me one particular question, and she elected her friend Rebecca to do it. Brenda had sent me out with a shopping list, and Rebecca was there when I returned. "Can I talk with you?"

Rebecca was a close double to my mother: Like Gloria, she was a sixty-eight-year-old, short, Jewish, formerly married lesbian who was a retired Gestalt therapist. In my early twenties, long before she had been friends with my mother, she'd been my therapist for a time. Small world. "I'm sorry for what you're going through," she began. "This just has to be awful. For you and Gloria. It's just that Gloria wanted me to ask you something."

"Yes?"

"Well, you know how much she's suffering. And, well, she wants to know if you'll agree to help her. Help her end it—I mean—the suffering. By taking pills."

"Oh." My stomach knotted in a fist. Somewhere over my head, the shadows of the three Furies hovered, flapping their great wings—those primal goddesses with mud-streaked faces and hissing snakes for hair, those avengers of matricide, baring their fangs.

"What do you think?" Rebecca prodded me from my glazed-eyed reverie.

No pondering was needed on the unthinkable horror of giving my mother pills to hasten her death. We'd come so close, so many times.

"My God, there's no way, Rebecca. I understand her wanting that—I'd probably want it myself—but you *know* my history with my mother and drugs and suicide. *Even* if we could get away with it, having all these hospice people around, I can't help her die of an overdose. It would haunt me the rest of my days. Killing my mother . . ." My voice trailed off. "We'll just have to go the natural route."

"Sure. Of course. I'll tell her."

THE HOSPICE NURSE CAME by at least once a day, sometimes twice. She and I were at odds. She kept turning up the morphine pump dial. Her goal was to help my mother drift off to her death. I wanted bedside talks, heart-to-hearts, last memories, conversations with as alert and coherent a mother as I could have. Balancing that with pain relief was tricky business.

Having no prior experience to guide me, I often deferred to the nurse. Yet I was horrified that my mother would end her days doped into a stupor. It was too reminiscent of the early years, with her stoned on psychiatric drugs. What complicated medical decisions further was that my role wasn't just to voice my own needs, but to speak for my mother, for what she'd want, and she'd asked for drugs. What to do?

For a time, I lost the morphine war. A week after her return home, Gloria spent a day completely snowed, breathing shallow breaths with long pauses before the next inhalation. It scared the hell out of me, and I was numbed into inaction. That day, a new social worker came to see me. He and I sat in the kitchen. We could hear my mother's rasping inhalation from there, followed by a gust of out breath, then the long silent pause.

He asked me questions and wrote down the answers. I told him some of my history with my mother: about her addiction to psychiatric drugs in my childhood, and how, after I'd left for college, she'd gotten off drugs and reclaimed her vitality. I was trying to get him to understand the context of why I didn't want my mother overly sedated, but as I spoke, I felt barely present, rambling, and unfocused. Part of me was hovering, disembodied, in the direction of my mother.

Finally he said, "Let's go see what's happening with her."

We leaned over her bed, listening to the long pauses between each breath. I found myself silently counting: *one thousand one one thousand two one thousand three . . . please please inhale.*

He shook me out of my frozen stupor with the simple statement "I think you should call the hospice nurse."

When I got the nurse on the phone, she said that was just how it needed to be. Nothing to be done. But now that I had mobilized myself to action, I wouldn't accept that answer. I showed the social worker out and called our family doctor, Dvora. She told me how much to turn down the morphine pump.

After several hours, Gloria finally came to. She raised her head and looked around. "I couldn't wake up," she rasped. "I thought I had died."

I took her hand. "No, no," I soothed, "you just had a bit too much drugs."

Chapter 49. Submarine

FOR A FEW DAYS, I had my mother back.

One afternoon, she said, “Something, something I have to tell you.” She was short of breath, struggling to get the words out. “Something about Happy.”

“About Happy?” I echoed.

Of course she meant my childhood dog.

My mother’s words were a bit slurred from the morphine. “’Member when we talked about giving Happy to the farmer?”

“Yes?”

“There was no farmer . . . a story I made up.” Her voice caught. “Juz couldn’t handle him anymore. I had him put to sleep. Sorry, so sorry. Can you forgive me?”

I laughed at the shock of it, all these years kept secret by my mother. In the immensity of my mother’s dying, Happy’s death seemed far away and small. Absurd, almost. I dismissed its meaning, giddy in my present sorrow. I was quick to reply, skimming the surface, too overwhelmed with grief to excavate below.

"Of course, Gloria, of course," I soothed. I wanted no regrets between us, and so I overlooked my own.

SOMETIME AFTER HER death, I wondered at her decision to put Happy down all those years earlier and felt the stirrings of fury. Was there no other way to tame Happy's wildness than the injection of a lethal sedative? My mother's choice had found no way to leave me one of the few solaces in my childhood, a companion who eased my loneliness and gave me joy. She robbed me of that.

And what of my mother's shame, like a boulder between us? I thought we had told each other everything after we both came out and were beyond the silence of her suppressed lesbian years. How terribly guilt-ridden she must have been, to never speak of what had happened.

But then I thought further. There were my own silences, the taboo learned early on—from whom, I'm not sure: Don't be angry with your mother; it's not her fault she's sick. My fury had leaked out toward her in mean and scornful remarks like plutonium from a sunken Russian submarine, unacknowledged but still lethal.

I imagined another conversation. *My mother tells me about putting Happy to sleep. "Can you forgive me?" she asks.*

I reach toward my mother, take her face between my two hands, hold us eye to eye. It is time for naming.

I tell her, "Mom, I have hated you. This moment, I hate you. Can you forgive me?"

Chapter 50. Sinai

BY THE MIDDLE OF her second week home, my mother was becoming more agitated and incoherent. She whispered, she muttered, she yelled sentence fragments over and over.

I leaned over the side of her hospital bed, stroking her hair. "Shhh, shhh, it's all right, Momila." I tried to make eye contact, but her pupils were dilated and she seemed to have gone some manner of blind. She was far from me; I could not find her.

Her arms raised, her hands fluttered in the air. Although her words formed no sentences, I could hear her distress, feel her deep restlessness.

Brenda came into the bedroom and checked the catheter bag. "You won't be able to speak with her," she said flatly. "She's too far gone." When Brenda left, I closed the bedroom door.

I knew there was a place beyond words, this ancient connection between my mother and me. I began to sing, simple songs, singing the words over and over:

We all come from the Goddess,
and to her we shall return
like a drop of rain flowing to the ocean.

MY MOTHER QUIETED, her arms lowered, her face relaxed. She joined me in singing, not word for word, but humming, singing one word now and then . . . *goddess . . . ocean.*

I reached my hand toward her and laid my palm and spread fingers on her breastbone. "My heart to your heart," I said. "My heart to your heart." She whispered, "My heart. Your heart."

Then I sang to my mother the names of all the women who loved her, and the names of all the women she had loved. "Chana loves Gloria . . . Dana loves Gloria . . . Arlene loves Gloria . . . Reva loves Gloria . . . Carol loves Gloria . . . " on and on. She sang her name, drawing out the syllables, "GLOR—I—AAA."

I sang her Hebrew prayers and Yiddish *niguns,* wordless tunes whose nonsense syllables vibrated with memories, with meaning and meaninglessness.

Hida hida hi diddy di da hida hida hida . . .

There was life between us, my mother and me. We found a place to meet when spoken words were no longer possible. Beneath words, behind naming, lived something else.

THE NEXT MORNING, I arrived to find my mother muttering gibberish and sentence fragments, sometimes in a whisper, other times shouted. Most of the time her eyes were closed, but when she opened them, they were unfocused, not recognizing what was right around her. Not seeing me, sitting right there next to her. She didn't respond to my voice or my singing. She would open her eyes and stare off into some unfathomable distance. I wondered—where was she journeying? What wilderness called her?

Amidst her muttering, two sentences, so potent with history that they were in some ways a life summary. I could make out each word clearly: *"Abe is not good for Gloria. Gloria prefers women."*

Later that day, she whispered, *"All the wild things, wild, beautiful things."* Repeating it over and over, *"Wild things, wild, beautiful things . . . "*

Where was she traveling? I wanted to go with her, like we had on that camping trip in the Sinai Desert. I wanted to lie back in our sleeping bags laid out on warm sand, staring into a desert night ablaze with stars.

My mother, whose spirit was like an elf's, with her twinkling eyes, her wild-hearted lust for women—that desire that would not be crushed by the modern-day Inquisition of electroshocks and psychiatric drugs. My mother, who loved the wild places of the earth—the sea, the mountains, the forests—and the wild places in our hearts; who danced with abandon in lesbian bars; who laid her body in the roadway, protesting nuclear bombs; who meditated to Ram Dass tapes and introduced me to sunflower sprouts; who looked me in the eye when she asked, "Am I dying?"

She was leaving me. Standing on the wild threshold, saying goodbye.

Chapter 51. Shiva

AFTER MY MOTHER died, I dreamed of her each night and woke with a start to a motherless morning.

Grief descended on me with its thick animal musk, a beast with ragged, muddy fur, muffling all my senses. My mouth was dry, my chest hollow. I covered every surface of the living room—mantel, coffee table, end tables—with photos of my mother. I was nearly blind to the friends who came and went, bearing casseroles and soup, barely noticed Dana's presence or absence. I knew that visitors were supposed to be a comfort, but it strained me beyond capacity to turn my face toward them.

It was a chilly, damp fall. I kept a fire going in the stone fireplace, its flames an orange haze. I sat in an armchair. Nothing warmed my bones.

On the eighth day after Gloria's death, close friends gathered in our house for a small private ritual. I felt like a groundhog poking my head up above its hole to check: *Is it spring yet? No, snow all around.* But now, just a bit, I could take in the comfort of being surrounded by those who loved my mother or me or both. We shared memories and stories of Gloria, sang together.

A few days later, I drove up into the Berkeley hills. I parked the car at an overlook, got out, and stood on the edge of the precipice. The entire Bay Area spread out beneath me: the flatlands, the gray metal of the Bay Bridge bisected by the knob of Treasure Island, the bay itself ringed by the skyscrapers of San Francisco and the silhouette of Mt. Tamalpais, and, spanning the bay's entryway, the Golden Gate Bridge. Below me, waitresses were serving meals, executives were sitting at board meetings, prostitutes were turning tricks, women were giving birth, people were falling in love, being mugged, painting on huge oil canvases—I knew all this, but it seemed inconceivable, bizarre. Didn't they know the world had been rent asunder?

OVER THE NEXT FEW months, every now and then, I'd get this irresistible urge to pick up the phone and dial my mother's number. I would hold the receiver tight against my ear, leaning in. Always, now, the same female computer voice stiffly intoned: "You have reached a number that is no longer in service . . ." The sinking feeling. The weight of my arm, lowering the phone.

Then, one day, the inevitable. I called and a voice said, "Hello?" She sounded young. I wanted to cry out, *This used to be my mother's phone. Who* are *you? What matters to you?*

I remained silent. She repeated, "Hello? Hello?" There was a *click,* and then a dial tone.

Breathe in, breathe out. Another motherless day.

Chapter 52. Thermals

IN EARLY OCTOBER, as the first anniversary approached, it was as if my body were remembering each day of the year before, each stage of those last weeks of my mother's dying: *This is the day she came home from the hospital, this is the day she could no longer speak, this is the day I sang to her.*

Our living room was no longer covered with her photos. I'd condensed her tribute to an altar on a side table. Candles, photographs, seashells, and a small owl statue were arranged around the ceramic vase that still held her ashes. Although I'd gone to Hawaii the past spring, I hadn't brought along her ashes. I wasn't ready to feel her sifting through my fingers, couldn't yet bear to let her go.

Now, each day for a bit, I would sit in a rocking chair facing the little altar, memories flashing through my mind.

On the anniversary of my mother's death, Dana and I drove up the Berkeley hills to Tilden Park. We took a long walk on a trail that looped over a ridgeback, through stands of eucalyptus and bay laurel, their fragrant leaves crunching underfoot. As we hiked, I calmed and loosened, the hills under my feet grounding me, the pungency of eucalyptus in my nostrils bringing me into the present. I felt how I loved my life, my life with Dana.

On the drive back, we pulled into an overlook and shut off the engine. The city and bay spread beneath us. We were quiet for a long while, just looking down at the Bay Area pulsing below, the sun lowering toward San Francisco Bay, sky glowing orange, lights just on the edge of blinking on.

The hills here were steep, dropping to the flatlands of Berkeley and Oakland. I sat wondering if the warm air currents called thermals rose up these hills, as they did in Calistoga, as they had that time they held me aloft. And then I was lost in memory:

One year, after Gloria's move to California, she and I are driving north to the Napa Valley town of Calistoga, known for its hot springs, to celebrate my birthday. Along its one main street are the spas boasting various treatments—mud baths, hot whirlpools, massage—but we have not come to seek the waters. I long to soar, to lift into quiet far above the world's din, and my mother is giving me the gift of flight: a glider ride in one of those motorless little planes.

My mother has never gotten over her fear of heights. She no longer goes into the panic that would overcome her driving when I was a child, but any precipice, cliff, grandstand, or steep balcony seat makes her hyperventilate, stiffen, and sweat.

Nonetheless, my mother wants her daughter to fly. At least, she makes a brave show of it, smiling at me before I walk off toward the plane. I know her fear lurks underneath, but we both ignore it as she says cheerily, "Have a great time!"

I walk onto the tarmac, where the pilot waits next to the glider. It looks like a blown-up toy, a narrow white fiberglass body with long thin wings and a domed clear hood. The pilot adjusts something in the tiny cockpit, then ushers me into my seat directly in front of him, gets in, and closes the Plexiglas lid that bubbles over our heads. The clear nose of the glider encases my legs. After I strap myself in, I can't even turn to see the pilot behind me. It's just me and this tiny bubble of plane.

The small twin-engine aircraft that will lift us aloft taxis into position in front, and with a rough tug pulls us down the runway. I watch the tow plane lift, and then we rise. Just before the hills, the plane cuts us loose and banks away. We're catching the thermals that let gliders soar, those warm pockets of air that rise from the valley up the mountainsides. The noisy plane disappears, leaving us in the quiet, the hills green and brown below me.

The whoosh *of the air currents over the wings is the only sound. I know my mother is down there on Earth, waiting for me, but as the glider dips, sensation roars through my capillaries—drowning out anything but the moment. To be free to forget my mother is her greatest gift to me. She has reclaimed her own happiness, and I have let go of constant vigilance toward a depressed mother. Now, she's been well for over ten years, though her phobia of heights remains.*

Hawklike, we swoop and glide, taking in the hills below, the tiny rows of vineyard grapes, the dots of houses. I am filled with wind, sound, and light. I must have laughed, the joy bursting out of me. The pilot, who has been respectfully silent, asks, "Would you like to do some stunts?"

"Sure," I blithely respond.

Barely a beat passes, and the pilot puts the plane into a full dive. The Plexiglas nose in front of me is now headed directly for the earth. Nausea lurches in my stomach. My intestines are both jelly and hard knots. If my chest belt is digging in, I don't feel it because I am screaming like a middle-schooler on a roller-coaster ride, full-out roaring. When I find words, I yell, "Stop, stop!" *The pilot pulls us out of the dive.*

"I guess-that's-why-I've-never-been-on-a-roller-coaster," is all I manage to choke out. I think of my mother then, her breathless terror of heights, the silence of it. There were never any screams. I have a sense of it now: how it must have felt in her frozen body, stiff and sweating, with her choked breath, her panicked eyes. I remember the sour smell of her fear. Oh, Mom. *My banging heart regains some of its steadiness as the glider resumes its gentle arcs. I release my own breath, come back to pleasure in the soaring.*

Mom is waiting for me. She is standing next to her car in the parking lot that butts right up against the airstrip. One hand is shading her forehead, as if she has been squinting into the distance for a long time. A lit cigarette dangles from her other hand. When she sees me coming toward her, she drops the cigarette and stomps it into the gravel, then smiles at me. I can tell from her smile that she did not see the plane suddenly dive toward the earth.

"How was it?" she asks.

I hesitate, just for a moment. Then I tell her the truth: "It was the most amazing thing ever."

Her face breaks open, fully lit, and we stand there beaming at each other. "I'm so glad, sweetheart."

Across the bay, the skyscrapers of San Francisco were backlit by the last vestiges of the sunset. The lights of the Bay Bridge were sparkling against an indigo sky. Late in life, but not too late, my mother had arrived, fed me meals, listened to my troubles, and, with her joy, launched me into a realm that was further off than she could go.

I emerged from my reverie. "Dana?"

"Yes?"

I started up the car. "Let's go to Saul's for dinner, and eat soul food for Gloria."

Dana reached over and touched my arm. "Sure, let's go."

Epilogue

IN THE YEAR AFTER my mother died, my father had what I've come to call a transcendental stroke. Perhaps it was the struggle back from near death, the complete loss of speech, and a paralyzed left side that spurred his transformation to a self more openhearted than before.

Miraculously, after months of rehab with his wife's support, my father got on a plane and came for a visit. He was so much more expressive now. Everything delighted him; it was all "terrific." He let me know how much he enjoyed being with me. And some closed-down part in me softened to this changed dad.

When I started to work on the memoir a couple of years later, my father and I began a new dialogue: talking about our family and all that had happened. He believed in my writing and was willing to excavate the past, as he'd never been before. It took time for us to process, many years of going into it bit by bit.

Together we came to a more complex understanding of how Mom, Dad, and I had all suffered. I realized how painful the marriage had been for my father, what it must have been like to be told by your wife, "Let's live as brother and sister." Dad saw how trapped Gloria had been, how society had offered her no possibility for happiness. I braved telling him what it had really been like for me the year he left me with my suicidal mother and went to England. It was radical for me not to protect him anymore.

Some years into our new phase, on my visit to New Jersey, I was surprised and touched when Dad took me to a gay-themed art exhibit. Dad was an art hound who loved museums, and this was a way of showing me his acceptance. As I was flying home, he called Dana. "I just want to tell you how happy I am that you have each other," he told her. He went further, "I think you have a wonderful relationship. I love you."

On May 15, 2008, the very day the California Supreme Court ruled that same-sex marriage was a constitutional right, Dana and I booked our appointment to be married at San Francisco City Hall. We chose the day in August that would be our twenty-fourth anniversary. Same-sex couples were jamming to fill the slots before the November elections, when Californians would vote on Proposition 8, which, if passed, would ban further unions.

The day we arrived at the marble rotunda of city hall, ceremonies were taking place simultaneously on the stairs, in corridors, on the second floor. The hall vibrated with tremendous elation, radiance glowing on the faces of the marrying gay men and lesbians, that jubilation mirrored in their children, friends, and family gathered around them.

During our ceremony, I looked into Dana's face, feeling our love and something larger: how profound it was to be welcomed into a common humanity. I wished my mother could be here to see how far we'd all come. Could she have even imagined this?

By then, my father was ill and unable to fly to our ceremony, but he'd kept getting my reports as the day neared. The day after our wedding, he called.

"Are you married?" he asked, delight in his voice. "Did you get the flowers I sent?"

"They're beautiful, Dad. Just beautiful."

Reader's Guide

QUESTIONS FOR DISCUSSION

1. What do you think are the different meanings of the title, *Riding Fury Home?*

2. Gloria has a secret underlying her depression that Chana won't know until she reaches age twenty. What was the impact of keeping the secret on the mother, the father, and the daughter?

3. What is the difference between secrecy and privacy? In your family, were there any stories that were kept secret and later revealed? If so, how did that revelation help you understand your life?

4. What were the historical and cultural forces at play in Gloria's depression? In what ways do you think an individual's mental state and cultural forces interact?

5. How did social stigma, taboos, and shame play out in the Wilson family? Is there anything you somehow knew you weren't supposed

to talk about without having to be told? What have you been able to speak about in your life that was formerly taboo?

6. How did you respond to Chana's childhood struggle to take care of her mother? In what ways do you think this role reversal affected Chana?

7. When Chana's father went to England, he made a choice to leave Chana with her troubled mother. Gloria chose to put Chana's beloved childhood dog, Happy, to sleep because Gloria was unable to deal with him. How did you react to these actions? Have you ever been torn between your own well-being and that of your child or someone who depended on you?

8. Both mother and daughter became involved in the Women's Movement of the 1970s, whose slogan was "The personal is political." How did the interaction of the personal and the political play out for Gloria and for Chana? Are there ways in which the personal and political interact in your life today?

9. The narrative covers the time period from the mid-'50s to the '90s, with the epilogue continuing up to 2008. Discuss the cultural changes that happened in those eras. How have those changes influenced your life?

10. Throughout the story, Chana describes herself from childhood on as an outsider. In what ways? How does her sense of being an outsider shift over time? What are your experiences of feeling like an outsider?

11. As Gloria becomes ill in her sixties, first with rheumatoid arthritis, then with cancer, there are instances in which her illness recreates the dynamic of Chana's being her mother's caretaker. How were the interactions between mother and adult daughter similar to those in the past, and in what ways were they different?

12. How much do you think mother and daughter resolved in their relationship with each other? What remained undone?

Acknowledgments

RIDING FURY HOME was shepherded to completion by many.

I am indebted to the teachers who helped me hone my craft. First and foremost, Monza Naff, in whose classes the book took shape. Her teaching offered the potent combination of rigor and support. She dared me to write beyond the safe and easily known with challenges such as: "What's the thing you most don't want to write?" Monza welcomed me into a community of writers and saw my project through as writing coach and editor, encouraging my unique voice all the way. Over time, our connection deepened into a lasting friendship.

Gracias to Andy Couturier and his classes at the Opening. Andy's in-class exercises gave me permission to take risks and play, adding richness and emotional depth to the narrative. Sandy Boucher's autobiography class was among my first stabs at the memoir. Judith Barrington, who taught memoir at Flight of the Mind, the writing workshop where I crafted the first chapter, insisted it was good enough to read onstage in front of all those *real* writers.

Joelle Fraser, workshop instructor at the Truckee Meadows conference, gave me critique that solidified the structure of the memoir. Ani Mander, in her creative writing class at Antioch College, ushered me through my writer's block.

My long-standing gratitude to the writers who've been so generous with their feedback. My Sunday writers; group: Teya Schaffer, Helen Mayer, and Susan Schulman who've been with me since the very beginning. The Tuesday writer's group: Jeanne Courtney, Camille Escudero, Chantal Rohling, Helen Greenspan, Rose Wood. Thanks to Jayne Schabel, writer friend and partner in our weeklong writing retreats, whose crazy ability to sit in the chair, writing for umpteen hours, helped me stay the course. Helen Zia, who encouraged me after a rejection to stick with and believe in my narrative. Thanks to the members of Redwood Writers for warm camaraderie and lively salons.

Thanks to my fellow therapists for their support, especially Esther Lehrman, who believed in the story's relevance to healers and nominated me to present at the Psychotherapy Institute. And to Rebecca Silverstein, who invited me to give a dramatic reading from the memoir-in-progress at Gaylesta's conference Queer Families = Healthy Families. Much gratitude to Laura Pilnick, who accompanied me on the healing path.

Deepest thanks for help along the road to publication. Caroline Pincus, who practiced midwifery on my manuscript through the proposal process with her book-biz wisdom, good cheer, and belief that books that matter will find a home. Judith Cope, the brave editor who tackled my behemoth and wrestled one hundred pages out of its length. The path-to-publication support group: Julia Hutton, Martha Snider, Katrina Alcorn, and Phil Lapsley. Thanks to Linda Wattanabe McFerrin for her fierce advocacy for fellow writers, and to the members of Left Coast Writers, Linda's baby. *Gracias* to Book Passage Bookstore in Corte Madera for hosting us, and to bookstore manager Tina Vierra.

Appreciation and thanks to Brooke Warner, my editor at Seal Press. Her keen eye for what was chaff and her astute insight into what was missing so enriched the book. To the staff at Seal Press and Perseus Books—thanks for believing in the relevance of the narrative and for getting behind it with zest and skill.

Thanks so much for the sustenance of friendship: Iris Stallworth-Grayling, Rebecca Silverstein, Linda Gebroe, Frayda Garfinkle, Vicki dello Joio, Joyce Wermont, and Doug Beaton. Thanks to Carolyn Brandy, maestra of Sistah Boom, for the wild joy of polyrhythms. To all the Sistahs as we drum in the streets and chant, "Work for peace in the belly of the beast."

Most of all, thanks to my wife, Dana, who, in addition to all her other endearing qualities, is a terrific editor. She knew me and the story deeply enough to read a piece and say, "It's not there yet; go back and do it again." I would sigh and trudge back to the studio, knowing that in the end, her loving push would get me there.

About the Author

© Irene Young

CHANA WILSON IS A psychotherapist and a former radio producer and television engineer. She began her career in broadcast journalism as a radio programmer with KPFA in Berkeley, California. Her work hosting the KPFA program *A World Wind*—in which she interviewed poets, musicians, writers, and activists—sparked her desire to work with people on a deeper level. Now a psychotherapist for twenty-four years, she credits the extraordinary courage of her clients for inspiring her to write.

Wilson's writing has appeared in the print journals *The Sun* and *Sinister Wisdom*, in the online journal *Roadwork*, and in several anthologies.

Since the mid-'80s, Wilson has been playing percussion with the women's samba band Sistah Boom. She resides with her wife in Oakland, California.

Visit Chana online at www.RidingFuryHome.com.